"Funny, frightening, ironic, and de[   ] engrossing thrill ride through the l[   ] espionage. . . . A wonderful book."

> —RICHARD NORTH PATTERSON, *New York Times* bestselling author of *Degree of Guilt* and *In the Name of Honor*

"Propulsive momentum . . . the authors give a good sense of the improvisational nature of the CIA. . . . Both Baers write affectingly of their experiences."

> —*Kirkus Reviews*

"Provides a spot-on and compelling portrait of real life inside the CIA: periods of boredom and frustration loudly punctuated by fast-moving and sometimes frightening, sometimes amusing, intelligence operations. Bob and Dayna Baer are the real deal and they beautifully capture the murky world they lived and worked in for years."

> —VALERIE PLAME WILSON, *New York Times* bestselling author of *Fair Game*

"A revelation . . . [shows] how spies operate in the field, the personal costs they pay for the exceptional lives they live, and the way fate can deliver up redemption . . . I loved this book."

> —BARRY EISLER, *New York Times* bestselling author of *Rain Fall* and *Fault Line*

"An emotionally candid memoir of a life few could imagine, juggling terrorists and dictators with all-too-real family dramas . . . describes how two accomplished spies trained in shooting for the heart improbably found their own."

> —JANE MAYER, National Book Award finalist for *The Dark Side*

"After twenty years as the CIA's best and most adventurous spy, Bob Baer has established himself as America's go-to writer on espionage and the Middle East in the age of 9/11. Now he and his wife, Dayna, have added a heart-stopping new chapter, revealing how a couple caught up in the dark world of CIA intrigue try to balance romance and gunplay while building a relationship on the jagged edge of undercover work. . . . *The Company We Keep* will make you ask, who needs Brad Pitt and Angelina Jolie?"

—JAMES RISEN, Pulitzer Prize–winning author of *State of War*

"Engrossing . . . filled with juicy, personal, on-the-job details . . . [an] exhilarating tale of geopolitical love and peril."

—*More* magazine

"A cross between John le Carré and Erich Segal . . . Told with flair, intelligence, and emotion—and often diary-like detail."

—LESLIE STAHL, CBS News

"Extraordinary . . . shows the Baers' ultimate triumph over the isolation inherent in their professions and the banality of bureaucracy worldwide."

—LINDSAY MORAN, author of *Blowing My Cover: My Life as a CIA Spy*

"Will illuminate the dark world of intelligence gathering that very few people ever see. It's filled with ground truth, tradecraft, and operational details. . . . You will not be disappointed."

—FRED BURTON, VP Intelligence, STRATFOR, and author of *Ghost: Confessions of a Counterterrorism Agent*

"A cross between voyeurism and adventure, this book takes us through the emotional, poignant, and often dangerous lives of two CIA operatives: the fear, the violence, the requisite suspicion, and the tenuous friendships. . . . It's especially intriguing to follow a woman into dark corners, thrilling missions, and psychologically difficult moments."

—RITA GOLDEN GELMAN, author of *Tales of a Female Nomad*

"Vivid and revealing . . . A look inside the real CIA."

—DAVID WISE, author of *Spy*

THE COMPANY WE KEEP

THE COMPANY WE KEEP

A HUSBAND-AND-WIFE TRUE-LIFE SPY STORY

Robert and Dayna Baer

Broadway Paperbacks
New York

Originally published in hardcover in the United States by Crown Publishers,
an imprint of the Crown Publishing Group, a division of Random House, Inc.,
New York, in 2011.

Library of Congress Cataloging-in-Publication Data

Baer, Robert.
The company we keep / Robert and Dayna Baer.—1st. ed.
    p. cm.
1. Baer, Robert. 2. Baer, Dayna. 3. United States. Central Intelligence Agency—
Biography. 4. Intelligence officers—United States—Biography. 5. Spies—
United States—Biography. 6. Husband and wife—United States I. Baer,
Dayna. II. Title.
JK468.I6.B33 2010
327.12730092'2—dc22
[B]   2010019829

ISBN 978-0-307-58815-9
eISBN 978-0-307-58816-6

Printed in the United States of America

Book design by Lauren Dong
Map by Mapping Specialists
Cover design: © Pete Garceau
Cover photograph: (feet running) © Henriette v. Muenchhausen; (map) © istockphoto.com

10 9 8 7 6 5 4 3 2 1

First Paperback Edition

AUTHORS' NOTE

All events in the story are true. However, to protect "sources and methods," the names of operatives and informants have been changed, and their identities blurred beyond recognition. For instance, we describe the organization that "Yuri" works for as the Russian KGB, although by 1991 the KGB had been dissolved into multiple organizations. The term *parabolic mic* substitutes for a device that is still classified. The names of the people who helped with the adoption have been changed because they belong to Pakistan's imperiled Christian minority. Special thanks goes to our editor, Rick Horgan, who first saw the possibility of this book, and whipped it into the shape it needed to be in. The CIA has reviewed the book to ensure that it contains no classified information.

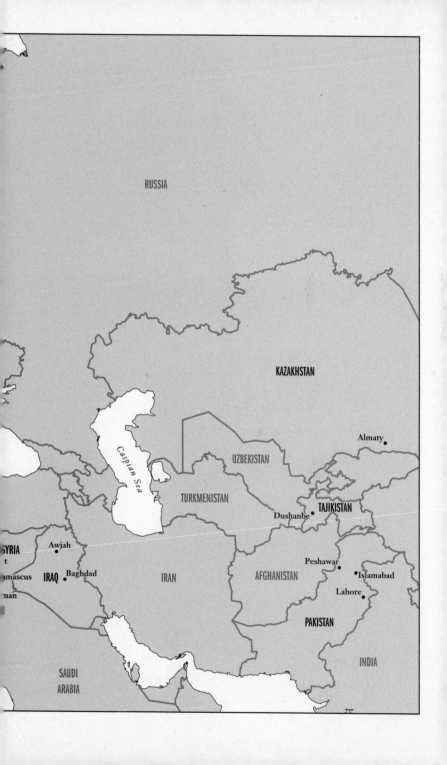

The bottom line is: There aren't any textbooks on spying, you have to invent as you go along.

—Robert Littell, *The Company: A Novel of the CIA*

PROLOGUE

<hr>

Split, Croatia: DAYNA

think Bob's joking when he points at the station wagon parked
out front of Split airport, the one we're about to drive into
Sarajevo. It's lime green with a tangerine *Orangina* painted
down the side. What's worse, it's right-hand drive, a British Vaux-
hall. Bosnia, Croatia—everywhere in the Balkans—is left-hand
drive. It just makes no sense to me, driving a billboard on wheels
into a city the Serbs have been pounding with artillery and sniping
at since the civil war started in 1992. Does he want to give them
something to shoot at?

Bob catches my look and asks if it's a little too early for me. I
can't tell if he means it sarcastically. But it's only six thirty, and I
decide to keep quiet and let him think I'm sleepy. Anyway there's
nothing I can do now. Although I don't work for him, he outranks
me. And that's not to mention that I don't have another way to get
to Sarajevo.

I tell myself it'll be fine. We'll part ways as soon as we get to
Sarajevo. But the car does break every rule in the book. From day
one, they drilled into our heads never to drive a car people will remember. You drive something plain vanilla, like a dirty, dinged-up
brown sedan. People forget plain and ugly things. This station
wagon is definitely ugly, but it's a car no one will ever forget. An
ice-cream truck, bells jingling, would attract less attention.

Truth is, I think Bob's a little nutty. I met him in Sarajevo the
first time when Washington cabled us to meet an operative going
by the name of Harold. "Harold's an alias, right?" I asked Charlie,
an ex-Marine pilot I work with. We both wondered who'd agree

to an alias like Harold. The only other thing the cable said was that he'd wait for us at eleven at a fish restaurant on the Zeljeznica River, ten miles outside of town.

It was a soft spring day. Small, fluffy clouds drifted across the sky, and the leaves were just coming out. The restaurant was packed with locals drinking and chain smoking. "Riley, Charlie!" a voice called out. It was obviously Harold. He stood up, motioning us to come over, like he was berthing an airliner. He was at a table with a half-dozen men, talking and waving a half-defoliated cigar. Charlie and I didn't move, so Harold got up, said something to the men that made them laugh, and threaded his way through the tables to join us.

He stuck out his hand. "Hi, I'm Bob," he said. So much for the Harold alias. We found a free table in the corner. Washington hadn't told us what we were supposed to do for Bob, only to hear him out. Bob said we should have lunch, and recommended the grilled trout. When we told him we couldn't stay, he got right to it: headquarters had sent him to Sarajevo to go after Hizballah, the Lebanese militant group backed by Iran. It had set up in Bosnia at the beginning of the civil war to fight with the Bosnian Muslims—at the behest of Iran. "Done right, we'll pin 'em down like butterflies," Bob proclaimed.

Out of the corner of my eye I saw Charlie concentrating, making sure he'd heard right. I was sure he was thinking the same thing I was: it was Hizballah operatives that were hunting us, rather than the other way around. Three months ago we'd caught Hizballah planning to kidnap, torture, and kill a CIA operative here. We pulled him out in the middle of the night, right before Hizballah's plan was to be executed. Bottom line: we were playing in Hizballah's backyard.

Bob must have seen the expression on our faces. "Invisibility," he said. "We become invisible."

He talked about the stuff he'd learned in Lebanon during the civil war—from Hizballah itself, how Hizballah created their own protective covering by constantly moving between houses, changing cars and routes, staying off the telephone and radios, and never patronizing any one establishment exclusively. "Why can't we do the same?" he said, smiling.

Bob relit his cigar, sending up a fat column of smoke that crouched over the table. The cigar looked Cuban. I wondered where he'd gotten it. Probably in Sarajevo's black market, where you could find anything from machine guns to stolen cars.

That was pretty much it for the first meeting. I wouldn't see Bob again until this day: in front of Split airport, leading me toward a car you can see from the surface of the moon. I throw my bag into the back of the station wagon and climb in the passenger side. So much for being invisible, I think.

We start the five-hour drive to Sarajevo not saying a word. Bob breaks the silence by telling me how he's rented the car from a British former military officer who owns a small travel agency in Sarajevo.

"What does he think you do?" I ask.

"It doesn't matter. The point is, *he'll* catch any flak the car draws, not us."

I nod my head, letting him think he's convinced me of the logic of it, and we fall into another long silence. As he darts in and out of a British tank convoy, I can't figure out how he sees to pass.

I wonder about the butter-yellow houses we are passing, with their red tiled roofs. How was it that an incredibly bloody war started in a place like this? These people are modern Europeans, and then one day, I don't know, sitting around watching a national football championship on Eurovision, they picked up axes and started killing each other, Croats slaughtering Serbs, Serbs slaughtering Bosnian Muslims. Aren't they all Slavs? And don't they look alike and speak the same language? It just doesn't make sense to me. But headquarters doesn't really care if I know next to nothing about Bosnia. My job is to surveil the Arab Mujahidin, who showed up here at the beginning of the war. Period.

At Sarajevo's outskirts I point to a trolley stop, telling Bob I'll get off here. He shakes my hand, and I watch his lime-green station wagon as it disappears into traffic. I don't mind when it starts to rain and I reach to pull up the hood of my parka. The fresh air and uncomplicated anonymity feel good.

A week later, headquarters cables that Charlie and I now work for Bob—chasing Hizballah. We're immediately to cut all contact with the embassy and scatter to different houses and apartments around Sarajevo. Charlie finds his own place, and I'm to move temporarily into the safe house Bob works out of until I can find my own apartment.

Charlie drops me off at a two-story house in a village near the airport, a place called Butmir. The house is overgrown with trees and shrubs. One side faces the "green line"—the confrontation line between Serbs and Muslims. It's pockmarked by bullets. The fields around the house are bordered by blue tape with little skulls and crossbones—land mines.

Bob comes out of the dark house and grabs my duffel bag. Inside, he gives me a quick tour. The owners fled at the beginning of the war, he says, which explains the thick coating of dust everywhere. The food in the refrigerator is calcified. A couple of the windows are shot out. You can see where a bullet came through a window, ricocheted off the ceiling, knocked over some knickknack on the shelf, and lodged in the wall in the living room. There's an upstairs bathroom, but the water's shut off, just as it is to the rest of the village. Bob takes me back downstairs and points at a hose coming through the window of the downstairs laundry room. It's connected to an irrigation pipe off Igman, the mountain that sits just southwest of Sarajevo. He says the showers wake you up fast. I turn it on. The water's icy. The hose is the only way to flush the toilet.

It's completely dark now. Bob turns on the light, but tells me not to get used to it. The electricity goes off in a half hour, and there's no generator or flashlights. I say good night, go downstairs to my bedroom, pull the dusty sheets off the bed, and spread out my sleeping bag. As Bob promised, the lights flicker off, and I lie there in the black. Just as I close my eyes, a machine gun fires in the distance, from the direction of the green line. An angry fusillade answers. I sit up expecting Bob to come out of his room. But there's not a sound. A rocket explodes in the direction of the airport. I wonder if this isn't the start of something serious, like a Serbian attack on Sarajevo. I don't hear a sound from Bob's room, and can only think he's sleeping through it.

I zip up my sleeping bag. If it isn't going to bother him, it's not going to bother me. After an hour the shooting tapers off and stops. The last thing I remember before falling asleep is that I haven't seen the lime-green station wagon. It seems to have been replaced by an old Toyota Land Cruiser with rust-chewed doors and a cracked windshield. That's a start.

ONE

General Aoun took refuge in the French Embassy in October 1990 after Lebanon's Government called in Syrian air and ground forces to flush him out of his bunker at the presidential palace in Baabda, a suburb of Beirut. About 750 people were killed in the battle, one of the worst in Lebanon's 15-year civil war.

The defeat of General Aoun and the 15,000 men in his Christian faction allowed the Government to begin restoring peace and reaffirmed Syria's role as a powerbroker in Lebanon.

—*New York Times*, August 30, 1991

Damascus, Syria, October 1990: **BOB**

When the Lufthansa plane comes to a stop in Syria's capital, Damascus, half a dozen passengers stand up—German businessmen, I'm guessing, trying their luck at selling the Syrian regime something. The rest of the passengers stay put. They're on their way to Jordan's capital, Amman.

Two men in overalls push a rickety stairway across the tarmac. It's late, and most of the lights are off in the squat terminal. I stay in my seat. I know how slow they are here.

As the stewardess starts to crank open the cabin door, the captain comes over the intercom. "Would everyone please retake their seats, and would Mr. Robert please come forward."

The Damascus passengers look at each other to make sure they've understood, and then sit back down, their cabin bags in their laps. I know what they're thinking: Damascus is an exotic place and anything's possible. But it's not a place where you defy authority.

This is clumsy. They should have met me at Immigration,

pulled me aside. But I hurry down the aisle. In my Levi's, V-necked sweater, and T-shirt, I don't look like even a shady businessman. All I can think is that I'm happy Lufthansa wrote down my first name for my last when I boarded in Frankfurt.

A man in a grease-stained blue smock stands at the bottom of the stairs and motions for me to come down and get into his beat-up Syrian Air Peugeot station wagon. I climb into the passenger seat, Mr. Blue Smock behind the wheel. He doesn't say a word as we slowly round the terminal, pass through a cargo gate held open by two Syrian soldiers, and pull up beside three identical black BMWs. A man standing near the middle car opens the rear door, takes my bag, and I get in. In the backseat is a man I know from Geneva—a friend of Ali, the one who set all this in motion. The man shakes my hand, welcoming me to Damascus. To the driver he says, *"Yallah,"* Arabic for "let's go."

It's a little after midnight.

Once we're out of the airport, the three BMWs take off. They've got to be doing ninety, maybe a hundred. We slow down when we come to Damascus, but then, once past the city center, pick up speed again on the Beirut highway. My Geneva friend doesn't say anything, and I look out the window at the passing darkness, thinking about the chain of events that got me here.

Ali had once been a Syrian general. Now he's a very rich businessman with a grand villa above Cannes, a spectacular Geneva mansion, and elegant stopping-off spots all around the world. I'd phoned him out of the blue in Geneva two years earlier, not expecting he'd give me the time of day. Almost ever since, he's been tutoring me on the nuances of Syria and its secretive president, Hafez al-Asad.

Ali's own village had been within walking distance of Asad's. His father knew Asad's father well. Ali said that unless I understood these small villages in the Alawite mountains, I could never understand Asad's Syria. "It's all relationships, loyalty, trust."

Only a few days earlier, I'd stopped by Ali's Geneva place just as the news arrived that the American embassy in Beirut was closing because of a flare-up of fighting in Lebanon—and Syria's threat to intervene with its army to stop it. Ali sighed, saying a renewal of Lebanon's civil war was in neither America's nor Syria's interest. It was rare that our two countries shared a common interest, he said. This was one such time.

Ali explained to me something I already knew: that the man intent on dragging Lebanon into a new civil war was General Aoun, a Maronite Christian and the former commander of the Lebanese army. As we spoke, Aoun was trying to enlist his fellow Christians in an all-out war against Syria. In particular, Aoun wanted the backing of the commander of the Lebanese Forces, a Christian militia. Aoun had told the Lebanese Forces commander that the United States fully backed him. It wasn't true, but, as I told Ali, there wasn't anything the United States could do about it now because we no longer had an embassy in Beirut to tell the Lebanese Forces commander differently.

Ali asked me if I'd go to Lebanon to tell the Lebanese Forces commander that Aoun was a liar. He'd believe an American official. At first I didn't think Ali was serious. The airport was closed, and the Syrian border tricky to cross. But Ali said he could arrange it. He'd been true to his word.

Sometime after one in the morning, we begin to ascend into the mountains between Syria and Lebanon. At the border, the convoy veers to the right, onto the military road. A soldier watches us silently. As soon as we're through, I turn around and see him closing the gate behind us.

The Lebanese side of the border is empty, a no-man's-land,

and now it's a straight shot through the Biqa' Valley. At a little after 2:00 a.m, we start up a narrow road into the mountains. We go only half a mile when the first BMW stops, and my traveling companion finally breaks his silence. He tells me he'll soon leave me, and a Captain Walid will take me the rest of the way.

Another mile up the road we stop again, at the edge of a village.

Before I can get out, an old Mercedes pulls up next to us. A man in jeans and a collared shirt gets out and introduces himself to me as Captain Walid. He doesn't say it, but I know he's Syrian intelligence. He opens the back door of the Mercedes, and I get in. Captain Walid gets in the front, next to the driver. The driver doesn't look at me, and we start.

The road up into the mountains is one lane, large stretches of it rough. It's too dark to see if the villages are inhabited or even where we are, but the shelled-out buildings say we're close to the confrontation lines. After a mile the driver gets out to push a couple of boulders off the road, the only thing that separates the Syrian army from the Christian Lebanese Forces militia. There has been fighting along this front since 1975.

We stop at the far edge of an abandoned village. "Here we wait," Captain Walid says. So I doze off.

When I wake up, it's dawn. The driver is gone, and Captain Walid's staring straight ahead. I've no idea what he's looking at, and I close my eyes to see if I can get back to sleep. Maybe five minutes later, Captain Walid says it's time for me to go. He gets out and opens the door for me.

Above us on the road, about 50 yards away, is a white Isuzu, with a man behind the wheel. I walk toward him. The fresh air wakes me up. I can see down in the Biqa'. It's hard to tell, but I think we're in the mountains across from Tripoli.

I climb into the passenger side of the Isuzu. The driver asks if I'm hungry. Not waiting for an answer, he hands me a *manoushe* wrapped in paper—flat bread garnished with olive oil and thyme.

He finds one for himself in the bag between his legs, and we eat. He starts the car and we take off.

By eight, we're climbing up through a steep pass. At the top there's a sudden expanse of water, the Mediterranean. Tiny fishing boats are coming back into port. The villages we drive down through are now awake, people talking in front of grocery stores and bakeries. Every village has a church and a small, neatly kept municipal park with swing sets.

Another hour later, we reach the coastal Tripoli-Beirut road. We're only on it ten minutes before the Isuzu turns back up into the mountains at the sign to Laqluq, a small summer resort in the mountains.

The chalets and hotels in Laqluq are closed for the season. The driver turns down a gravel road lined by pine trees, and we stop in front of an A-frame house with a Lebanese Forces radio jeep parked outside. When I get out of the Isuzu, I can hear the heavy artillery from the direction of Beirut.

The Lebanese Forces commander—hollow cheeks, bald, dressed in olive green—opens the door for me. "Thank you for coming," he says, shaking my hand. He shows me into the living room, where a beautiful woman in Spandex and a sheepskin vest waits. "My wife," he says. We shake hands too, and the three of us sit in front of the fireplace.

I start. "The United States in no way supports General Aoun. No matter what he says about secret emissaries and a back channel to Washington, there isn't one."

The militia leader's wife interrupts. "If this is to be believed, you know what it means."

"This is strictly a Lebanese affair. It's the Lebanese who must decide what to do with Aoun, follow him into a war with Syria or remove him. Either way, expect no support from the United States."

Just then, we stop to listen to a volley of artillery coming from the mountain above us. To have the range to hit Beirut from here, the guns must be 155 mm.

"Why is he saying he has American support?" the militia leader asks.

"He's a liar."

"Can we trust you?" his wife asks.

"You'll have to decide that on your own."

When we finish, the Isuzu is waiting outside. If I'm lucky, I'll make it back to Damascus by dark.

I don't know if my message had anything to do with it, but a week later a battle erupts between the Lebanese Forces and army units loyal to General Aoun. Aoun loses and takes refuge in the French embassy. The U.S. never lifts a finger to help either side.

It's odd. In this business, we lie all the time, live with false identities. We suck the lifeblood out of our sources, pillage our contacts. Every arrangement has a twist; every favor comes with an IOU. But in the end, it all comes down to what Ali was talking about in a slightly different context: relationships, loyalty, trust. You have to tend to the human element. Without that, there's nothing.

TWO

Did that James Bond movie marathon have you dreaming of being a secret agent? If you're a U.S. citizen, and want to work with the nation's top career choice for aspiring spies, read on. But first, however, there is much to know. First, the Directorate of Operations, or "clandestine service" (the branch that includes spies) makes up only a small percentage of the CIA; most employees hold fairly mundane office jobs. Second, the selection process for any job there is rigorous, and even if your experience and education qualifies you, you can be turned down for many reasons. Still want to give it a go? Here's how!

Stay squeaky clean. The CIA requires security clearances for all positions, and you'll need to pass a very thorough background check to obtain this. It's not public exactly what the background checks entail, but generally, you must be a model citizen starting quite young. Avoid criminal activities; be responsible, ethical and dependable at work; maintain good credit; avoid gambling; be trustworthy; and be faithful to your spouse and the United States. You don't need to be perfect, but the CIA places very high importance on personal integrity, sound judgment, and loyalty to your country. Your parents *and* friends must also be as squeaky clean as possible!

—www.wikihow.com/Become-a-CIA-Agent

Los Angeles, June 1991: DAYNA

Two months after I start working for the CIA in Los Angeles, I decide that it's crazy the way they have us racing all over L.A., going from one background investigation to the next. Wouldn't it make a lot more sense to assign interviews near where we live?

It would cut down on the driving by half and, I don't know, double the number of cases we clear in a month.

I live in Corona del Mar, a beach town an hour south of L.A., or at least when there's no traffic. Logically, my cases should be in Orange County. But the way they have it, I'll catch a case, say, in the San Fernando Valley, three hours away. The next day it's Santa Monica, which puts me on the freeway almost as long. In the meantime, an agent who lives in North Hollywood is assigned a case in Laguna Beach. He ends up making the same slog I do, only in the opposite direction.

True, I know L.A. freeways better than the people who built them. In my sleep I can navigate the 5, the 405, the 605, the 110, the 710, the 91, the 10, the 134, the 101, and the 210. I can tell you exactly how many minutes it is from the chalk-colored Best Western Royal Palace on the 405 to the Garden Grove exit. I know every off-ramp to Redondo Beach, the shortest way to TRW, every backstreet to Northrop Grumman and Lockheed. I still laugh at the stale office joke that if you can't drive, read a Thomas Guide to L.A., and eat an In-N-Out Burger at the same time, you're not working hard enough. I can do all that, but do I want to?

At first I thought screening people applying for a CIA job would be interesting. But soon enough I found out that the job comes down to looking for the unappetizing mess in people's lives. Like a lot of other outfits, the CIA attracts misfits along with very bright, talented people. My job is to dig deep into an applicant's life, find out if there really is a mess, and then let Langley decide whether the mess is going to lead to stealing or spilling the nation's secrets.

I interview their bosses, co-workers, friends, and ex-friends, as many as I can find from the last fifteen years of their lives. I run police checks in every city in which they've lived, worked, or gone to school. It helps that people will tell you all sorts of things when you flash a badge at them, things they wouldn't tell anyone else.

Maybe they think you can arrest them or something—I can't—or maybe they're just scared of the CIA. It helps too, that I'm a girl. Women are more disarming when they ask the hard questions.

Usually the first thing I do in a background investigation is talk to the applicant's boss, even though I know bosses are uncomfortable offering the unvarnished truth. Who wants to admit they have a lousy or crooked employee working for them? Of course, sometimes they're happy to try to foist off their losers on the CIA.

Neighbors are more forthcoming, and so are teachers and co-workers. But the real gold mines are ex-spouses and ex-lovers. They're more than happy to talk about their exes' dirty secrets. By now I'm pretty sure I've seen it all: alcoholics, pedophiles, adulterers, wife beaters, tax cheats, embezzlers. I've come across perversions so strange I have to look them up in the dictionary.

Another class of people the CIA won't hire is congenital liars, the kind who lie about the size of the fish they've caught. I can't miss the irony that an organization that lies for a living won't hire men and women born to the task, but I guess the CIA prefers to train its own to lie.

The main objective of my job, of course, is to keep foreign spies—moles—from infiltrating the CIA. Moles are as rare as a black swan, but CIA security has caught its share.

One of the more notorious cases before I was hired was that of Edward Lee Howard, an operative who was on his way to Moscow when the unexpected happened. Like anyone assigned there, he was administered a special polygraph—"hooked up to the box," as we say. The agent asked Howard if he'd committed a crime since joining the CIA. Howard said no.

The polygraph measures heartbeat, blood pressure, and perspiration. Howard sent the needles quivering on all three fronts, up and down the rolling graph paper. The agent watched the needles for a second and told Howard that he seemed to be having a problem with the question. Howard asked if he'd unhook him so he could talk off the record.

Howard told the story of how, a couple of weeks before, he'd been on a plane, a domestic flight. A lady sitting next to him got up to go to the bathroom, leaving her purse on her seat. Howard looked around at the other passengers, made sure they were deep into books or nodding off, then reached into her purse and grabbed her wallet. He took out a twenty-dollar bill, pocketed it, and put the wallet back in her purse.

The agent couldn't believe what he was hearing. "Why would you do that?" he asked.

The question surprised Howard. He saw absolutely nothing wrong with stealing the money. It was only twenty dollars. But the real point was that he'd soon be on Moscow's streets, watched every minute of the day by the KGB. Howard said he'd needed to steel his nerves, and this had been the perfect opportunity. The money was nothing when it came to America's national security.

The conversation, of course, wasn't off the record. There's no such thing as off the record in the CIA. Howard was fired, and he later volunteered to spy for the KGB. When the FBI found out, Howard fled to Russia, where he died of a broken neck. But that's another story.

Edward Lee Howard, though, was the exception, not the rule. Most people get through a background investigation fairly smoothly, which leaves me, aka CIA security, in the uncomfortable position of living for a "Denial"—the turndown of a top secret security clearance. A denial is where recognition comes in, and promotions. But, as I said, denials are few and far between, and short of that, it comes down to the number of cases you clear in a month—in other words, how efficiently you get around the L.A. freeways.

❖

I finally get the nerve to bring up all the pointless road time with my boss, Ed. "Is there some reason we do it this way?" I ask, plopping down in the chair in his cubicle.

Ed's a big guy with a surly baby face. He's always been frank with me, and I like him. I have the impression he knows his way around the government. His father worked for the State Department, and he grew up in Washington, D.C.

Ed agrees with me that it doesn't make any sense. He tells me to bring it up at the next staff meeting with Carol, the agent in charge in Los Angeles. Carol is a pinched woman of few words, and I've never really talked with her, but Ed tells me not to worry. He'll speak up too.

I watch nervously as the twenty or so agents in our office start gathering in the pen. It's not just Carol I've been quiet around. I've never said a single word at any of these meetings. Today I stand in the back as usual. Carol walks in, says good morning, and starts in about keeping better track of mileage, auto maintenance, coordinating leave, and some other bureaucratic ministering from Washington. As she gets to the end, I'm even more anxious.

"Any questions?" Carol asks. It's the way she lowers the boom on every staff meeting—more a dare than a question.

I wait to see if anyone's going to say anything and then raise my hand, at half-mast. I'm surprised she even sees me. "Yes?" she says. Carol stands up on her toes to see me better.

"Carol, do you think there's a possibility that cases could be assigned nearer to where we live?" I say. Carol cups her ear as if she can't hear me. I force myself to raise my voice. "To cut down on driving time?"

Carol's face is a clenched fist. It's as if I'd asked her why her shoes don't match her purse. She turns around without saying a word and goes back to her office. When she reappears ten seconds later, she has a piece of paper rolled up in her hand.

"I don't see why you are complaining," she says, sweeping

the room with a gaze rather than looking at me. She unfurls the paper and holds it between her forefinger and her thumb, waving it in my direction. "From what I can see of your caseload, it looks pretty doable to me."

That's not what I asked, of course, but I don't say anything. Instead, I wilt into the fiberboard wall behind me, my face on fire.

Afterward I go into Ed's office. "I'm sorry I told you to bring it up," he says. "I guess it's always been done this way, and it always will be."

I want to ask him why he didn't say anything at the meeting, but I let it go. As Lieutenant Escobar says in the great Robert Towne script, "Forget it, Jake. It's Chinatown."

THREE

Cannabis in Europe is usually available in the forms hash and marihuana. Although marihuana is gaining in popularity, hash is still predominant in Europe. A substantial part of hash on the European market originates from Morocco. Traditionally, the mountainous Rif area in northern Morocco has been a production region for cannabis, mainly destined for local consumption. Since a nearby European cannabis market became accessible, the acreage under cultivation in northern Morocco has grown considerably. In 1993 it was estimated that between 64,000 and 74,000 hectares of cannabis were under cultivation in northern Morocco. This would imply the acreage increased tenfold in the period of ten years. Today, Morocco is considered as the world's main cannabis exporter. The potential of Moroccan hash production is estimated to be around 2,000 metric tonnes a year.

—Tim Boekhout van Solinge, "Drug Use and Trafficking in Europe" (1998), www.cedro-uva.org/lib/boekhout.drug.html

Salé, Morocco: **BOB**

Vera, my secretary, is waiting when I come outside, sitting behind the wheel of her Peugeot 505. When she sees me, she flicks her cigarette out the window and waits for me to get in before starting it. She wheels it in a half circle, the tires slithering in the damp sand.

"Which way?" she asks.

I tell her I don't care. She already knows the routine: she drives me north of the capital, Rabat, and drops me off. The more circuitous the route, the better. The trick is to see whether we've picked up a tail or not.

Vera heads north on the beach road, turns right on a road called Tareq el Marsa, and then left on the N-1, the highway to Tangiers. We immediately get stuck behind a file of trucks. She lights a cigarette, rolling down the window to let the smoke out. She asks how far I want to go. I tell her Kenitra, the first big town between Rabat and Tangiers. She doesn't say anything, but I can tell she's pissed. It's bridge night, and now she's going to miss it.

I've always suspected that Vera thinks a spy's craft is hocus-pocus. Do the Moroccans really care about the CIA that much? I don't know, but I don't intend to find out by getting followed to a meeting with an informant.

I slump down in the seat so I can get a better angle on my side mirror. The line of lights behind us is what you usually find on the Tangiers road this time of night—trucks moving when it's cooler. A car comes out from between the trucks, ducks back to avoid an oncoming truck, and then comes back out to pass. It's now right on us, flashing its light. Vera moves over a foot and it passes. And then it's back to only us and the trucks again.

At Kenitra, Vera takes the airport road. She stops by the side of the Oued Sebou, a rotting estuary. I get out, and the stench almost floors me. In the dome light, Vera's eyes look like they're frozen open wide. She once told me it was from a cheap face-lift in Bombay. I let her turn around and drive away before I walk back toward Kenitra.

The town's quiet, a few people cutting through the small streets, shadows on shadows. I take a narrow road that runs parallel to the airport road until I come to the first big street, Beni Hssen, where I start to look for a taxi. A block from the Safir Hotel, I wave one down and open the front passenger door. The driver moves his dinner off the seat and puts it in the back to make room for me. I tell him to take me to Salé, Rabat's old sister city, which once was ruled by Barbary pirates.

There are fewer trucks on the road back to Rabat, but more

cars. I tell the driver to slow down, and he doesn't ask why. When we get to Salé, a mile from where this all began, I direct the driver on to Sidi Moussa, then tell him to stop a quarter-mile down the road. I leave the money on the dash, paying him too much so he won't argue with me. I hurry across the street and walk down a few short steps into Salé's old city, the medina. With its twisted, narrow alleys, anyone who did not want to lose me would have to keep right on me. I zigzag along a route I know as well as the inhabitants do. I come out on the N-1 side of the medina and cross the road to the Salé train station. The old Fiat's there in the parking lot where it's supposed to be. I fumble in my pocket, find the keys, unlock it, and get in. It coughs and starts on the third try.

The beach road is quiet except for couples parked facing the ocean. I park as close to the water as I can, turning the Fiat so the breeze off the Atlantic passes through the open windows.

I pull the Pepsi out of my coat, and a bar of Toblerone chocolate. It's melted and I lick it off the tinfoil wrapper. The Pepsi is warm. I check my watch. He's late. I turn the radio on, and listen to an imam extolling the promise of the hereafter.

I don't see Salah until the door opens, and he climbs in the passenger side.

"*C'est bien passé?*" he asks. Did everything go OK? Salah's French is good. He went to college, but I don't remember where.

I tell him next time we'll meet farther outside of Rabat, but still along the beach

"So what did they say about it?"

"It's good stuff, you know."

I can't see Salah's face, but I can tell he's happy. I never had any doubt the cocaine was good, pure. After all, it was for resale.

Salah has a pouch over his shoulder. He pulls a plastic shopping bag out and opens it. In the phosphorescent light off the Atlantic, I can see it's white, cellophane-wrapped.

"That's not more, is it?" I ask.

"A half kilo."

"I told you to stop."

"It's from last night's Caracas flight."

"They don't want it."

I think about telling Salah the truth, about how the cable from headquarters told me to cease and desist—we aren't authorized to collect intelligence on narcotics in Morocco. And that's not to mention that no one wants to hear that the king himself is trafficking in it, ferrying tons of coke from Caracas to Casablanca on Royal Air Maroc flights and sending it on to Europe by small airplanes. I decide on a useful lie.

"Salah, we have it covered with someone else. I don't want you thrown out of a helicopter over the Atlantic for nothing. I need you for more important things."

And that's exactly what the palace would do if it caught him spying for the CIA. No one would ever find his body, just one more among the tens of thousands of Moroccans gone missing.

"What do I do with it?" Salah asks.

"Throw it in the ocean when we get done."

"Then what do you need for me to do?"

"There's a lot to do. We'll talk about it at the next meeting."

But the truth is I don't know what to do with an informant inside the palace who's bent on doing something for the United States. In fact, I'm not sure what the CIA is even doing in Morocco. The country's a backwater. And headquarters is right about the cocaine—it's not news about the Moroccan royal family and narcotics. They've been trafficking hashish out of the Rif mountains in northern Morocco for centuries.

I don't say anything, and neither does Salah. We both look straight ahead. I think about how Soviet Central Asia is opening up, a place I have to admit really intrigues me.

❖

I joined the CIA in 1976, served mostly in the Middle East, and somewhere along the way became addicted to political upheaval—civil wars, revolutions, coups d'état, armies on the move. I was in Damascus during a failed coup in the early eighties, and then in Khartoum for a successful one. I was in Lebanon during the civil war. There's nothing more fascinating than seeing a house come down, and the fight to rebuild it.

The chances of anything like this happening in Morocco are zero. In the early seventies, the Moroccan army tried to overthrow the king, but failed. To prevent another attempt, the king eviscerated his army, and so today Morocco is as stable and boring as Switzerland. True, the king is old, but when he dies, it's a given that his eldest son will succeed him. A state funeral and a coronation are as complicated as it's ever going to get here.

It seems to me that what my job is about is trying to understand the messy, unpredictable parts of the world and the raw political passions that drive them, the kind that change history. It's with that in mind I've asked for an assignment to Tajikistan, a small ex-Soviet republic nestled up against the borders of Afghanistan and China. There have been stirrings of an Islamic revolution there. I'm also attracted to the place because mountains cover more than 90 percent of it. The roof of the world, as Tajikistan is called. If it doesn't get too messy, I'll spend my downtime hiking and skiing in them, my favorite pastimes.

Something else you should know about me is that my marriage is going through a dead spot, and my wife and I have decided to live separately. She and our three children will live in France, where we've just bought an old house. The place is pretty much a wreck, but the way it sits in the grapevines on a steep hill, it has real potential. The extra money I make in Tajikistan will go to fixing it up. My wife and I believe that with time and distance, things will work out between us.

On the other hand, I never imagined it would come to this.

When we first met in 1982 in Damascus, Syria, she was a secretary at the embassy, working for the State Department, a real trooper. We both loved Syria and talked about going to more places like it together. But three children quickly followed—two born in Washington, D.C., and the last in Paris—and, well, life changed. Now my onetime would-be partner in seeing the world is completely consumed by them, as any mother would understand. And although she never puts it in these terms, she doesn't care where I go or what I do. Coincidentally, Tajikistan is what's called a "separation tour"—spouses and children can't come along or even visit. It's too dangerous.

FOUR

Typical duties of the Protective Agent include deploying worldwide to perform sensitive operations in support of protective requirements. Protective Agents are consistently called upon to deploy and participate in training and operational assignments, and are expected to work long hours and deploy for periods from 45 to 60 days in length. Minimum requirements include a high school diploma or the equivalent, and applicants must be at least 21 years old, physically fit and possess a valid driver's license. Extensive military, security, or law enforcement experience, preferably in a military special operations branch, protective operations, or as S.W.A.T officers, with a minimum of 7 years combined experience. A bachelors degree or higher is preferred. Applicant should possess excellent oral and written communication and analytical skills, have high levels of integrity, trustworthiness and loyalty to the United States.

—www.cia.gov/careers/opportunities/support-professional/
protective-agent.html

Los Angeles: **DAYNA**

One morning I'm at my desk, planning my day with the Thomas Guide close at hand, when I look up to see Carol standing over me. "You got a second?" she asks. She's looking more irritated than usual. As I follow her into her office, I search my mind for what I could have done wrong.

"Close the door," she says.

I sit down.

She picks up a cable from her desk and reads it silently as if seeing it for the first time. "If you don't want to do this," she says, "just tell them no." She hands me the cable with two fingers, as if it were a dirty Kleenex. Before I can even start reading, she says, "You know you'd have to leave L.A."

I read the first line and my heart starts to race. It's from headquarters, asking if I want to go to the CIA's basic training for bodyguards and shooters—six months of grueling day-and-night drilling in pistols, shotguns, automatic weapons, hand-to-hand combat, high-speed driving, killing someone by shoving a pencil up through their hard palate. It's all the guys in the office can talk about, and what most of them joined the CIA for in the first place. At the end it means a posting to Washington, along with a lot of travel overseas. Unlike the FBI, the CIA is all about going overseas.

I understand what Carol's getting at when she says I'd have to leave L.A. I'm married, and the job that comes out of this course won't be the kind where a spouse can exactly tag along. And even if my husband could, I know mine wouldn't. He's a municipal court judge, not exactly a portable job. In other words, I'll either be going alone or not at all.

Carol taps her desk with the eraser end of a pencil to get my attention. I'm about to ask "Why me?" when Carol answers the question herself.

"We nominated you because *they* asked us to nominate another woman from this office. Do you want it or don't you?"

The other woman Carol is talking about is Lara, who went to the same course last year. A tough, energetic blonde, Lara met her husband, Brad, in the L.A. office. She took Brad with her when she left. Since they both worked for the CIA, it made perfect sense. But that didn't stop Carol from complaining about losing them.

I take a quick glance around at the scuffed brown Formica tables, the mismatched chairs, the dusty Wang computers, the IBM Selectric typewriters, the shabby carpets, the piles of telephone books, the tattered maps on the bookshelves, the grimy windows that look down on an auto mall. *Yeah, I want it*, I think. *I want it very badly.*

I'm not about to say this to Carol, but I wonder if I can really do this. The only time I held a real gun was when I first went to Washington right after the CIA hired me. They took us out to a range and had us fire at a target. But no one cared if we hit it or not.

"Well?" Carol says.

I try to hide my excitement, not sure she doesn't have some way to spike it, out of spite or something. Who knows what she would do not to lose another agent?

Just as Carol reaches to take back the cable, I pull it back. "Yes. I'll do it."

I leave early, walking out into the gray-glazed sun, looking for my government sedan parked in among the discounted Toyota Corollas, overflow inventory from the dealer next door. I'm still trying not to think about what it means for my marriage and how unfair it is that I got the training instead of one of the guys. Instead, I wonder whose idea it was to put us at the back of an auto mall. I guess something to do with hiding behind bleak anonymity.

I get home before my husband. I put my briefcase down and go out in the backyard to feed my two turtles. As soon as they hear me, they come out from behind their pond and waddle over. I have lettuce for them.

There's almost a view of the ocean from here. If you walk a block toward the beach you can see sailboats coming back down the channel at the end of the day. At night you can hear the bell buoy and the seals barking. It's six blocks from my parents' house, and a five-minute walk to the yacht club where my husband and I first met. It's a beautiful house, one my husband owned before we married.

Corona del Mar is the only home I've ever known, a magical place. I grew up on the water, racing up and down the Balboa Channel in my seven-foot Sabot sailboat, darting between the moored boats, sitting on the docks eating lunch with my friends, our feet dangling in the water. By high school, if we weren't sailing or in school, we were hanging out at Lifeguard Station Number 5, across the jetty from the Wedge, maybe the best bodysurfing beach in the world.

My husband spent most of his life here too, and we share a lot of friends from before our marriage. He loves to golf, and spend his vacations close to home, usually in Palm Springs. He's always told me he'll never move; it's just too nice here.

I myself could see settling down in this place, at least when I'm older. But frankly, life right now feels a little too scripted, too predictable, and, well, maybe just a little too comfortable. Every time I walk up to Albertson's, the grocery store on the Pacific Coast Highway, and talk to the checkers—many of whom I went to high school with—I'm reminded of how self-contained the world I live in is. I know there has to be more out there.

When I was at graduate school at UCLA, I interned as a social worker counseling gang members locked up in juvenile hall. Their childhoods were a nightmare of abandonment and hopelessness, and many were in for rape and murder. One was only eight. Another told me how his father had punished him by attaching jumper cables to his nipples. Like people who slow down to look at a car wreck, I was transfixed, and reminded of something I should have known a long time ago: not everyone grows up as comfortably as I did. What else didn't I know?

I'm not sure what I imagined when I first picked up a CIA application at the job fair at UCLA. Working in some exotic foreign place where the dogs bark all night and the moon is always full?

Well, I wasn't *that* romantic. But I did think of CIA work as intriguing, maybe even vital. At the very least, I expected a world less tidy and confined.

But working for the CIA in Los Angeles turns out to be all about looking into lives that aren't a whole lot different from mine. It's like boarding a bus expecting to wake up in a new city, but instead making it only to the end of the block.

When my husband comes home, I wait until he gets his drink and sits down in the lawn chair where he likes to read. I sit in the chair next to him, pick up a magazine, and then put it down.

"They offered me a new job," I finally say.

He looks over at me. "That's interesting."

As I tell him what I can about the course, he listens, nodding his head. Every once and a while he stirs his scotch with his finger.

At one point I pause to see if he wants to ask me anything. But he only keeps looking at me, waiting for me to finish. I don't know what I want him to say. Tell me not to go and stay here with him?

He smiles when I'm finished. "That's fabulous." I can tell he's genuinely excited for me.

"Maybe I should just go to law school here," I say. It's something I've thought about for a while.

"Trust me, you don't want to go to law school, and besides, you'd be miserable to live with."

I finally get out what's been nagging at me since I found out about the course this morning. "It would mean I'd be based in Washington."

He laughs, good-naturedly. "Well, I can visit, right?"

FIVE

The Republic of Tajikistan gained its independence during the breakup of the USSR and is part of former Soviet Central Asia nestled between Kyrgyzstan and Uzbekistan to the north and west, Afghanistan to the south, and China to the east.

Covering an area slightly smaller than the state of Wisconsin, Tajikistan is home to some of the highest mountains in the world, including parts of the Kunlun, Himalayan, Tienshan, and Pamir Ranges. Ninety-three percent of the country is mountainous with altitudes ranging from 1,000 feet to 25,000 feet, with fully 50 percent of Tajikistan's territory at elevations above 10,000 feet.

Within the Tajik population, important social divisions exist according to an individual's place of origin. Tajiks separate themselves into Kulyabis, Gharmis/Karategins, Khojandis, Pamiris, Bukharans, and Samarkandis, as well as a host of other names based on location of origin. The Kulyabis, who were not a powerful group during the Soviet era, provided the muscle to win the civil war. Since 1993, they have dominated the government, and there has been a steady migration of Kulyabis from the underdeveloped south to the capital. President Rahmonov is a Dangaran Kulyabi. Conversely, the traditionally powerful Soghd group experienced a decline in power in the central government.

—www.ediplomat.com/np/post_reports/pr_tj.htm

Dushanbe, Tajikistan: **BOB**

Beware of what you wish for. It's a little after nine when a friend with the UN knocks at my door, breathless. "There's been an attack on the airport," he says. "A bad one."

I immediately call up a contact at the ministry of the interior to ask what he knows about it. He's heard the same thing, so I try calling some other people, but can't find anyone in.

I have a C-130 transport plane coming in this afternoon. On board are two pallets of food, books, and other stuff to get us through the next month. The plane is supposed to be on the ground for no longer than an hour, but now I can't risk letting it land, even if the airport gives permission. I run upstairs to the communication center and type out a one-sentence cable to my counterpart in neighboring Tashkent, Uzbekistan, where the C-130 is waiting to take off: *There has been an attack on Dushanbe airport and we cannot allow clearance at this time.* Five minutes after my communicator sends the cable, a return one from Tashkent confirms that the plane has been diverted.

I run downstairs and jump into my car to have a look for myself. Even if I can't make it all the way to the airport, I'll be able to tell from the smoke how bad the attack was.

As I get closer, it strikes me as odd that there are no police, fire trucks, or ambulances racing down the road. When I stop and roll down the window to listen, I hear a plane taking off. I keep driving until I come to a policeman standing by the road. I ask him what happened with the attack. "What attack?" he asks, genuinely puzzled. I drive into the airport and stop in front of the terminal, where people are coming and going as usual.

I never do find out how the rumor started.

I've been in Tajikistan nine months now, and still live in Dushanbe's old Communist Party hotel, the Oktyabrskaya. It's off-the-rack Soviet sixties architecture, constructed of cheap concrete. Water streaks and cracks run down the side. And it's an even bigger dump inside. The wallpaper's bubbled, the curtains filthy. Plaster crumbles off the walls. There's a plague of cigarette burns on the furniture. The city water goes off for a week at a time, and there never is any hot water. Mornings I don't bother pulling the curtains in my room because the view is a dusty park with scorched grass and a couple of dead maples and poplars.

My room is on the third floor, at the end of a corridor I share with the Russian embassy. Two Russian soldiers with automatic weapons sit behind a desk at the stairwell. Every couple of weeks I give them a carton of Marlboros, and now they know me by my first name. The Russian diplomats I pass in the hallway smile at me, not seeming to mind my living in their midst. The bloom isn't yet off glasnost.

I'm still struck by the irony of holing up in the back of a Russian embassy. Since its founding in 1947, the CIA spied on the Russians. They were *the* enemy. We spent our lives trying to recruit them as moles, and they us. And now all of a sudden we're on the same side, in my case I'm practically a roommate. We depend on the Russian division here to stanch the chaos sloshing across the border from Afghanistan. The dumb fear is that if the Russians fail, one Central Asian country after another will fall to the Mujahidin. An Islamic domino effect.

Still, things are pretty calm these days. The occasional tank rumbling down Dushanbe's main street is about the only reminder that Tajikistan is in the middle of a civil war. Russia's 201st Motorized Rifle Division is gradually retaking ground, one village at a time, moving up into the rebel sanctuaries high in the Pamir mountains. But the rebels keep moving up higher and higher. Now it would take a three-day climb just to reach them, too high even for Russian helicopters.

The Russian soldiers call the rebels the *dukhi*—the ghosts, the same word the Soviets used for the Afghan Mujahidin, who also had a knack of disappearing into thin air. The Russians can't even tell me who the rebels' commander is. You know it's a messy war when you don't even know who the king of the barbarians is.

When I first got to Tajikistan, "Central Asia" for me was shorthand for "exotic." All I had to do was close my eyes, and I could conjure up the steppe empires, the Silk Road, Alexander the Great's marches up and down the Pamirs. It was here that Alexander found a wife, Roxanne, one of history's great beauties. Bucephalus, Alexander's horse, died not far north of Dushanbe, and the myth is that at midnight, if you're lucky, you will see its ghost running around a certain mountain lake.

I needed only a day walking around the capital to figure out that I got the "exotic" wrong. There is no old Dushanbe. There's no trace of the Silk Route, or of Alexander the Great and the other ancient empires that once rivaled Greece and Rome. I drove up to the lake where Alexander's horse supposedly died. But there wasn't an epigraph or anything else to mark it. History deleted Central Asia's empires, and no one more efficiently than the Soviets.

That's what I've really learned here: what great haters Marx, Lenin, and Stalin were. They hated Central Asian culture, its babel of languages, its religions, and in particular Islam. No doubt they hated the mysterious East itself. The Marxists believed that before they could build their delusional utopia they had to efface from the earth every trace of ancient Central Asia. Over the years, Soviet proconsuls flattened the old Mogul forts, the mosques, the bazaars, and the caravanserai, and turned the ancient cities of Samarkand and Bokhara into cheap theme parks.

Now the Soviets are gone, but the ex-Communists have kept their grip on Dushanbe. Like the old Soviet apparatchiks, they race around in their Zils and Volgas, tailed by police chase cars with flashing blue lights on the top. They all live in a party compound. In their dull, somber suits they remind me of Brezhnev. I once sat next to the Tajik president at a state dinner. A taciturn, colorless man, he said maybe two words the entire time. I caught him pouring his vodka into the planted palm behind him so he wouldn't get drunk like everyone else.

I'm starting to have my own idea why Dushanbe's water shuts off, and it has nothing to do with the government's explanation about routine cleaning and flushing. I suspect deeper machinations at play. In Central Asia, he who controls the water is he who rules. That once meant the ancient irrigation canals, but now it's a city's water supply. My theory is that the rebels sabotage Dushanbe's water to undermine the legitimacy of the ex-Communists. If they can turn it off permanently, the city falls.

Granted, it's a theory easier to believe than to prove, but I've been flying by the seat of my pants ever since I got here. The fact is, I have only the haziest understanding of Central Asia, or even of Tajikistan and its civil war. The place is a spy's nightmare; American baseline knowledge is zero.

As an example, we're not even sure who the important political players are in Tajikistan. We know who the president is, of course, the man I sat next to at dinner, and the ministers. But there's a small, secretive clique that really runs the country. A Central Asian scholar at Harvard, Richard Frye, calls these cliques "charismatic clans"—tight-knit extended families who ruthlessly look to their own for survival. Nationalism and ideology come into play only when it serves the interest of the clan.

So far, so good, but all we know about the charismatic clan that runs Tajikistan is that it can be traced to Kulyab Province, or, to be precise, a village called Baljuan. The president is only the clan's face, while a handful of members in the shadows run the army and the security services. Kulyab was the site of a former Tsarist penal colony, and today many Tajiks look at the Kulyabis as a band of unreconstructed criminals.

From time to time I stop by the door of the Russian political officer, hoping he can clear up the question of the Kulyabis for me. After all, the Russians have been here for more than a century, while I'm still short of year one. But all I get out of my visits is a cup of tea and a cookie.

The fortunate side of it all is that Washington doesn't really care whether I understand the place or not. I don't have a shred of evidence for it, but my hunch is that James Baker, George H. W. Bush's secretary of state, opened our embassy in Dushanbe solely to remind the Russians that Tajikistan is no longer a piece of their empire. An embassy here is an act of pure defiance. The fact that the Russian 201st is all that keeps the peace and prevents our plucky embassy from being sacked and burned to the ground is a detail Washington doesn't like to consider.

SIX

Most of the highly experienced officers in the study, in contrast, concentrated their visual focus on the target/suspect, catching only a fast glimpse of their sights in their peripheral vision and relying primarily on "an unconscious kinesthetic sense to know that their gun is up and positioned properly."

In the recent study . . . elite officers were able to read danger cues early on and anticipate the suspect's actions ahead of time so they could stay ahead of the fight. They knew where a gun was likely to appear and were focused there before it did. So they were able to get protective rounds off sooner than the suspect and sooner than the rookies.

That anticipatory skill can only be developed through experience. At the training level, that means extensive experience with dynamic force-on-force encounters and realistic simulations in which you learn by "being there" over and over again in a wide variety of encounters what to expect and how to look for and recognize danger cues.

—Force Science Research Center

Northern Virginia: **DAYNA**

t's still dark when a white van with government plates drives under the Marriott's portico and pulls up next to me. The driver's window slides down a couple of inches. "You Dayna?" It's dark, and all I can see of him is the Oakley wraparound sunglasses cocked on his forehead. He doesn't wait for my answer. "Get in. We're late."

I walk around and open the panel door to find nine guys asleep, backpacks and duffel bags piled everywhere. The only place free is occupied by a leg. The guy it belongs to wakes up and looks at me blankly. He doesn't move, and I look at the driver for help. Finally the guy grumbles and moves his leg. I squeeze in, but there's no place for my duffel bag, and I hold it on my lap.

As we drive away from the Marriott, someone in the back tells a crude joke. I don't laugh, and no one else does, either. I can only think it was meant for me. I close my eyes; this is going to be a very long one-and-a-half-hour drive, and I don't even want to think about the coming months. I try to occupy my mind by going through the list of things they told me to bring, from a web belt to polarized shooting glasses. I also brought one of those all-in-one pocket tools, a Leatherman. I'm definitely my father's daughter, the civil engineer who never went far from home without some sort of tool.

We drive west on Route 50 in silence until the driver starts flipping through radio stations, probably more to keep awake than anything else. Just as it turns light, he stops in front of a grim little McDonald's in a mini-mall. I let the guys go ahead, watching them stretch and walk across the parking lot. Their patched and sun-bleached fatigues and scuffed desert boots make them look like stragglers from some defeated army heading home. In fact, many of them were in the Gulf War.

I wince when I catch one of the guys studying my laced Timberlands. I bought them the day before at the Tysons Corner mall, and there's not a scratch on them. I'm already self-conscious about my hair pulled back in a ponytail, my new black military-chic rollneck sweater, and my tan cargo pants. The darts I sewed in the butt to hold them up make it look like I'm auditioning for a slightly more rugged J. Crew catalog.

After another thirty-minute drive, the van turns off Route 50 onto a two-lane rural road. We pass a few white clapboard houses with enclosed porches and American flags out front. It's late October, the trees are bare, and piles of copper leaves blow across the road. The van startles a deer that bolts into the underbrush.

We turn down a gravel road where there's a neatly painted sign that says simply PRIVATE. A mile farther down, the van comes to a guard blockhouse with a ten-foot drop barrier, a spinning yellow light on top. On either side of the blockhouse runs a chain-link fence with razor wire on the top. You can't mistake the place for anything other than a government base.

A guard in a camouflage uniform opens the van's panel door, and we hold up our blue badges for him to see. He first checks to make sure the badge numbers match the numbers on the paper on his clipboard. (There are no names on CIA badges.) Then he matches the pictures on our badges with our faces. From somewhere on the base I hear a slow, throaty *dah-dah-dah*. A heavy machine gun.

We drive into some pine woods and stop in front of a rickety wooden building with dirt floors. A wooden overhang serves as a roof for an outdoor classroom set with high metal chairs and waist-high tables.

There's a clump of students out front talking, Styrofoam coffee cups in their hands. In the middle of them is a girl in faded camies, her boots as scuffed as the guys, with a pair of yellow range glasses on top of her head. The only thing that sets her off is a pair of pearl earrings. It's the first familiar thing I've seen all morning, and my nerves ease up a bit.

I walk over, and she sticks out her hand to me. "Hi, Sunshine, I'm Cheri."

I must look at her a little funny. "Oh, sorry," she says. "I got 'Walking on Sunshine' stuck in my head. So, where'd you learn to shoot?"

She walks over to the coffee urn to get me a cup of coffee, and I follow her.

"I have no idea what I'm doing here," I say, in a voice only Cheri can hear.

Cheri puts her hand on my shoulder. "If you need help, just ask."

Cheri tells me she's here only for a refresher. For the last three years she's been overseas, training foreigners to shoot. This course is like a vacation for her.

Jeff, the head instructor, looks up and down at our tables to make sure we each have a holster and a Glock 9-mm semiautomatic pistol. He's about forty, with a receding hairline, hollow cheeks, and a pair of cold, silver blue eyes. He has a briskness that tells you he's run this course more times than he cares to remember.

"Small-town cops wear their weapons on their hips," he says. "It's not the way we do it here. You holster your weapon on the small of your back."

I watch the others as they undo their web belts and thread their holsters through them to the back. I do the same. I remember my Leatherman, take it off, and thread it back on my belt on the left side.

I wait until everyone else grabs his Glock off the table before I pick up mine. I follow suit as they pop out the magazine, rack back the slide, and hold the weapon up to show that the chamber is clear.

"It's a hot range," Jeff says. "Get your ammo."

We line up in front of a table set with boxes of ammunition, and cram fistfuls of rounds into our cargo pockets. Walking to the range, we load fifteen rounds into each of our magazines. Jeff takes us to a ten-foot-high berm with twenty-five black-and-white silhouette paper targets lined up in a row. It's quiet except for the wind whistling through the metal frames. We spread out to pick a target. I take the last one at the end.

"You may dry-fire before you qualify," Jeff shouts.

I've never drawn a gun from a holster, and for a few seconds I watch the others draw their pistols, cup them in their hands, aim, and squeeze the trigger. They do it all in one smooth, even motion, and all very quickly. I try to imitate them, only a lot more slowly. Thank God no one is looking at me.

"Load and make ready," Jeff yells. "One round, two seconds. On the whistle."

Please, please, please, I tell myself. *Just get them all on the paper.* My hand shakes, and my heart pounds. What if I do something really, really stupid—like hit someone else's target.

Jeff blows the whistle, and loud pops fill the range. I force myself not to close my eyes, and concentrate on squeezing the trigger rather than jerking it. It's the one basic I can't forget. The Glock bucks up when I fire, but I bring it back down, and then holster it. I look at my silhouette, but it's too far to see what I hit.

We do this five more times and then move back ten feet and do it again. We shoot from behind a barricade, on both the right and the left. The last thing we do is shoot with our weak hand.

"Unload and show clear!" Jeff yells. We take out the magazines, pull back the slides, and hold our Glocks up in the air for Jeff to see. "Downrange!" he yells.

I walk toward my silhouette with my eyes on the ground. When the time comes for Jeff to count the holes in my target, I hold my breath and stare at his back.

"All there," he finally says.

I look up and count them. I can't believe it. They're all there on the paper! Who cares if half are outside the man's silhouette.

"Next time put them here." Jeff makes a fist and puts it in the middle of the man's torso. "Center mass."

Cheri walks over. "You'll get there, Sunshine. Just a little practice."

And practice is just what we get for the rest of the day, the next day, and the day after that. For a few minutes each morning we start by drawing our unloaded Glocks from our holsters. It's to get a feel for the weapon. Jeff watches, prodding us to move faster and faster. "It's either you or them," he says.

Then there's a live qualification on the silhouette targets. Almost everyone passes on the first day, except for me and a couple of others. "We don't move on to higher-speed stuff until everyone qualifies," Jeff says.

We settle into a routine. Mornings are "live fire" on the paper silhouette targets, and afternoons are on the "pop-up" range—metal targets that only go down when you hit the figure's torso or head. We shoot standing, kneeling, and on our stomachs. One afternoon it rains, but we keep at it. By day three, the Glock starts to feel like an extension of my arm, and I finally qualify, the last to do so.

On Friday morning the Glocks are gone, and 12-gauge shotguns are waiting on our worktables. "One chance to qualify, people," Jeff says. "You won't need more than that anyway." I have no idea why we only get one chance, but from the way everyone stands around joking, planning their weekends, I can tell they all agree this is going to be easy.

I've never picked up a shotgun before, and the moment I fire it, I hate it. It's heavy, loud, and obviously determined to dislocate my shoulder when I pull the trigger. I don't have the strength to hold up the shotgun with my left hand while I fumble in my pocket for shells to reload. It's not like you can set it on the ground to do it.

Jeff tells us we will shoot three rounds (slugs) at twenty-five yards. We then reload three more shells while holding the shotgun pointed at the target, a "combat load," and then fire them. Finally, we will move up to "cover the threat," firing a final three shells at fifteen yards.

Jeff blows the whistle, and I pull the trigger. But the gun doesn't fire. I realize too late that I didn't flick off the safety. My first shot goes way wide, missing the target altogether. I get off the next two shots and then try to reload, but drop a shell on the ground. When Jeff blows the whistle to change position, I haven't even finished loading the third shell. I move forward with everyone else to the fifteen-yard line and shoot three shells. But now I have to combat-load four to make up for the one I dropped. I don't even have time to aim, and can't see if I hit the target. When the whistle blows to fire the last three rounds, I realize too late that I've miscounted, leaving one unfired.

Jeff comes over and takes the shotgun from me. I follow him as he walks up to my target. All my slugs went wide except one. Jeff doesn't need to tell me that I didn't qualify. Or that everyone else has. I already know there's no half-passing this class, and I walk back to my room thinking about the prospect of being sent back to Los Angeles.

There's a knock at my door. It has to be Jeff. I don't answer, and there's another knock, then a girl's voice. It's Cheri.

"I heard," she says, sitting down, one leg over the chair's arm. "Can I tell you a story?"

Two years ago Cheri was in Kuwait on a protection detail. The VIP she was protecting was in a meeting, and she asked a local policeman where the bathroom was. He pointed her down the hall. Rather than a toilet, it was a "Turkish bomb sight"—a hole in the floor with two ribbed places for your feet. When she finished, she pulled the chain hanging from the tank to flush, but instead of flushing, it dumped a gallon of water on her! It was a shower. Her new Ann Taylor suit dripping wet, Cheri was mortified, unsure of what to do. There wasn't even toilet paper to dry off. So she did the only thing she could: she went back and pretended nothing had happened.

"Everyone was too polite to say anything," Cheri says. "And

the moral of the story, Sunshine, is never let them see you sweat. Pretend it never happened."

It's pretty clear by the next week that the idea is to turn up the heat, see who cracks and who doesn't. Today it's high-speed driving.

As I watch the speedometer edge over seventy, the Jamaican instructor, George, says, "Go, girl." George is short with thick glasses and a floating eye—I wonder where the CIA found him. When I hit eighty, he gives me the thumbs-up. "Now we're cooking with gas!"

The car, an old government Crown Vic, loses its footing as we make the first bend. It just wasn't meant for high-speed driving on a racetrack. At the straightaway I pick up speed again, noticing out of the corner of my eye George pulling something out from under his seat. I concentrate on the road, preparing for the next turn, when the windshield goes blank—George has thrust a piece of cardboard in front of me so I can't see the track!

When I hit the brakes, George yells, "Keep your speed, girl." I take it back over seventy, George watching the speedometer. Without warning he pulls the cardboard away, and in front of me is a stack of baled hay. I hit the brakes hard, sending the car sliding sideways into the hay. The Crown Vic comes to a stop in a cloud of straw and dust. "Next time, drive around, girl," George says. "One day there will be a car there."

George then teaches us to run a moving car off the road by driving up alongside it and swerving into its rear quarter panel. At sixty miles an hour, the other car instantly loses traction and spins down the road in a 360-degree circle, the tires smoking. We do that four or five times, and then we take our turn in the car getting run off the road.

There's a week of bailing out of a moving car, rolling across the ground, coming to a stop on your stomach, drawing your Glock, and firing at metal pop-up targets. We learn how to ram cars to smash them out of the way, and drive backward at sixty miles per hour before cranking the wheel over and slamming the car into forward. By the end of two weeks we must have gone through a dozen cars. I wonder what the salvage yard thinks about them when they arrive.

While almost everyone drives back to Washington for the weekends, I stay on base. So does Cheri, and it's not long before we're friends. We spend Friday nights in the Jacuzzi singing country songs at the top of our lungs. Sunday morning we play football with a couple of the guys. My spiral pass isn't bad and wins me points. Cheri and I go off base Sunday afternoons to go shopping.

Sometimes I look at Cheri and wonder if one day that's going to be me. For the last three years she's been traveling around the world teaching foreigners to shoot, sometimes working with the Secret Service, sometimes with the CIA's paramilitary group. She tells me she loves it and can't imagine what else she'd do in life that would interest her as much. Part of it is that she's good, a better shot than many of the guys. She's modest about it, though, trying to convince me that video games honed her hand-eye coordination. Maybe. But what I really admire about Cheri is her raw confidence. "I'm not afraid of shit," as she puts it.

One Monday morning, three bosses from Langley come down to see how the class is doing. Over breakfast, the rumor starts flying that they're here to select a couple of us for an assignment at the end of training. They want to see who can shoot and who can't.

After we run through a quick requalification on the Glock, Jeff and the bosses walk down the silhouettes examining our groupings, the tightness of our shots. When they get to mine, Jeff says

something to them, and they look over at me. I know my groupings are now pretty good, but I'm sure he's just told them I didn't
qualify on the shotgun.

Jeff then takes us to the pop-up range, where one of the instructors can't make a metal target go down. Jeff walks downrange
to help, bends down to take a look, but he can't fix it, either. He
looks up and asks if someone would drive back for a toolbox.

I hesitate a moment and then take my dumb Leatherman off
my belt and hold it up. "Will this help?"

Jeff looks at me with my silly drooping cargo pants, my
Leatherman held high, then motions for me to bring it to him. It
takes him two minutes to fix the target with the fold-out pliers and
screwdriver.

At lunch in the cafeteria, one of the bosses comes by our
table. "Hey, girl with the multitool, hope one day we get to work
together."

It all comes back to guns, who can shoot and who can't. But the
ability to put a round in a paper target's bull's-eye doesn't neces-
sarily make you good with a weapon. The only way to find that
out is by mixing it up. Some nights it's live fire where we have to
reload our magazines in pitch blackness, by feel. Just as we start
to feel comfortable, they start throwing flash-bang grenades and
shooting blanks above our heads. Other nights we simulate a fire-
fight with paintball guns from moving cars. One night they send
us solo out on the track to practice high-speed turns in the dark.
As I'm driving a straightaway I see a guy on the side of the road
frantically waving his arms for me to stop. As soon as I slow down
and pull off to the shoulder, four instructors with paintball guns
ambush me before I can even draw my weapon. Point taken: Don't
stop for anyone or anything.

They leave the hardest for the last—"the shoothouse." A shoothouse is a one-story structure built of stacked old tires filled with sand, thick enough to stop a bullet. Plywood inner walls give the sense of a real house. There are even windows and doors, furniture and appliances.

Jeff stands at the front door. "We're going through one by one. Take down the bad guy and don't shoot any women or children unless they have a weapon."

We put on our bulletproof vests and load our Glocks. Jeff follows the first guy through the door. The rest of us wait outside, trying to imagine what's going on inside. After a couple of seconds there's a muffled yell, followed by two gunshots. It's silent for a couple of minutes, and then two more shots.

One of the guys in the class walks up to me. He's a DEA agent on loan to the CIA, a nice guy who's helped me with my shooting. He's six-four, and standing next to him I feel like his little sister.

"Lookit, I've worked with petite girls like you before. The only way they can do this is if they go completely out of character."

I'm not sure what he means.

"Scream as loud as you possibly can, use every swear word you know. Coming out of someone like you, it'll throw them off guard. Trust me, it gives you an edge."

When it's my turn, I walk in trying to ignore the Glock shaking in my hands and Jeff right behind me. I crouch low at the first door, listening. When I don't hear anything, I swivel into it, my Glock sweeping the room. No one's there. At the kitchen door I do the same thing. There's a paper mom in a blue ruffled apron standing at the sink and a little girl in a pink jumper behind the table. I whisper at them to get in the closet and stay there. I continue down a hall and wait at the door of the back bedroom. I listen. There's no noise. I swivel into the room. I don't see anything, but then a paper man with a gun in his hand swings out from behind a cupboard.

I don't pause even a beat, and yell at the top of my lungs, "Drop the *fucking* gun and get your *fucking* hands in the air, or I'll blow your *fucking* head off!"

The silhouette doesn't move and I put two rounds into its forehead, less than an inch apart.

When I come out of the shoothouse, everyone's laughing—I could be heard swearing as clear as a bell. Several of them come up and pat me on the back. Later I learn that a few of the guys took out both the mom and the little girl.

As with the rest of the course, they constantly raise the shoothouse ante. They move furniture around to confuse us, leaving toys and junk in the darkened halls to make us trip. Sometimes we do it after running an obstacle course, our heart rates up over 140, sometimes to deafening music, sometimes in the dark with night-vision goggles. Cameras mounted on the wall record our every mistake. But at the end of three weeks I feel pretty good and move a lot faster than when I started. I can almost sense in which room they have a paper bad guy.

One day it's a dry-fire exercise—pulling the trigger with no bullets in the weapon. I stand outside with a couple of the guys, laughing. I've almost managed to put it out of my mind that I haven't qualified on the shotgun. At least they know I'm as good as everyone else in the shoothouse.

It's my turn. I crouch in the first door, listen for a beat, and peek in. Mom isn't in the kitchen today. I back out, turn, and cross the hall to the next room. I crouch and listen again. There's not a sound. I swivel into the room crouching. I'm just about through the door when I sense something behind me. It's too late. It's a man. He hits me with the full force of his body, hurling me to the floor, knocking the air out of me. He pins me to the ground with his knee. He's big, heavy, and I can't move or breathe. He yanks my left arm behind my back, the one without the Glock. Then he grabs at the gun. I pull my arm free, stick two fingers through the trigger, and wrap both hands around the barrel of the pistol and hang on. We roll across the floor, with him yanking at the barrel of the gun. I manage to pull it away and shove the gun between my legs, my hands locked around it. He gives my right arm a hard yank, but can't pull it away. He jumps up and runs out of the room. "Fantastic!" a voice exclaims over the intercom.

I walk out of the shoothouse shaking, trying to get my breath. Carlton, a very large African-American instructor who's helped me all through the course, walks up to me. He's breathing hard too. He says I'm the last one he would have thought he couldn't take a Glock from. He shakes my hand. "You'll do well in a bar fight."

The last day of the course we sit at our tables cleaning our Glocks. Jeff comes over and tells me to go outside and see Carlton.

Carlton is standing there with a 12-gauge shotgun and a box of shells. He says that if I can keep him from grabbing my weapon, I can do this. He knows I haven't picked up a shotgun since the day I failed to qualify, and I can only think he's counting on sheer confidence to get me through it now. I take the shotgun and the box of shells and follow him to the range.

I load three shells and put six in my pocket. Carlton blows his whistle. I take a deep breath, point the shotgun, and squeeze the trigger, evenly and steadily. I fire all three and combat-load three more. I walk up to the fifteen-yard mark and fire three more shells and reload. I walk to the ten-yard mark and "cover the threat." Carlton blows the whistle a last time, and I fire the last three.

Carlton walks over and looks at the slug holes in the silhouette. "Nice. All center mass."

I notice Jeff has been watching the whole time, and he walks over.

"I've got the first assignment, and it's yours if you want it," he says.

I'm sure I've misunderstood him. "Excuse me?"

"Ever been to Texas?"

It's not exactly overseas, but I spend the next ten days in Houston with Jeff and Carlton, guarding the queen and a princess of an Arab royal family. We drive in a motorcade formation, weaving in and out of traffic, blocking cars coming up on our rear. One day I escort the queen and princess to tea at the Ritz Carlton. Another, I shop with the princess for lingerie at Nieman Marcus. I stand behind the queen as she gets her hair blown out, my hand on my back around the Glock. One evening I sew a button on a dress for the princess. I would like to see any of the guys try that.

In the CIA, training never really stops. It seems like I'm in some course every couple of months, either on a range requalifying or blowing something up. But somewhere along the way I realize that all the training is not just about learning how to shoot, but as much about building confidence in yourself, learning things you never thought you could. It's also about bonding, not a whole lot different from military basic training. They want to see if you can work in a group, follow orders, get along, and think on your feet. It's all a safe way for them to see who has common sense and who doesn't. Better to find that out in training than in the field.

I would carry guns overseas when that was what the orders said. But like everyone else I work with, we consider them a liability, a constant worry hanging over your head that you'll get stopped and searched. And the fact is that without a weapon it's a lot easier to talk your way out of a tight spot. You just look more innocent.

Anyway, what I end up doing has nothing to do with banging down doors and firefights. The CIA doesn't try to turn me into some *femme Nikita*. Instead, I join a deep-cover team that travels the globe, trying to stay out of trouble rather than get into it. I know all of this goes against the myth of CIA ninjas roaming from hot spot to tinderbox, assassinating people and rendering justice. As it almost always is, the truth is a lot blander. The CIA's rock-cut ethic is never to leave a fingerprint behind, let alone pull the trigger on a gun. The moment a gun comes out, the mission is compromised.

SEVEN

Before coming to Tajikistan, please visit your dentist, optometrist, and any health care professionals you see regularly. Bring a spare set of glasses. Contact lens wearers should bring a supply of cleaner and soaking solution, which may not be available locally throughout the year. New arrivals should bring an ample supply of all prescription medications, since pouch deliveries take several weeks.

Some Russian and Turkish crackers and cookies can be found, but you take the risk of them being stale. If you do not want to bake your own, we advise that you include these in your consumables. A variety of jams can be found. There is no peanut butter. Canned goods such as tuna fish are sometimes available and sometimes not. Bring your own favorite condiments (ketchup, mustard, mayonnaise, etc.) and pickles, baked beans, and other canned goods as well as marinades, barbecue and spaghetti sauces and so on, and your favorite salad dressing, in your household shipment or order them as a consumables shipment. Some of these items can be found on a hit-and-miss basis, and you can try the Russian versions of salad dressings and sauces, if you like, but these are sometimes expensive and whether you like the flavor is a personal choice. Frozen vegetables sometimes disappear from the store freezers for several months in the winter.

In general, you can get along without bringing the above named items with you, but your quality of life will probably suffer and you will spend a lot of time going from store to store to try and find which one has the items you need in stock. There is nothing you can do about the quality and selection of meat, cheeses and fresh produce you can find here, but if you send yourself the usual spices and other products that you like to use, you will probably save yourself some frustration at the least.

Very limited veterinarian care is available. The usual process

is for surgeries etc to be carried out on your kitchen table with
rudimentary equipment.

—www.ediplomat.com/np/post_reports/pr_tj.htm

Dushanbe, Tajikistan: **BOB**

It takes an abscessed tooth for me to find out there isn't a dental
X-ray machine in the entire city of Dushanbe.

"You see, come," the nurse at Dushanbe's main hospital says.
She motions me to follow her. We walk through dark waiting
rooms, corridors, and wards. People stand and lie everywhere, two
to a bed, some on filthy blankets on the floor, others squatting
against the walls. They're eerily silent, as if they know the hospital
is a place to die rather than be healed. There's spalling from shrap-
nel on the wall, blistered paint from a fire. I'd heard about an attack on the hospital last month, and it's only now that I believe it.

The nurse stops at a small room in front of a hulking X-ray
machine. She flips on a switch, but nothing happens. "See. Broke,"
she says. She flips the switch up and down in rapid motion. Still
nothing.

I point at my tooth, telling her in Tajik again that it really, really hurts. She shrugs and takes me to a waiting room, where I sit
on a hard wooden bench next to a young boy who stares at me, a
glass eye rolling in its socket.

Half an hour later an Uzbek man in his sixties comes to see
me. He tells me he's a dentist, and has me stand up so he can stare
into my mouth. I point below my cheek, where pain radiates like
a glowing ember. He reaches into my mouth with his index finger
and thumb and starts shaking my lower jaw. It feels like he's just
yanked out my tooth.

"I will pull all these," he says. He adds that he's very good at making gold teeth. I believe him; his own mouth is full of them.

He sighs when I say no, looks into my mouth again, and offers to drill around until he finds the abscess. It takes me a moment, but I understand what he's proposing are three root canals.

I'm about ready to leave when he tells me he has another idea. "A Soviet miracle that will fix our tooth for good." I know he means *my* tooth. But I'm curious now.

I follow him out the back of the hospital, up an outside stairway, along a catwalk, and into a room furnished with a daybed. He sits me down and leaves. A bleached-blond Russian woman in an apron arrives a few minutes later. She attaches two metal squares on the end of an electrical wire to my lower right gum where I tell her it hurts. She tells me to hold the plates in place and attaches the other end of the wire to an electrical box on the wall with a blinking emerald light.

"*Kharisho,*" she says. Russian for "good." I notice she too has solid gold grillwork like the dentist's.

She flips the switch, and a shock runs through my jaw and races around my head as if I'd plugged my nose into an electrical socket. I grip the side of the couch. She stands there watching for ten minutes before unhooking me. My entire face is numb, but not numb enough to know the abscess is still there. I hand her the equivalent of a dollar and leave.

Back at the Oktyabrskaya, I take more antibiotics, but they only dull the pain. I decide seeing a real dentist isn't to be put off any longer. I can catch a ride on a C-130 to Frankfurt next week. But that means three days of flying. And what if I have to wave off this C-130 too? There's no way I can wait for the next one. It leaves me with the only other option, a commercial flight to Moscow.

Thirty minutes out of Dushanbe, the pilot announces we're making an unscheduled stop in Aktyubinsk, Kazakhstan. There's not enough fuel to make it to Moscow, he says. I look down, but I can't see a runway, only snow. It crosses my mind that an abscessed tooth is going to get me killed.

The plane hits hard, snow billowing in its wake. Before it can turn and taxi to the terminal, we're surrounded by police cars and fire trucks, forcing the plane to stop. The lady next to me says she's seen this before—we don't have permission to land. The Kazakhs don't trust anyone or anything that has anything to do with Tajikistan. She says we could be here for hours. Resigned that I'm going to miss my dental appointment, I watch a dog wander down the aisle and take a pee on the side of a seat.

I make it to the dentist at the last minute, and he takes care of my tooth. But as soon as I check into my hotel room, the phone rings. It's Leah, a Russian fixer I've cultivated in Dushanbe. She tells me the Dushanbe airport is closed. She doesn't know whether it's because of fuel shortages or fighting. Either way, I'm stuck in Moscow.

I have an idea. A while ago I heard from a Russian friend that Leah's mother was a KGB officer, a general assigned to Moscow. She might know another way to get back to Dushanbe, like a Russian military flight.

"Isn't your mother in Moscow?" I ask.

"Don't go anywhere," Leah says. "I will call you back in an hour."

She calls back in ten minutes. "Tomorrow, go out to Domodedovo and ask at the Aeroflot freight counter for Natasha. She's a good friend of my mother's."

Domodedovo is Moscow's domestic airport, which serves Dushanbe.

"But I thought you said there were no flights," I say, trying to elicit what she has in mind.

"Natasha knows what to do."

Now I get it. It crosses my mind to ask whether Natasha is her real name or her KGB alias. But even now, after the breakup of the Soviet Union, you don't talk about the KGB on the phone.

The next day I present myself at the Aeroflot freight counter at Domodedovo. "Natasha?" I ask the squat lady on the other side of the counter. She looks at me uncomprehendingly. "Na-ta-sha," I say slowly. The woman continues to look at me stupidly, then turns around without saying a word and disappears into the back.

Just as I start to think this is a wasted taxi ride, another lady, with thick rouge and brass hair, appears at the counter in front of me.

"I'm Natasha," she says. "So?"

I explain that I would like to go to Dushanbe, but there are no planes. She looks at me as if she doesn't understand a word I'm saying. I decide this must be the wrong Natasha. There could be dozens of Natashas at Domodedovo. I wish I knew Leah's mother's name because I definitely would drop it now.

For some reason there's finally a look of recognition on Natasha's face. She comes out from behind the counter and leads me to a bench under a set of stairs. "Go sit. I come get you," she says.

It's as cold inside the terminal as it is outside. I put on my polar expedition gloves, an extra pair of socks, and a wool watchman's cap. I'm still cold, so I cover myself with my duffel bag. A blown-out speaker above my head announces arrivals and departures, but there's nothing about a flight to Dushanbe. For all I know, I'm meant to spend a week waiting here. I lie down and try to catch some sleep.

When I open my eyes, Natasha is standing above me. "Come," she says. I follow her outside. The tarmac is slick with an inch of new snow. We walk past a blackened plane, the landing gear on one side collapsed, the wing dipped in the snow. I've noticed it before on other trips. It's been there a year, ever since it burned up in an electrical fire. I follow a few steps behind Natasha as she threads her way through half a dozen airplanes. At last we come to one with its engines running, the cabin lights on. I can see passengers in the windows. Natasha points at the stairway leading to the back door. "Go," she says. "Go to Dushanbe." It sounds more like a curse than a farewell. I do as I'm told, though, and Natasha turns around and walks back the way we came.

As soon as I step into the plane, I'm surprised to see it filled with blond and blue-eyed Russians, a third of them children. Many are in short-sleeved Hawaiian shirts and straw hats. I can't see a single black-haired Tajik.

The stewardess has decided I'm the one who's held up her plane, and she's not happy about it. I try to look as stupid and innocent as I can, and follow her to the back of the plane, where she points me to a jumpseat.

I don't know why, but I get this nasty, unfounded suspicion that Natasha, the KGB, maybe even Leah, have deliberately put me on the wrong flight, to the Black Sea or whatever beach resort these people are going to, someplace from which it will be almost impossible to return to Dushanbe. Explaining this to headquarters is going to be tough.

Then, ten minutes after the plane takes off, the pilot comes over the PA system and announces there will be an unscheduled stop before we get to—*Bombay, India!* When he says the stop is Dushanbe, a wave of consternation passes through the cabin, something between disbelief and terror. Everyone talks excitedly. One man shouts something toward the cockpit that I don't understand. It takes the stewardess ten minutes of running up and down the aisles to calm everyone down.

I finally understand what's happened. The KGB has commandeered the plane, a vacation charter. And now the passengers, rather than spending tomorrow on an Indian beach, face the prospect of getting caught in a civil war. I put my head against the bulkhead pretending to sleep, as if none of this has anything to do with me.

I wake up as the plane starts to descend. It's dawn, and I can see the pink tips of the Pamirs. The other passengers are mostly asleep, seemingly at peace with their fate. A couple of minutes later there's a hard bump and the roar of the reverse thrusters. The plane turns around and taxis to the terminal. No one's in sight, and there isn't a light on anywhere, including in the control tower. Leah was right about the airport being closed.

Without saying a word, the stewardess opens the rear door for me. I throw my bag down on the tarmac and jump down after it. As soon as I'm clear, the plane lurches forward, heads down the runway, and takes off. The airport's now as silent as the grave.

The terminal doors are locked closed, as are the perimeter gates. I find a low section of the fence, throw my duffel bag over, and climb over after it.

As I walk to the Oktyabrskaya in the breaking dawn, I decide two things: one, Tajikistan is like riding a roller coaster in the pitch-black dark of night; two, the KGB is connected to the machine. Unless I intend to leave this place as blind as when I arrived, I need a KGB officer to educate me.

EIGHT

Over the years . . . when circumstances permit, the CIA *has* publicly identified Agency officers who have been killed in the line of duty. There are currently 78 stars etched on CIA's Memorial Wall for Agency employees who have died in the line of duty, and of those, fully 43 have been identified publicly and are included in CIA's Book of Honor. Of those 43 brave Americans, more than 30 served in the Directorate of Operations, the Agency's clandestine service. Among the heroes named in the Book of Honor are Richard Welch, the CIA official assassinated in Athens in 1975, and William F. Buckley, the Agency officer who was tortured and died in captivity in Beirut in 1985. When an officer under cover dies in the line of duty and there is no capability or reason to preserve their anonymity their names have been released.

—Statement by CIA spokesman Bill Harlow, December 3, 2001

Athens, Greece: DAYNA

As soon as we're through the door of the seedy little taverna, Jacob and I spot our inside officer. He's twenty-something, sitting at a table in the back, facing the entrance. In his penny loafers, white button-down oxford shirt, and khakis, he looks like he was recruited at a frat party. He introduces himself as Tom, but why believe that?

He looks at us as if he's fallen in with bad company, and I suppose we do look the part. I'm in ripped and mended jeans and a faded T-shirt; Jacob, a lanky blond Dutchman with dirty hair, is wearing some sort of weird smock and a pair of filthy sandals. A bandanna is tied around his neck. Although Jacob lives in Washington when he's not on the road, married to a prominent lawyer, he easily and convincingly slips into rootless Eurotrash. The two of us must look like we've just hitchhiked across Africa or something.

When the waiter comes over, Jacob and I order souvlaki, Tom a coffee. Tom doesn't say anything, but I can tell he's irritated we ordered lunch. He looks from Jacob to me and says he wants to make it short because he needs to get back to the embassy for some meeting.

Tom pushes his coffee aside without taking a sip and leans across the table so there's no possibility anyone can hear us. "Can you watch this place?" he asks. He pulls a piece of paper out of his pants pocket and turns it around so we can read it. "It's a house in Koukaki."

Jacob and I memorize the address.

"Stay as far away from the house as you can. Like about five blocks away. This is very much a go-easy thing."

"And do what?" Jacob asks.

Tom turns around to watch as a couple walks in the door. They look English. He waits for them to sit down out of earshot before he starts again.

"And whatever you do, don't take pictures. Don't even take a camera with you. Just find out what the neighborhood's like. But no, repeat no, pictures—17N are cold-blooded murderers."

I bite my tongue. This is what we do for a living: take pictures without anyone seeing us do it. It also annoys me that he talks as if we don't know what November 17 is, the Greek terrorist group that assassinated a CIA operative here in 1975. I concentrate on my souvlaki.

It was a little after ten on December 23, 1975, when the driver pulled up in front of the Athens villa of Richard Welch. Welch told the driver he and his wife would walk the rest of the way. The driver got out to open the gate for them.

The Welches were coming back from a reception, happy that the Christmas season was winding down. It had been pretty much dinner parties and cocktails every night for the last month. They still had not gotten used to the Greek custom of eating late.

A Harvard-trained classicist and fluent in modern Greek, Welch had joined the CIA when America's elite still believed in careers in intelligence. Now his star was on the rise. Athens was an important assignment. Two years here, and he could pretty much count on getting a flagship posting.

Just as the driver swung the gate open, a car pulled up behind the Welches. Two men got out. The chauffer would later say one was tall and the other short. But that was all he could see. They were just shapes, dark on dark. The tall man walked toward Welch and told him in Greek to put his hands up in the air. The short one covered Mrs. Welch with his pistol.

The tall man fired three quick shots into Welch's chest. He and the other man walked back to their car and drove away. Welch died on the spot. The police found casings on the ground but none with a fingerprint.

A group calling itself November 17, or 17N as it would become known, claimed responsibility in a communiqué. No one had heard of the group, but the communiqué made it clear from where it took its name: November 17, 1973, the day the Greek military junta violently put down a demonstration at Athens's polytechnic school. Subsequent communiqués led to the belief that 17N held some odd Trotskyite ideology, and, needless to say, the United States was its main enemy.

Welch was the first of more than a dozen similar assassinations, many with the same .45 semi-automatic, which put 17N near the top of the CIA's target list. But we are still struggling to know just the basics, even the name of 17N's leader. Each and every lead, no matter how tenuous or implausible, has to be followed up on. That's what Jacob and I are here to do, all the while trying to make ourselves as invisible as 17N.

The next morning Jacob and I start out for Koukaki early enough so people will still be on the street going to work, but we catch rush-hour traffic on Konstantinou Avenue and end up lost. By the time we get to the 17N house's street, the neighborhood is quiet—we don't have the protective screen of people on the street we were counting on. The only person in view is an old woman in a black shawl hanging laundry on a second-floor balcony of a house next to the 17N house. There's an occasional passing car, but that's pretty much it.

Jacob finds a parking place fifty yards down the street from the 17N house, but a truck partly blocks our view. Jacob starts to move the car, but I tell him to let it go. We should do what Tom said, and only get a feel for the street. I watch the house for a while and then notice that Jacob has his camera out, loading it with film. "Come on, no pictures," I say. I look around to make sure no one is looking at us.

Jacob mumbles something in Dutch about Tom and clicks the camera shut, the film loaded. He's fiddling with a jacket on the dash, which he's going to use to conceal the camera, when I see a flatbed truck backing down the street, loaded with twenty sacks of something. The truck stops in front of the 17N house, and someone comes out to help unload it. Jacob sees it too. "I thought this was just a house," he says. He starts up the car and drives around the block to get a better view from the opposite end of the street.

Jacob pulls halfway into the drive of a shuttered garage, giving us a good view of the house and the truck. We're too close, but the men unloading the truck are too busy to notice us. "It's fertilizer,

I think," Jacob says. It's the same thing I'm thinking. The stuff is spilling out of the seams, a burnt umber.

Fertilizer is the main ingredient for the homemade explosive known as ammonium nitrate fuel oil, or ANFO. The first time it was used as a terrorist bomb was in 1970, when a part-time student at the University of Wisconsin blew up the physics department, killing a researcher and knocking down half the building. The bomber had found the formula in the *Encyclopaedia Britannica*. Since then, ANFO has become one of the cheapest and most lethal terrorist explosives.

Jacob puts a telephoto lens on the camera while I lean back as far as I can to give him a clean shot of the writing on the bags. A shadow falling across the car and my body block anyone from seeing the camera.

The next day I hand Tom a roll of Agfa color film.

"What's this?" He holds it in his hand as if it were a vial of poison.

"There wasn't a choice. We think the house just got a load of fertilizer."

"I told you *no* pictures." Tom tugs at his earlobe, obviously dreading how he's going to explain this to his boss. He looks at the film roll in his hand. "What am I going to do with it?" The question is directed more at himself than at me.

"Did anyone see you taking the pictures?" he asks.

I tell him we'll only know if it's fertilizer when we develop the film.

Tom pockets the film. "I sure hope it's fertilizer, or we're all going home."

The next morning Tom tells us to settle in for a very long stay in Athens. They want full coverage on the Koukaki house. Tom won't confirm that what we photographed was fertilizer, but I've learned to live with the CIA belief that the fewer people who know a secret, the less chance it has of slipping out the door.

◈

Spend enough time on the road, and you learn to improvise. If you need a clean phone line, you grab a pair of alligator clips and a spare phone, go down in the apartment's basement, and borrow a neighbor's line. Or if you need a clean license plate for a car, you borrow it, returning it before the owner knows it's gone.

You also learn how to do things yourself. Even the hard ones. If a kitchen pipe breaks and you don't want a plumber to see the inside of your place, you fix it yourself. It's not much of a problem for me. As a girl I used to stand behind my dad at his workbench, watching him fix things, and he could repair pretty much anything. I'm a whiz at using Bondo, wood glue, and clamps to repair doors after we change a lock and need to cover up our handiwork. I can make it look as if it has never been touched.

The thing is, our lives are completely unplanned. One week we're in a fabulous five-star hotel, the next in a flophouse with a communal bathroom. I've had bosses hand me $75,000 in a plastic sack so I could go on a shopping spree and turn a complete dump into a reasonable facsimile of a four-star short-term business rental, and I've had other bosses whose motto was the sleazier, the better. There's no way to predict. Every job is different.

We don't keep office hours, or obey any sort of workweek. We go for days waiting for an assignment, just killing time. But no one feels guilty. Sooner or later we'll catch a job pulling eighteen-hour-a-day shifts. And anyhow, downtime is rarely just sitting around a hotel swimming pool. There's always something to do. For me it's learning to disappear—blend in with the locals.

My mentor in all this is Jacob. The first time I worked with him and he saw me in a pair of white Keds, he shook his head as if to say, "Absolutely not." He pointed at my feet. "Only Americans wear white tennis shoes," he said. "It's black, brown, or nothing."

He took me shopping that very day, picking out a cheap

European-cut black leather coat that would fit in anywhere in the world. In Vienna he helped me find a black wool woman's bowler with a bow, and a long brown wool bouclé coat. I laughed at it at first. Back home, it would look like I'd shopped at a costume store. But in Vienna I can stand at a tram stop on the fashionable Ringstrasse for hours on end and no one notices me. It took me a couple of months under Jacob's tutelage to go from posing in Paris as a chic *parisienne* shopping in Galeries Lafayette to mastering the art of dressing German Gothic, making it look as if I had nothing better to do than hang out in front of Frankfurt's Bahnhof, the train station.

Another discipline we learn is living for a long time in a hotel and going unnoticed by management. You can count on the staff of any hotel in Europe reporting to the police. It's all pretty much common sense. No parties, one person to a room, no equipment left around for the maids to find. And of course nothing with your true name on it. That comes down to no calls home, no letters, postcards, or e-mail, nothing that could in any way link your alias with your true name. There's no diagonal parking in parallel lives.

At one point Langley considers telling the Greeks about the 17N house, but just as quickly changes its mind. There's a real risk 17N has sympathizers inside the police. That leaves us to do everything ourselves, from identifying who lives there to finding out what's going on inside.

One thing I learned early on about intelligence is that it's not so much connecting the dots as it is deciding what's a dot and what isn't one. The case in point is that we're still not sure the house really does belong to November 17. It could just as easily be a bad lead. Until we nail that down, the fertilizer could mean anything. For all we know, someone in the house owns a farm and is just storing it here.

That's the first hurdle. The second is that there's no place to park a van without attracting someone's attention. There isn't an apartment for rent anywhere on the street, or even a café for one of us to hang out in. We're reduced to walking by the house, noting new details, but this gets us only so far.

It turns out the house is actually a building containing several apartments around an interior courtyard, but there is no panel outside to tell us who lives where. And what did happen to the fertilizer? It doesn't look like there's a storage area anywhere.

One morning I find Jacob working on a small cargo box, the kind that sits over the back wheel of a bike or a motorcycle. He's making a pin-sized hole in it. When I ask him what it's for, he says for a video camera to put on a motorbike. When I ask him what happens if someone steals the box, he says we'll chain it to the motorbike. And if they steal the motorbike? We'll chain that to a pole.

That afternoon I go out with Jacob to rent a 65-cc Suzuki, common as dirt in Athens. It's beat up, the gas tank caved in on one side and handlebars rusted. The glass on the headlight is cracked. This is the last motorbike anyone would ever steal.

We stand in our backyard and admire the dirty, dented bike now fitted with a camera.

"So who rides it in?" I ask.

"You ride, right?"

Sort of. When I was fifteen my dad and my brother both had dirt bikes, and I often tagged along on their trips to a dry lake bed near our house. When they got tired they'd let me ride around. It's not going to give me a mastery of Athens traffic, but it's a start.

The next day Jacob coaches me, riding the bike in the alley behind our apartment. When I'm more comfortable, I venture out into the street and drive around the block three or four times.

The next morning I push the bike to the street, put on my helmet, and tuck my hair up inside. I look like any other Athenian on her way to work. And when I hit traffic three blocks away, I start to drive like one too, weaving through traffic to be the first at the signal.

When I turn onto the 17N house's street, I deliberately take the sidewalk to get around traffic. Anyone following close on me would have to do the same thing—and I would see them. I park in front of the house, chain the bike to a lamp pole, and walk away. I stop two blocks away at a café for a cappuccino and then make three other stops to make sure I'm clean. Finally I go look for Jacob, who's waiting on a corner in a car.

I do the same thing for a week, every evening picking the bike up and riding it to an underground parking garage where we keep it at night. Jacob pulls out the film, and late that night I hand it off to Tom, who then takes it to the embassy.

To this day I have no idea whether anything Jacob and I did, any of our film, any of our surveillance, helped bring down 17N a decade later, in 2002. The people in the Koukaki house might well have been innocent. Not knowing is pretty much par for the course. A guy I worked with tracked Carlos the Jackal, the Venezuelan terrorist, in Khartoum for weeks. One day they called him in and simply told him it was time to leave the Sudan. No one said why. Not until weeks later did he read about Carlos's arrest and realize he had helped pave the way, providing information about his car and his house.

In my job you soon get used to living with little pieces of the truth. Spying is like keeping a giant accounting ledger. You collect a fact at a time, a name at a time, tiny pieces of insight. Collect enough of them, collate them, and you might end up with a big payoff, or with nothing. Meanwhile, you live on the faith that Washington knows what it's doing.

NINE

When Tajikistan was part of the Soviet Union, the republic's Committee for State Security (KGB) was an integral part of the Soviet-wide KGB. Neither the administration nor the majority of personnel were Tajik. When Tajikistan became independent, the organization was renamed the Committee of National Security, and a Tajik, Alimjon Solehboyev, was put in charge. In 1995 the committee received full cabinet status as the Ministry of Security.

—The Library of Congress Country Studies

Dushanbe, Tajikistan: BOB

A few months after I get back from Moscow I run into a Russian walking out of the American embassy. He introduces himself as Yuri. With thick folds under his eyes and a slight, gun-dog physique, he looks more Chinese than Russian. His English is cultivated, peppered with distinct Americanisms. We talk for a while about the civil war in Afghanistan. As we say good-bye, he invites me to drop by his place.

As soon as he's away, I stick my head into the political officer's office. "Who's that?"

"Yuri. He's KGB. He's my contact, so let it go."

Three days later in the evening I knock at Yuri's apartment door. Yuri is in the back, changing out of his suit, but his wife insists I stay. I sit on the sofa waiting for Yuri, watching her set a place for me at the table.

Yuri comes out in loose-fitting pants, a T-shirt, and a traditional *chopan*—a stiff, tube-shaped embroidered robe. As he pours me a cup of unsweetened green tea, I ask him about some reports of recent fighting in the Garm Valley, less than fifty miles from Dushanbe. He laughs, shaking his head. "Where do these stupid rumors start?"

Over dinner we talk family, schools, weather. His two teenage daughters both speak fluent English, and Yuri has to hold them back from overwhelming me with questions about the United States. Both of them want to go to college there.

I sense Yuri's reluctance to talk about local politics, and I don't press him. That can come later. But as I'm ready to leave, I can't resist asking if it's wise to drive up to the Garm.

"Definitely not."

"So there is fighting."

"I worry about the criminal gangs there."

This is a typical Soviet non-answer answer, and we both know it. As the Soviet Union collapsed, the official explanation for every problem was that "criminal elements" were behind it rather than people with genuine political grievances.

"Where's it safe?" I ask, still hoping to elicit at least something from Yuri.

"I'll tell you what. You and I'll take a trip outside the city sometime."

Two days later Yuri and his driver pull up in front of the Oktyabrskaya to collect me. As I climb in the backseat, I see a Kalashnikov assault rifle on the floor beneath Yuri's feet. He follows my gaze. "Don't worry. We're going someplace safe."

Instead of the main road out of town through the Hissar Valley, the driver takes the backstreets north of town, through a neighborhood of stale yellow houses and poplar trees. People are starting to close up their metal shutters against the night and the criminals. There's a murder almost every night in Dushanbe.

Yuri half turns in his seat. "We'll have a pleasant dinner. Just friends." He reaches across the seat with an open pack of cigarettes. I decline, and he lights a cigarette for himself and the driver.

By the time we find our way back to the main road, it's dark. There's almost no traffic. Just outside town we come to the first roadblock. The driver slows, pulls a pistol out of his belt, points it at the side of the door, covering it with his jacket. He shows his KGB ID to the soldier, and we're allowed to continue.

Forty miles west of Dushanbe we come to a small village without lights. Shadows move between the houses. Yuri and I get out. He points into the sky, and only then do I see it—a monstrous smokestack attached to a giant factory encased in steel scaffolding.

"It's our aluminum factory," Yuri says.

I realize where we are: Tursunzade, the fourth largest aluminum plant in the world. I've never seen it in the dark. Closed for the last two years, it's now just a carcass.

I follow Yuri around the factory until we come to a run of stairs down to a sublevel. Scaffolding above drips water. Yuri opens a door that lets us into the guts of the factory. I can barely see Yuri in front of me as he feels his way down a pitch-black corridor until he comes to a padded door, which opens into a room lighted by smoky kerosene lanterns.

There's old rattan furniture and a pool table, and what looks like a raised dance floor. The walls are covered in varnished papier-mâché fishes, mermaids, and seaweed. At the far end is a black pool. I walk over to look at it. Scum and a patch of some sort of oil cover the surface. It's too dark to see how deep the pool extends.

Yuri pours us vodka in shot glasses, and we down them. "I told you," he says. "No one will bother us here." We sit down at a table that has been set for dinner. The driver comes in with an armful of more vodka bottles, fills a large tumbler for himself, and throws his head back, finishing it.

"You want to know about Tajikistan?" Yuri says. "Here there are no issues. Only ambitions. You people see sides, secularists against Islamic fundamentalists, Communists against capitalists. But you are people who live somewhere else and don't know."

This almost sounds rehearsed. I don't say anything, and Yuri pours us another vodka. A man I haven't seen before comes in with a platter of pilaf, rice cooked in cottonseed oil, and pieces of grizzled lamb. Yuri pours us more vodka. I decide I need to start asking him questions before this stuff hits me.

"What do the Kulyabis want?" I ask. The fortunes of Tajikistan's charismatic clan are critical because if they fail, the country collapses, throwing it wide open to Islamic fundamentalism.

"Why do you care about Kulyabis? They're trash. They're destroying this country."

"You have to wonder if they're going to hold together through all of this."

Yuri turns to his driver. "Would you find someone to get the sauna ready?"

I've lost track of what toast we're on, but I can hear my words starting to slur. I get up for a walk. "Wanna get some fresh air, a walk outside?" I say. "Let's take a swim," Yuri counteroffers. Drunk as I am, I tell him no. Not in a pool I can't see the bottom of. We compromise on the sauna, and change in the dressing rooms into bathing suits.

The sauna's a bagel oven, sucking the air out of my lungs. But rather than sobering me up, it makes me sick. The room spins, and I hold on to the bench. It doesn't help that Yuri looks sick too. I'm thinking about getting up and leaving when a man I haven't seen before opens the door and dumps a pitcher of a yellow liquid on the rocks. Billowing clouds of steam engulf us. It takes a second for me to realize it's stale beer.

I jump up like the sauna's caught fire, push out the door, and jump into the pool. Thank God it's icy cold.

After our dinner at the aluminum factory, I see Yuri every couple of days. But his diffidence doesn't wear off, and I'm no closer to finding out what makes him tick, or getting him to answer my questions about Kulyab. He's seemingly unaffected by the collapse of the Soviet Union, the violence in Tajikistan, the empty markets. I know his KGB salary is small, and getting smaller with inflation. He's told me his friends in Moscow send him the necessities he can't find here. But can that be enough? He would like to send his daughters to school in Moscow.

A lot of spooks believe betrayal isn't bought and sold. People are led to it for reasons more complicated than money. They may be driven by revenge, or may be psychologically flawed or just stupid. Money is only an afterthought or the justification for what they do. Yes, there are operatives who will tell you they can talk the silver off a mirror, recruit someone with a smile and a few bucks, but I'm not one of them. Anyhow, every important mole I've ever known about was a volunteer. They've rolled the idea of betrayal around in their minds long before they've met their first operative. They're only waiting for the opportunity to spill their guts.

My problem with Yuri is that I can't detect the slightest inclination that he's prepared to betray his country. He doesn't express the kind of systemic doubt that would give me something to grab hold of. This leaves me with the default position, the one I don't have a lot of confidence in: find Yuri's price.

At our meetings I try to get him to talk about money, how the collapse of his world affected him. I tell him it has to hurt. As a KGB officer he was at the top of the *nomenklatura*, the Soviet Union's elite, with all the money he needed. Then one day he finds himself a poor civil servant, surely an incomprehensible fall. But Yuri only laughs at my questions.

I decide my best chance to close the distance between Yuri and me is to get him out of Tajikistan, give him a chance to let his hair down away from his KGB comrades. I cable headquarters to arrange an all-expenses-paid trip for him to the United States.

TEN

Geneva, Switzerland: DAYNA

I n the van's rearview mirror, I watch a woman come down the sidewalk. She's in a cream linen pantsuit and crocodile mid-heeled
sandals. She's accompanied by a black Labrador retriever on a
retractable leash. When the two come to the Hilton grounds, she
gives the dog slack, and it bounds over a low hedge and onto the
lawn. After a couple minutes the woman tugs the leash, the dog
jumps back across the hedge, and they continue down the street.
Who walks her dog in a cream linen pantsuit at seven in the morning? I wonder how it is the Swiss are so put together.

I've been sitting in this van every morning for a week now.
The shops all open precisely at eight-thirty, not a minute before
or after. Unerringly, the owners come out with a bucket of soapy
water and a stiff broom to wash the sidewalk. They follow it by a
quick polishing of the window, and then a stepping back to check
the window displays.

Swiss orderliness would just be a curiosity, but it's a bane for
anything we try to do here. A couple of months ago we put a concealed camera in the suit pocket of a man's jacket hanging in a car.
It worked fine parked in a two-hour zone for a couple of days. But

then one day we were thirty minutes late getting back to feed the meter, only to find the car had been towed. A 200 Swiss franc fine later we had our car back. The police didn't find the camera, but we learned our lesson about the Swiss.

It's hotter and more humid today than it was yesterday, a soupy haze rising off the lake. You can't even see the mountains. I never guessed it could get so muggy in Geneva. Every other time I've worked here, it was either fall or winter, when the place can really turn on the charm. There's that cosmopolitan allure combined with the feel of a small town on a beautiful lake.

Frankly, the tediousness of the job is starting to get to me—moving the van from parking place to parking place, sitting and watching. It doesn't help that I've yet to see the Russian mobster we're supposed to be on. Our inside officer assures us he's in Geneva, working out of an office at 14 chemin du Petit-Sacconex. But I'm starting to question whether he really exists. The only thing I can think is that if the Russian leaves his office, he's doing it in the middle of the night after we stop watching him. We've thought of testing that hypothesis, but the Genevois police would notice someone sitting in a van at night when most people are off the street.

I get to drive the van for the same reason I got the motorbike in Athens: girls are less threatening. They can sit in a car all day, adjusting their makeup, exploring their purses, fiddling with the radio, and no one thinks twice about it. Alan, an ex-Marine from Texas, was going to spot me this morning, but showed up in a Hawaiian shirt and flip-flops. Jacob sent Alan back to the OP, the observation post, because the way he was dressed, he wasn't about to go unnoticed. So Alan gets to spend the day in an air-conditioned suite on the seventh floor of the Hilton. Not that he's doing anything a whole lot more interesting than watching the street through a pair of binoculars.

Maybe this whole gig is bad karma punishing us for our downtime last month. We dubbed our latest swing around Europe the "Tour de Bally," in honor of the midsummer shoe sales at the high-end store.

Then, in the rearview mirror, I see a car pull out of the drive at 14 chemin du Petit-Sacconex. The angle's wrong to see whether our Russian is behind the wheel, but Jacob or Alan, whoever is on the binoculars, will have clear view from the 7th floor. I look at the radio crammed between the seat and the gearshift. *Come on, guys,* I whisper under my breath. *Is that him?* I pick up the radio and key it twice. Nothing. This time I hold the key down and ask, "Did you catch that?" No answer.

I make a half turn to get a look back down the street, but a delivery truck blocks my view. I look at the radio again. Why hasn't anyone called it out? Even if it's not the Russian, they should have said something.

Then the car goes right past me, and my heart pounds. It's the Russian for sure, the first we've seen of him in two weeks. *What's going on?* "Where are you two!" I half scream into the radio. I need backup, but there's no way I'm waiting another half month to latch on to him again.

The Russian is two blocks ahead of me, merging into traffic. I don't think he's trying to lose me—it's just that he's a fast driver. He's switching lanes back and forth to pass, gaining distance on me. I need a red light to stop him. One does at the next intersection, and I nose into his lane, three cars behind him. That's enough cover for right now. But I need Jacob and Alan to take over. Otherwise the Russian's going to pick up on me. The innocent-girl-in-the-van act can only go on for so long.

I keep the radio in my lap and key it twice to let Jacob and Alan know I'm still up on the network. But there's nothing in the way of an answer. Only static.

"I'm eyes on, east on Route de Ferney," I say.

Static.

The light turns green. "Crossing Chemin de sous Bois," I say. Static.

"I repeat. Crossing sous Bois."

I name each street as we pass them, hoping they're listening and will catch up. I know I can't hang on like this much longer, especially if this guy turns off onto a street with light traffic. He's an ex-intelligence officer, and there's no way he won't see me.

What I keep thinking is that this is our first break in two weeks. All headquarters wants us to do is to find out where he lives, or even goes. We'd settle for a nightclub, a bachelor's pad where he spends time with his mistress, the store where he buys his chocolate. Just as long as it's away from his office, neutral ground where later we can arrange for an operative to run into him. Recruiting a spy is a long, slow process, and my team and I are just the very start.

"Right on Giuseppe Motta," I say. "Hey, if you guys are out there, let me know!"

I take a left with the Russian. The street is deserted. It's just him and me. I can't follow any longer without getting burned, and make a right when the Russian takes a left.

I get back on the radio. "I'm heading back. I dropped him."
Silence.

It has to be the radio, I think. The repeater's down or something. There's no other explanation.

I let myself into our room on the seventh floor and stare daggers at Alan and Jacob. Alan's got a pair of binoculars in his hand; Jacob is on the sofa.

"What the hell happened?" I ask.

Alan looks at me sheepishly. "Where'd you go?"

"I looked away for less than one minute and when I looked back you were gone," Jacob says, getting up from the couch.

"Yeah, uh, we looked away and looked back and you were gone!" Alan says, sounding just as stupid but also just as guilty.

I drop it and don't say anything. But that night over beers it comes out.

"It's Jacob's fault," Alan says. "I was watching you, and Jacob wouldn't stop about the topless women at the pool. I went over to take a look only to shut him up."

"The radio was in the room," Jacob says. "When we came back to check on you, you were gone."

It makes me feel better they're both genuinely repentant, and we all laugh at the same time.

I never tell our inside officer about the slipup—I wouldn't think of it. Someone's always making a dumb mistake like this. I have, and will make more too. But what it really comes down to is that I've worked with Jacob and Alan long enough to know that they're really good at their jobs. I can count on them for anything. We're like a close family. Although we don't stay in touch between assignments, and a lot of the time we're on opposite sides of the world, I know I can take them at their word. If we're in Singapore and agree to meet two weeks later at noon in the southwest corner of Rome's Piazza Navona, they'll be there.

I travel with Jacob more than with anyone else. We're good as a pair because we never get on each other's nerves, and on downtime we do our own thing. Jacob sits for hours in his room, fiddling with computers and cameras. I cruise the streets, window-shopping. At night we usually meet up for dinner at some out-of-the-way restaurant. Jacob's told me more than once that it's easier to make plans with me in some obscure part of the world than it is to plan a dinner out with his wife in Washington, D.C. At the same time we know that even if we were single, we aren't meant for each other.

This isn't to say that all relations in this makeshift family I live in are platonic. Affairs do go on, though they tend to be discreet.

As I hear the guys say, if you can't carry on a secret, amorous liaison, you're not worth your salt as an operative. But some couples don't even bother hiding it. A pair I often work with actually fell in love, neither caring that the woman was already married and had no plans to divorce. No one complains, though, because they work so well together. There's nothing like a passionate embrace to cover up the fact that you're taking pictures with a concealed camera. Washington pretty much knows what's going on but looks the other way. It's the CIA's version of "Don't ask, don't tell."

One evening, completely breaking the rules, I go down to the lobby of the Hilton to call my husband from a pay phone. It's seven in the morning in California, and he answers on the second ring.

"How's it going?" I ask. I talk in a hushed voice out of habit, not because I'm worried about anyone overhearing.

"Fine," he says.

He doesn't use my name or ask me where I am or what time it is. I've told him enough about the way we work that I can't give up that kind of information on the phone.

We talk about the weather, friends, and golf, the same things we always talk about the few times I've ever called him. I wait for him to ask when I'm coming home, but he doesn't. I promise to call again when I can and hang up.

A month later, the first night I'm home on leave, my husband tells me that his father died while I was away. I calculate the days in my mind. He died two days before I called him from Geneva.

"Why didn't you say anything?" I ask, both shocked and hurt.

"You were busy."

"But he was your father."

"There was nothing you could do about it."

ELEVEN

Operations Officers (OOs) are focused full time on clandestinely spotting, assessing, developing, recruiting, and handling individuals with access to vital foreign intelligence on the full range of national security issues. This human intelligence plays a critical role in developing and implementing U.S. foreign and national security policy and in protecting U.S. interests. OOs employ sound judgment, high integrity, strong interpersonal skills, and ability to assess the character and motivations of others to establish strong human relationships and trust that provides the foundation needed to acquire high-value intelligence from foreign sources. OOs deal with fast-moving, ambiguous, and unstructured situations by combining their "people and street smarts" with subject matter expertise and a knowledge of foreign languages, areas, and cultures. An OO's career can include assignments in the NCS's three key areas of activity—human intelligence collection, counterintelligence, and covert action—on issues of highest interest to U.S. national security, such as international terrorism, weapons proliferation, international crime and narcotics trafficking, and capabilities and intentions of rogue nations. Operations Officers serve approximately 50–70 percent of their time in overseas assignments that range typically from two to three years.

Operations Officers are given great amounts of responsibility and trust early in their careers. While they work in teams, they often need to "think on their feet," using common sense and flexibility to make quick decisions on their own. OOs have demanding responsibilities, often requiring them to work long hours, so it is essential that they be psychologically fit, energetic, and able to cope with stress. They must know themselves very well, and a sense of humor is also a plus.

—www.cia.gov/careers/opportunities/clandestine/core-collector.html

Dushanbe, Tajikistan: **BOB**

One day my mother calls me in Dushanbe to tell me she'd like to see Tajikistan. When I don't immediately warm to the idea, I feel her irritation barreling down the line like a freight train. When she senses I'm not softening, she goes to Plan B. "You know I'm getting old, and this may be my last trip. I so want to see Central Asia before I die."

My mother coming here isn't a good idea. As I've said, my wife and children aren't allowed to even visit because it's too dangerous. But oddly enough—or maybe not—the CIA doesn't ban mothers.

I told her a long time ago about the travel ban, hoping it would be enough to dissuade her. But my mother, a stout, fearless woman, is determined to see the world. She gets off a plane in a strange place and immediately wants to start seeing things, no matter the hour or how long she's been sitting. Invariably, she's read up on the country and knows exactly what she wants to see.

I cast around in my mind for an unassailable reason she can't visit. But other than the obvious—getting killed—I can't think of one. "OK," I finally say. "I'd love to see you."

As soon as my mother sets foot inside the Oktyabrskaya, she sniffs in that peculiar way she has, letting me know the place isn't up to her standards. We're walking past the gloomy dining room where last night's dirty dishes are still on the tables. "We're not having dinner here, are we?" she asks. She ignores me when I tell her it's military rations, as it will be every other night.

My mother comes to terms with Dushanbe when I take her to my room and open a bottle of wine. For an hour she fires off questions about my wife and children, how they're doing in the new house in France, what I'm reading, what I think about one political scandal or another, when I'm going to get serious about life. By the second bottle she's ready to turn in and too tired to argue when I point to the bedroom. I tell her I prefer to sleep on the couch anyway.

The next morning I leave her reading a thick history of China, her half-moon glasses perched on the end of her nose, one leg up under her. She looks content, but I know it won't last. I picture her in midmorning, poking around my room, counting the number of shirts I own, looking for the suits she bought me, wondering what's happened to the pair of silver-backed hairbrushes she once gave me as a Christmas present. Somewhere my mother read that a gentleman *absolutely must* have thirty-six collared shirts. She'll be disappointed when she finds my dozen faded T-shirts, two frayed oxfords, and three pairs of Levi's.

My mother comes from that old mind-set that believes in thank-you notes, jackets at dinner, straight white teeth, and an expensive education. When she visits, she always arrives with a bag of books meant to improve me. And when she returns home to Los Angeles, she writes asking what I think about them. If I answer (as I almost always do) that I've been busy, I get another letter about how hard she's tried with me. You can almost hear the sigh of resignation in the pages. My mother is someone who pictures herself in the tumbrel reading Lucretius on the way to her beheading.

She's definitely going to be irritated when she finds the Kalashnikov, the rocket-propelled-grenade launcher, and the hand grenades under the bed. I'll tell the truth—that they're gifts from Russian army friends that came at the end of long drinking sessions—but she won't listen. Male bonding rituals don't amuse her.

When I first joined the CIA in 1976, I told my mother, but at the same time I admonished her that I was undercover and she couldn't tell a soul. It was a needless precaution because all of her friends were liberals, and she was too embarrassed to tell them anyway. She herself doesn't take espionage seriously. "Mickey Mouse" is the name she usually attaches to it.

When I get back from work at three, she's through with her book and bored. She complains that I've left her all day, so I propose a beer at the Tajikistan Hotel, warning that it's a worse dump than the Oktyabrskaya. "Of course it is," she says. "But do you think I'm going to sit in this room all night doing nothing?"

An hour later she follows me across the Tajikistan's dismal lobby at a half run and down a dark passageway that smells of urine and rotting carpet. When she says something I can't understand, I slow down to let her catch up. "I said you should really get out more, meet people," she says.

The hotel's terrace is positioned so a breeze can't get to it, and the sun this late afternoon is a hammer. There's not a drop of water in the fountain—instead, hedgehog-like steel quills poke up silently out of the cracked cement. We're the only customers, but it's ten minutes before the waiter wanders out from the darkness of the dining room. He's been sleeping, and rubs his eyes with the flat of his hands. Our choice is warm, canned Rasputin vodka or warm, canned Heineken.

We sip our warm beers and sweat in silence, watching the waiter fool with something behind the bar. A single stereo speaker crackles. It goes silent for a while, and then comes the wail of a woman who sounds as if she's mourning her village bombed into rubble. Even my mother's stubbornly chipper mood is dented. She lights a cigarette.

Three Russian girls walk in. I've seen them before. They're professionals, camp followers of the 201st. They sweat too, beads of pure alcohol running down their faces, their makeup melting. Naturally, Mother smiles at them as if we were all at tea at New York's St. Regis. They ignore her and turn away, but Mother gets up anyway, walks over to the girl who looks the friendliest, the only one without a black eye or a broken nose, and grabs her hand, "So delighted to meet you. My name is Donna."

These girls have seen a lot in their short lives, but now they're at a complete loss for words. They know they've met their match, and further resistance isn't worth it. They offer her a chair at their table, and my mother summons me to join them.

The afternoon turns decidedly merrier when we get into the Rasputin vodka. My mother wants to know all about the girls' lives, what they studied in school, whether they intend to marry one day. A few Russian soldiers wander in and can't help but notice our little *fête galante*. A couple of them pull up their chairs to practice English, and my mother orders rounds of vodka for everyone. Half a dozen times this happens, followed by half a dozen teary toasts to mothers and motherhood.

At around eight, even good old Mom has had it. She writes down her telephone number in Los Angeles, should any of them get that way, and then we have one last toast to eternal friendship between America and Russia.

I have to help her outside and into the car. I tell her a nice cold shower will make her feel better. She ignores me and asks me what we're going to do tomorrow.

Before going to sleep that night, my mother snoring gently in the next room, I tell myself there has to be a silver lining to her visit. It's a fact that anyone who makes friends in strange places with so little cause is by definition a good Trojan Horse. I stumbled across this piece of wisdom years back when I was in Damascus.

It was before I married, and my mother came to see me, but mainly to sightsee. Every morning at eight, she'd set out with a 1930s Baedeker guide and walk the streets of the old city, not returning until after dark. She'd demand a glass of wine, make me listen to stories of all that she'd seen, all wound around some great historical event, and chide me for not coming with her.

After three days of this, she'd seen everything there was to see in Damascus. The next morning, without saying a word, she went out as usual, but came back in the afternoon with a bus ticket to Palmyra, an ancient city in the Syrian desert, about 130 miles from Damascus. "You're not going alone, are you?" I asked. She rolled her eyes. "What could *possibly* happen to me?" I knew there was no use pointing out that the night before, the USS *New Jersey* had shelled Syrian army positions in Lebanon, or that the United States was all but at war with Syria.

Two days later the concierge came pounding at my apartment door. "Your mother is back," he said with great excitement. "With people!" I followed him down to the street to find her talking with a Syrian man and woman in their mid-forties, both well dressed. They were standing next to a late-model Peugeot, my mother's suitcase on the sidewalk. That was interesting, but what caught my eye was the *other* late-model Peugeot double-parked across the street. Three men in cheap Dacron suits and five-o'clock shadows were seated in it, staring at me—Mukhabarat, Syrian intelligence.

Unaware of the crowd she'd drawn, my mother introduced me to the Syrian man and his wife, and hugged them good-bye as if they were old friends.

"Who was that?" I asked, as soon as the couple drove away, the Peugeot with the three thugs pulling away after them.

"Such delightful people."

"But who are they?"

"I met them in Palmyra."

She told me how she'd run into the couple in the lobby of her hotel. They'd started chatting, which had led to dinner, which had led to an offer of a ride back to Damascus.

"But what do they do?" I asked. I was not going to let her off the hook on this one. Not everyone in Damascus has his own security detail.

She told me the man was a poet, but didn't really work.

I interrupted her. "And the wife?"

"Oh, she works for the president. She's one of his secretaries."

First, let me say that Syria's president is as remote and mysterious as a Ming emperor. Second, the main reason the United States had an official mission in Damascus was to try to crawl into his head. Since I'd arrived in Damascus, the closest I'd come to the presidency was walking by the front gate of the palace's compound.

I should have known that the moment I signed up for Tajikistan, my mother would show up. I'm her only child, and traveling is all that she has in life. I can even mark the day she became a traveler: the day my father left us. I was nine, she just short of thirty. She dropped out of graduate school, grabbed me, and the two of us headed to the airport to catch a flight to Europe—duration and final destination uncertain.

Years later, when I started to understand a little about marriage, I wondered whether my father, a Los Angeles businessman who'd never wanted to leave California, had held her back from the life she really wanted. Or maybe it was that his leaving had just snapped something inside my mother. I don't know because we never talked about it.

The trip to Europe was supposed to be a few months, but turned into something like three years. The only things I knew about friends, family, and home were written on the backs of postcards. My father never wrote, but I don't know whether it was because he didn't have our address or because he couldn't be bothered. And the longer we stayed away, the farther off the beaten path we got.

During the October 1962 missile crisis, when Kennedy put an

embargo on Cuba, we were in Berlin. One day the owner of the little pension we were staying in advised us to leave right away because the Soviets were about to blockade Berlin in retaliation. I was convinced, but my mother scoffed at the idea that anything would happen to us. That same morning we crossed over into the East and spent the day touring its monuments to socialism. Crossing back through Checkpoint Charlie, my mother spotted an East German soldier's helmet sitting on a wall, untended. She offered me five dollars to grab it and run back into the West with it. I was stung when she called me a bore for refusing.

My mother picked up friends on our travels, odd ones, from ski bums in Switzerland to poets in Paris. One snowy Christmas Eve in Rome, while, touring the catacombs, she attached herself to a couple of American priests who also happened to be archaeologists. She badgered them into Christmas dinner in order to interrogate them about some new dig she'd read about.

I have no idea if she missed my father through any of this. As I've said, she never talked about the man, and he dropped out of my life like a pebble into the abyss. I would see him once in 1990, but just for a day. She never asked how it went or what we talked about—which, as it turned out, wasn't much.

I didn't lure my mother to Tajikistan to do my dirty work, troll for sources, or make friends for me. I didn't even want her to come. But as long as she's here, insisting on socializing with the locals, can I pass up the opportunity?

Yuri is of course delighted when he hears my mother is visiting, and immediately invites us for dinner at his house. As I counted on, my mother is completely in character, instantly charming Yuri and his wife. They both roar with laughter when she recounts our night at the Tajikistan Hotel.

I let my mother monopolize the conversation over dinner, dazzled by how Yuri opens up to her. She's like a seasoned spy, asking why the Soviet Union collapsed, what's going to happen next, will Russia break up. Yuri is disarmed and amused, completely unable to fend off her questions as he does with me. He tells stories about the worst days of the civil war here. I wish I had mentioned Kulyab to my mother.

"You will of course come see me in Los Angeles," my mother says as we stand at the door to say good-bye. She looks at me and says to Yuri, "And don't bother bringing him. He's such a bore."

Yuri hugs her and promises that if he ever does visit the United States, he wouldn't consider not stopping by.

There's nothing like a mother to close the distance between you and your quarry.

TWELVE

Washington, D.C.: **BOB**

easily pick out Yuri in the flow of international passengers at Dulles. In his still-crisp, slate-blue suit, with a solid maroon tie, he's better dressed than anyone else.

"It's amazing," he says as he walks up to me. "They served meals on the airplane. Three of them!" He's like a child in an amusement park.

The first night we stay in Washington, but the next morning we fly to South Carolina, where I have a friend who's arranged two tickets in the president's box for Clemson University's homecoming game. I've already primed Yuri that my friend, a prominent Clemson alumnus, could get his daughters into the school.

In the morning, before the game, we walk around campus. There's a slight chill in the air, and the trees have just started to turn. I ask him if it wouldn't be wonderful for his daughters to go to school here, reminding him that this is something I could take care of.

We stop at a table where half a dozen coeds are painting Clemson Tiger paws on fans' cheeks. I persuade Yuri to get one. As a giggling belle paints one on, I take his picture, telling him it will look good on the Wall of Heroes at Lubyanka, the KGB's old headquarters.

Yuri watches the football game without saying a word, sipping a beer and eating popcorn. Every once in a while, after a big play, he asks me what just happened. At halftime, Clemson's chancellor comes over to introduce himself. He and Yuri talk for a couple of minutes, and the chancellor takes him around to meet some alumni. I wonder what Yuri thinks about all the pastels and plaids, and the easy, uncomplicated lives these people must lead.

By the second half, Yuri seems convinced he's stumbled on an American ritual he'll never understand. The game is lopsided in Clemson's favor. As the players walk off the field, Yuri asks me who won.

The next morning we fly to Los Angeles. Yuri thinks it's to see a different slice of American life, but what I really want is for him to spend more time with my mother.

We stay at the new Loews in Santa Monica. Five minutes after we separate to go to our rooms, Yuri is knocking at my door. "Can you believe it? There's a TV in my bathroom." I remind him not to be shy about sending down his laundry, not mentioning that it will cost more than he makes in a week.

After dinner we sit on the Loews terrace, drinking margaritas, gazing out at the Pacific. Toward the north, above Malibu, a faint reddish glow marks an out-of-control fire that has been all over the news. "Should we be sitting here?" Yuri asks. "Maybe we should drive there and help." I tell him there are fires like this all the time around L.A. "What about the people's houses?" he asks. He listens incredulously as I tell him that they will burn, and the owners will rebuild them with insurance money.

The next morning I take Yuri to see my mother, who lives in a one-story stucco house in Venice. She pulls him into the house with a hug. "I know you made my bad son keep your promise." As my mother and I catch up, Yuri looks around the house. He takes a picture off the shelf. It's my cousin Karen visiting us in Europe when my mother and I lived there in the early sixties. Karen, thirteen, is running down a flight of steps in old Geneva.

I pick up a framed photo of my maternal grandfather. I tell Yuri about him, how he lived until he was almost a hundred and how he helped raise me when my father left, and how he left small trust funds to his four children. Yuri takes the picture to get a better look. "He looks like a strong man," he says. I see it too. He died while I was in Beirut. I didn't attend his funeral. Whatever I was doing seemed too important to take the time to come home.

We go out back to sit in the bricked-in patio and drink tea. My mother quizzes Yuri about the latest news from Tajikistan. He's amused all over again by her rapid-fire questions, the way she keeps probing until she gets an answer that satisfies her.

I have to make a decision before it's too late. In the back there's a small guesthouse where Roy and Matt live. Roy is an artist, Matt an attorney for the City of Los Angeles. They are not so much renters as my mother's friends. I have no idea whether Yuri is offended by homosexuality.

I'm still pondering it when Roy lets himself in through the side garden gate. As soon as he sees Yuri, Roy puts his thumbs in his belt as if he's going for his six-shooters and challenges Yuri to a draw in a long-practiced, very good John Wayne imitation. Yuri loves it.

Roy grabs Yuri to show him his enormous train set, which occupies my mother's entire garage. I follow them in, watching as Roy points out the balsa-wood town he's made by hand, and the lakes and snow-covered mountains he spent months painting.

We spend the rest of the afternoon drinking wine in the garden.

Early the next morning I go back to see my mother. It's only today that I notice how much she's aged since she visited me in Dushanbe. She walks a little more slowly. There are more liver spots on her hands.

She lights a cigarette, coughing. "Is Yuri your friend?" she asks.

I don't answer because I don't know the answer. Where does my personal life end and my professional one begin?

I watch as she wipes down the kitchen counter. I suspect that she understands by now that I brought Yuri to the United States to try to recruit him. She must resent being used in this way.

When my mother goes out to the garden, I follow her. She fills up a water bucket at the faucet. I would help, but her garden is her only occupation other than reading and traveling. "I'm going to move to an apartment," she says, her back to me. "This place is too difficult to clean."

I can't remember how long ago she started complaining that her house is too large, or why. The place only has four rooms, and they're small. "I'm thinking about giving it to Roy," she says. She bends down and pulls out a dead geranium.

I've never imagined living in this house, or really thought much about inheriting anything from her. I think about asking why she wouldn't give the house to me, her only child, but we never discuss money. I've never really talked to her about Roy, either. I've just accepted that he's a friend. Now I wonder what exactly the relationship is.

But it's more than that. A couple of months earlier, my mother opened trust accounts for my children's college education. But rather than make me the trustee, she put them in my wife's name. She apparently didn't think I could handle the responsibility. I never could bring myself to ask her about this, either.

I hope she's at the end of the bloodletting. But she isn't. "Is your marriage really falling apart?"

The abruptness of the question surprises me. I wonder what I can say to make her stop. She looks at me, waiting for an answer.

"When has it never been falling apart?" I say.

A month ago I wrote her a letter telling her I intended to divorce. She wrote back a mortifying letter I couldn't finish.

She takes a step closer to me. She's angry now. "You will *not* divorce, and you will *not* abandon those children."

I think about telling her one more time that my marriage is a façade, empty, doomed. There's no intimacy between us, none. The French house did nothing for the marriage. My wife only lasted there six months before she packed up and moved to Paris with the kids, taking a temporary job at the embassy. But the real point is that I've now been away so long that the children consider me a stranger, unwelcome in the autonomous republic they live in with their mother. I don't say it, though. The words won't make the hopelessness of the situation any truer in my mother's mind.

I want to ask her why it was okay for her to divorce, leaving me without a father. Or why she never tried to put us together, even for short visits. She never even asked whether I wanted to see him. Why is not having a father unacceptable for her grandchildren, but all right for her son?

As I stand there watching her pick through her garden, I think about her running away to Europe when I was ten, and then dropping out in Aspen, Colorado, leaving me to conclude that it was acceptable to abandon people, sever bonds for no other reason than to make life more palatable. I don't know why she didn't think I'd do the same.

"I have to go pick up Yuri. I'm already late," I say. I turn to look at her before I leave, but she's pruning a bush, her back to me.

Yuri and I drive to Compton, a rough Los Angeles suburb, where I've arranged to spend a day with a police task force that tracks violent felons and gangs. (I've told the task force that Yuri is a Russian policeman on a courtesy visit to the United States.) I don't expect that any tricks our police know will be more sophisticated than the KGB's, but still he might find it interesting.

We sit at a wobbly wooden table across from two L.A. sher-iff's deputies who tell us how they monitor released felons. One explains how each of their unmarked patrol cars is linked to the task force's computer. Units check it for locations they have under watch, trace telephone numbers and license plates, and track out-standing warrants. For instance, if a recently released felon enters a house where they think he's going to pick up a gun or reconnect with his gang, they can instantly pull up everything they need on the house and its occupants.

As the deputy is talking, one of the units comes on the air. A just-released gang member has entered a house and come out with a gym bag. "Should we pick him up?" the unit asks. Their suspicion is that the felon has collected a gun. The deputy radios back. No, wait. The unit calls out its locations as it crosses South Central L.A.

Several cars suddenly come up on the net. "We have an inci-dent," the patrol car comes up. "We need backup right now."

Five minutes later a unit's on the net again to report that the just-released felon pulled up next to two men standing on the cor-ner. Without warning, he fired out the window at them, missing both. The felon gunned his car, but it stalled. Half a dozen people ran out of a house with guns, firing at the stalled car, killing the felon.

"It sounds like Tajikistan," Yuri says.

I have to wonder if it is a good idea to expose Yuri to my life and a Los Angeles ghetto shoot-out. But my read of Yuri is that if money doesn't interest him, then the truth does. And the truth I'm trying to convince him of is that he can't risk letting his daughters grow up in Tajikistan's violence and corruption. I want him to come to the conclusion that he needs to make a bargain with the devil, spy for the CIA to pay for Clemson. I'm counting on the briefings in Washington to push him over the edge.

Yuri isn't allowed in CIA buildings, so I rent two suites at the Sheraton at Tysons Corner. There, over the next two days, headquarters parades through a dozen specialists on Afghanistan, Russia, and Iran. It's a chorus of grim news. The Taliban's about to take over Afghanistan, chaos will migrate across the border into Tajikistan, Russia's too weak to hold it back, Iran's on the rise.

I've arranged the crucial briefing for last, about heroin smuggling. I already know the analyst will tell Yuri that commerce in the drug could very well bring Tajikistan down. I also know it's a message Yuri will listen to. He's told me before how heroin smugglers torture KGB officers by cutting off the tips of their fingers, and then keep cutting until they die from a loss of blood. Afterward, the smugglers throw the corpses, chopped up in a grain sack, on their families' front steps. Fear, I hope, will drive Yuri into the CIA's arms.

There's a knock at the door, the narcotics briefer. I let him in. He's a man I've seen around headquarters, but I can't remember his name. The man walks across the room to shake Yuri's hand. "Hi, I'm Rick Ames."

I go downstairs to make a call, while Ames gives Yuri the bad news about heroin.

Several months after I'm back in Dushanbe, my communicator hands me a cable from headquarters: The FBI's just arrested Aldrich "Rick" Ames for spying for Russia, betraying a dozen sources in Moscow, including KGB officers.

Yuri calls the same day the Ames arrest is reported in Moscow newspapers. "Did you hear?"

I pretend I don't know what he's talking about.

"The CIA man arrested," he says. I can hear the strain in his voice. "I know him."

"It's very unfortunate."

"Isn't he the one I met?" Yuri asks.

"Yes," I answer, with my head in my hands. If there were a hole nearby, I might climb in it and pull the dirt on top of me.

Yuri hangs up.

Shortly after Ames saw Yuri, Ames went to his last meeting with his Russian KGB handlers. Ames told them about Yuri, and about my intention to recruit him, and the KGB decided it couldn't take any chances. Although Yuri never betrayed a secret or ever intimated he would, he was recalled to Moscow and lost his job the following week. Langley knew about Ames and must have suspected he'd burn Yuri, but they never told me about the Ames mole hunt before his arrest, or tried to wave me away from having Ames and Yuri meet. Yuri was just a throwaway in the deal, but I suppose I should talk. I'd used my own mother to try to recruit someone who might have been a friend—if I knew for certain what that means.

THIRTEEN

The mandate of the Committee on Missing Persons is to establish the fate of missing persons: "The Committee shall look only into cases of persons reported missing in the inter-communal fighting as well as in the events of July 1974 and afterwards."

As a result of the violence generated during those times, a total of 502 Turkish Cypriots and 1,493 Greek Cypriots were officially reported as missing by both communities to the CMP. Following a number of recent identifications in the early 2000s, the total number of missing Greek Cypriots actually stands at 1,468.

—Committee on Missing Persons in Cyprus

Nicosia, Cyprus: **DAYNA**

I sit on the floor in a bathing suit, my back propped up against a cheap futon, sweat dripping off my face. It's only ten in the morning and already over ninety degrees. There's not a sound from the street, the Cypriots having fled to the beaches.

I pick up the muff earphones and listen to the static. It's just the usual forty-eight volts DC running down the line. I haven't heard the guy whose apartment we've wired for sound in the last twenty-four hours. I wonder if he's away.

I unplug the earphones and turn up the recorder enough to hear it in the kitchen while I make my second cup of coffee. I watch the kettle for a while and then lean over the sink to look out the window. At just the right angle, I can see his apartment. But his windows are closed, and I can't see in.

I've never seen the guy in person, although I've seen his photos. Someone else rented the apartment directly across the street so they had a full-face view when he came out his front door. He's a lanky, good-looking guy with dark hair and boyish features—nothing remarkable about him one way or the other. The fact is, he could pass as one of us in his scruffy chinos and knit polo shirts, and sometimes a fisherman's cap. In the photos it's all so nonchalant that it's hard to imagine he's a murderer.

The water boils, and I mix it with the last of my instant coffee. I'm going to have to go shopping. I remind myself that I don't want to forget anything and have to go out in the heat a second time. I look for a piece of paper and a pen to make a list. I'm also going to pass by the Europa Hotel. Maybe they've received some new magazines. I'd read about anything to get me through the rest of the day.

I try not to go out so much anymore. Last week when I was in Cyprus's second largest city, Limassol, I was parked only five minutes when a cop pulled up behind me. He got out and tapped on my window. The cop said something on his radio, then bent down to take a look around the inside of my car. I had a map on the passenger seat. Didn't I look like a tourist? He asked me if I'd accompany him back to the station. I didn't have a choice. There, he wrote down my name and passport number, and asked why I was in Cyprus. When I told him I was a film scout, he absorbed the information without comment. I expected he'd ask what studio I worked for or something. (I had a story for that.) But he didn't, and he let me go. Anyhow, it spooked me, and now I try to spend the least time I need to on the street.

Two days later something else weird happened. I was coming down the elevator of the Europa Hotel when it stopped to let someone in. I recognized the guy right away, a teaching assistant I'd known at Berkeley and a former Olympic swimmer. He held his head to one side, recognizing me. "Dayna?" Dayna is not the name I'm using here, and I panicked a little, but we were the only ones on the elevator. We got off at the lobby, and I had no choice but to talk to him. He told me he was in Cyprus working for Gatorade, although he normally lives in Holland. When he asked what I was doing here, I told him my cover story, film scouting. He nodded his head as if it made perfect sense. He gave me his card. I told him I didn't have one, but promised to get in touch when I was back in California. Fortunately, he was on his way to the airport and there was no more time to talk.

I can't decide what's flimsier—my using this film-scout cover, his working for Gatorade and living in Holland, or the crazy coincidence of running into someone from a past life in an out-of-the-way place like Nicosia. I don't know why, but it made me think about my last conversation with my husband. When I asked him what was going to happen to us, he didn't say anything right away, but finally said he guessed we'd just go along until one of us met someone else.

I sit back down against the futon with my coffee, and try to get into an old Italian *Vogue*. I put it down to listen to a noise in the hall, a door slamming and then a crying baby. It sounds like the neighbors are fighting again. I pick up the headphones to make sure the sound is still working.

It's two months now, and I still don't really have a good feel for the guy. All they told me about him was that he was behind a handful of political assassinations in Turkey. But you couldn't tell it from eavesdropping on him.

One time he called a taxi company three times, complaining about his car not coming on time. He kept calm, and if he was angry it was pretty restrained. Another time he called a woman. He was playful at first, and I thought for a minute it was a girlfriend. But the conversation turned serious, and I doubted there was anything going on between them.

Now he's gone silent, and I'm left wondering what anyone would learn by eavesdropping on me. I never call from the apartment phone. If anyone were listening to it, they no doubt would decide that I'm some sort of shut-in with no friends or family. And even if I could call home, what would I say? I spend my days spying on a terrorist. Nothing could be more foreign to my self-made engineer father or my homemaker mother. My dad thinks I work for the military, while my mother believes my paycheck comes from an international moving company. But I wonder how grounded any of us really is. Aren't we all some sort of phantom, not a whole lot different from the guy I'm eavesdropping on?

By two, I'm bored beyond endurance. I've got to get out. I turn the recorder's volume off and slide it into the concealment panel in the TV console, push it until it clicks closed, lock the windows, and quietly let myself out the apartment's door.

A couple of tourists are on the main street, Makariou, but the shops are all closed for the afternoon. I follow my usual route into the old city, passing through the old Venetian walls, cutting down a small alley that winds under latticed wooden balconies. In some places the sandstone walls are so close you can touch the houses on either side by raising your hands. I stop to smell the jasmine and bougainvillea from gardens I can't see. An old woman in black comes out of a door and dumps a bucket of dirty water into the street.

I take a left on the first street I come to, Artemidos, and walk down to the "blue line"—a UN-mandated separation line that divides the Turkish half of Cyprus from the Greek. I glance at the minaret of the mosque just on the other side, and then stop as I usually do to study a plywood board with pictures of missing people. No one new has been added.

On the way back, I make my usual stop at the little Greek Orthodox church on Stasinou Street. I don't know why, but recently I've started lighting candles for the missing. I light one now and sit in a pew in the dark, cool silence until a man comes in. He's young, in his twenties. I watch him as he lights a candle, putting it near mine. At first I think he's followed me here. But then he crosses himself and leaves.

When I come out, it's a lot cooler, and the shops are opening up. I stop at the gyro stand where they know me. A young boy who works there likes to practice his English. I order the same thing every day, and he starts making it when he sees me come in the door.

My final stop is the corner market. Back in the apartment, I put the things away in the kitchen and take a bottle of water out of the refrigerator. I take the recorder out and put on the earphones. I'm startled to hear two voices. Our guy is angry, the other defensive.

"You said that last time," our guy says.

"Yes," the other voice says. "But the envelopes are ready now." It's someone I've never heard before; his English is halting, searching for words, as if he learned it in school and never had a chance to practice.

"I need to see them now," our guy says.

"Tomorrow, maybe?"

"No, let's go now."

There's never been anything like this before. I quickly put the recorder back in the concealment panel and slam it shut, harder than I intended. I grab my cell phone and a wide-brimmed straw hat, even though it's dusk. I let myself back out and clatter down the steps into the street. I'm not sure exactly what I'll do. See the two meet and then follow the unknown voice home to see where he lives?

As soon as I step out of the apartment doorway and go around the corner, I catch sight of our guy walking down Makariou, alone. It's not even a decision—I follow him. I take note of what he's wearing, a bluish polo shirt and jeans. They are clothes easy to lose sight of at this time of the evening, so I'll have to stay a little closer to him than I normally would.

He stays on the same side of the street and then stops abruptly in front of a store window. I slow down and watch him as he pats his jacket. He finds what he's looking for, his cigarettes, and pulls one out to light it. He takes a deep drag, tilting his head back, exhaling up into the air.

He continues toward the old city, with me twenty paces behind him. By now I know every street and alley here. And that's what worries me. It's a labyrinth, and to follow someone you need dozens of people with radios. There's nothing I can do about it since I'm on my own. But I call my team leader to let him know.

"Hey, I'm with our guy," I say as soon as he picks up. "He's going to meet somebody."

I sense he's excited. "Stay with him as long as you can."

I hold back and keep my eyes on his shirt. I lose it for a second when he walks around a newspaper kiosk, and see too late that he's stopped on the other side, reading a newspaper clipped to its corrugated roof. There's no place to duck into, so I take out my cell phone again and pretend to dial, looking at the ground. If he notices me, he doesn't show it. He buys a newspaper, rolls it up in one hand, and taps the other with it.

Daylight is all but gone now, the store lights coming on. More people are out on the streets, escaping stifling apartments. I don't stand out as much, but now, with the streets alive, it's almost inevitable I'll lose him.

I close the gap a little, but he's still too far ahead as he turns down a small alley. I cross the street and follow him, but when I turn the corner, he's not there. There are three smaller alleys he could have taken. I take the one in the middle.

I'm halfway down when I notice that I'm in the red-light district. A child-size girl sits in an open window, curtains waving in the breeze, flickering lamps behind her. I keep walking, turn down another small walkway, but it's only more girls in more windows. I put my head down and walk back the way I came.

It was all so sloppy, following him like this, but there wasn't a choice. Just to make myself feel better, I stop for an ice-cream cone.

FOURTEEN

> Sheldon Kornpett: "You were involved in the Bay of Pigs?"
> Vince Ricardo: "Involved? That was my idea."
>
> —*The In-laws*, 1979

Washington, D.C.: **BOB**

Coming back to Washington from Tajikistan is like walking into your living room and finding all the furniture moved around. There are new Metro lines that go to places I've never heard of. Freeways have cloned themselves. Once-distant suburbs are cities unto themselves. Worse, maybe, no one much cares where you've been or what you've seen while you're away.

There's also the financial shock of having to live like everyone else. One day you're on Langley's tab; the next you have to pay your own rent, buy your own car, keep a regular business day, and wear a suit you have to take to the cleaners. You don't need long to get over the feeling that you can defy gravity. The Oktyabrskaya hotel starts to look not so bad.

I'm back living with my family, the divorce postponed. I need to get everyone settled before I leave, and at the moment we can't afford to live in two places. But I do manage, with my mother's help, to put the kids in a French school to keep up their French. My wife's in touch with the State Department to get back her job.

And then there's the rest of my family. It never seems to sit patiently waiting for you to return.

Two weeks after I'm home from Tajikistan, a hospital in California calls me at home. The woman on the other end of the line tells me that my father is dying. She's his nurse.

She has an efficient voice, no trace of urgency or pathos. I wonder how many calls like this she makes a day.

I ask her how long it will be. She says soon—that's why she called. She is standing next to my father, who would like to say good-bye.

A cousin had called me two months ago to tell me my father's lung cancer was back. But I never suspected it was this advanced. I told myself there would be time to fly out to California to see him. There's always time.

I hear the nurse tell my father his son is on the phone.

I wait, but no one says anything. "Hello?" I finally say. There's a faint rasping. "Can you hear me?" I ask. There's a longer rasp this time, forced and painful.

"I love you," I say. Although I barely know the man, that's all I can think to say.

There's only silence now. I wonder if he's understood me. Has my father lost his mind as well as his body?

"I love you," I say again.

There's no answer. I don't know what to say now. It must be five minutes before the nurse comes back on the phone. "Your father's been taken away."

Something else I soon have to wrestle with is that my career abruptly turns toxic. It all has to do with a National Security Agency message, Z/EG/00/60-95, and a CIA "criminal referral" to the Department of Justice. Translation: Six months after I'm back from Tajikistan, I'm sent to northern Iraq on a temporary assignment to work with the Kurds. But within days of my arrival I'm caught up in a plot by a handful of Iraqi generals to oust

Saddam Hussein. Their plan hinges on a classic military coup d'état—a dozen tanks boxing in Saddam at his palace in Al 'Awjah, a village just south of Tikrit. But Langley loses its nerve and cuts the knees out from under us all, and the generals abort their coup. A senior American military officer later would describe it as the "Bay of Goats"—a reference to the CIA's disastrous attempt to invade Cuba in 1961 at the Bay of Pigs. But I myself think the coup stood a chance of succeeding.

I thought being called back from the field after Iraq and chained to a desk would be punishment enough for trying to do what I understood my job to be. (I thrive best at the outer fringes of bureaucracies, not at their core.) But the FBI has other thoughts. It's investigating the coup attempt to see if there is enough evidence to prosecute my team and me for the attempted murder of Saddam Hussein.

All this puts me in a kind of limbo. The CIA will almost certainly let me limp into retirement five years from now, but my corridor reputation—always shaky—is mortally wounded. I can see it in the way colleagues avoid eye contact, in the lack of meaningful work. If I wait out the five years I have until retirement and grab the pension, I'll become one of those Incredible Disappearing Employees, hidden in an office somewhere behind the copying machines.

On the other hand, if the Justice Department decides to prosecute me for the attempted murder of a foreign head of state, I'll need the CIA. In an investigation like this, it's better to be a federal agent than not. I'm fairly certain that the Company will stand behind me, if only because we're at almost constant war with the FBI, and they can't let one of their own go down just like that.

But if I'm cleared and left alone, I'll ask myself every day whether I want to hang on until I retire. The Middle East is in my blood. And no one has to tell me that there's little chance the CIA will ever send me back there. I suppose I could move there after I retire, but it strikes me as sad, the old ex-spook holding on to stale memories.

In the meantime, I live for visits from my friends from the Middle East.

I stand in the window of our Arlington apartment looking out, and watch what's predicted to be the biggest blizzard in decades roll down the deserted street. The snow only started this morning, but already it's hard to tell what's a drift and what's a buried car.

I should stay home, but an Iraqi, Marwan, has flown down from Toronto the night before to see me. He's only here for a day, or at least until he can fly back out. Normally I'd stay in, but Marwan is a friend—a real one. We make an effort to keep up the relationship: we promptly return calls, go out of our way to see each other, ask after family. Marwan knows my mother, but I did not introduce them as a ploy to enlist Marwan in the CIA's service. Marwan is not recruitable.

I figure I have maybe four or five hours before they close I-66, enough time to go see him for an hour or two. I find my son Robert playing in his room and ask him if he wants to take a ride with me. He says no; he wants to go sledding. I tell him we'll sled later, that he should go find his coat while I look for a shovel.

Only a few cars brave I-66, and even the four-wheel-drives move at a snail's pace. Oddly, our front-wheel-drive Toyota Tercel does fine. "Nice ride we have," I say, trying to make conversation. Robert doesn't answer and stares straight ahead. He trusts his mother's driving more than he does mine. She would never go out in a storm like this.

The snowplows are not out yet on M Street in Georgetown. We pass four people on cross-country skis coming down the middle of the street. I wonder if we're going to be able to make it back home. I don't say anything to Robert, but I actually would look forward to getting stuck, the two of us staying at a hotel, giving me a chance to connect with him away from his sisters and his mother.

A great bank of snow almost makes me miss the turn into the Four Seasons. The Ethiopian doorman inside the front entrance doesn't see us until we pull up under the portico. He looks at us in disbelief as Robert and I climb out in mountain hiking boots and down parkas, like some advance party of refugees come to squat in his hotel.

Marwan is downstairs in the lounge, sitting at a table by the piano, a pot of tea in front of him. Dressed in flannel slacks and an expensive cashmere sports coat, he looks at home here, as if he spent his life in luxury hotels. A successful, globe-trotting oil-man, he probably has. We're the only ones in the lounge. Marwan is delighted I've brought Robert along, shaking his hand and asking him about school. He's known Robert since he was one year old. I haven't yet told Marwan about the divorce, or the FBI investigation.

Robert sits on the floor and reads a book while Marwan and I talk about Iraq. From time to time Robert looks up to gauge whether we're finishing or not. I order him an orange juice and a piece of chocolate cake. After it comes, he finds a notebook and a pencil in his knapsack and starts writing. I've never seen him take notes before, and tell myself I should ask him about it when we're back in the car.

The big picture windows are glazed with snow. It melts at the top in rivulets, but then freezes midway down. The waiter comes out to tell us that half of the staff is going home and the lounge is closing. We can move to the dining room if we like. Robert asks whether we shouldn't leave too.

When Marwan offers to take us to lunch, I take my opportunity to ask Robert if he wants to spend the night here at the hotel. He looks at me hard to see if I'm serious. When he thinks I might be, he says no. I tease him again, saying that tomorrow we'll rent cross-country skis and tour around Georgetown. "I want to go home," he says. "I told Mom I'd come home early."

I gather up our things, promising to come back and see Marwan after the snow stops and the roads are plowed. Robert is halfway across the lobby as Marwan and I make our way to the front door.

I'm not sure why now, but it just comes out. "I'm going to resign."

Marwan stops. "You've found a new job?"

"Change every once in a while's a good thing."

"Come work with me."

"It would be a pleasure."

We both understand we're just making conversation. I can't work with Marwan because his business is in Iraq, a country under UN embargo. In fact, I have no idea how I'm going to make a living after I leave the CIA.

FIFTEEN

Thursday evening, May 25th, 8:30 p.m. The Day of Youth in former Yugoslavia. Everything has been quiet for more than a week in Tuzla. The weather is perfect: a late spring day, with lots of sun and a nice temperature. A perfect day for a stroll in the old centre of town. Lots of young people meet in this centre: they don't have the money nor the opportunities to do something else. Discotheques are closed, other facilities not available. As always, Kapija is the centre of activity. This old square, that used to be the eastern entrance of Tuzla (how cynical), is filled with people, most of them between 18 and 25 years old. There is no indication whatsoever that a disaster is about to happen. Of course, you can hear the shelling in the distance (Tuzla Airport was hit by 13 grenades), but that is nothing unusual anymore.

Six persons are having Bosnian lessons in the HCA office, only twenty meters away from Kapija: we want to learn something about Bosnia. Around 9 p.m., there is a big bang. Everybody throws himself at the floor. Panic. Only seconds later, you can hear the screaming, the moaning. People are coming into the office, most of them hysterical. A girl is brought in: she is wounded at her left leg. Fortunately, it is not a severe injury. She's been lucky. But a lot of others were not. Slowly, information is dripping in. A grenade fell in the middle of Kapija. A grenade, fired by the Bosnian Serbs on Mount Majevica, some twenty kilometers east of Tuzla. Don't let anybody tell you something else. Of course, there will be rumors again from the Bosnian Serbs, saying that the Bosnian Muslims did it themselves. Don't believe it: the shellings is the reaction of the Bosnian Serbs to the bombing of Pale by NATO forces.

A long time it is uncertain how many people have been killed or injured. Ten, maybe even twenty people are killed, and a lot more wounded. But after one and a half hours, when I have gathered enough courage to take a look outside, I can easily see that these are low estimates. Kapija is covered with white sheets, stained with blood, which are used to cover the dead. I count at least forty of them.

—Eyewitness report of the Tuzla massacre, May 25, 1995, by Andre Lommenbr, International Liaison Officer of the Helsinki Citizens Assembly, Tuzla; accessed at www.barnsdle.demon.co.uk/ bosnia.tuzla5.html

Split, Croatia, **DAYNA**

By Tuesday the snowplows are finally out, clearing the roads in northern Virginia. At the Tysons Corner Marriott, where I'm staying, guests in the parking lot help each other dig out their cars. As soon as we're all dug out, I head off to work to check in.

The secretary looks at me oddly, I'm sure forgetting I'm back from my last assignment in the Philippines and about to go to Bosnia. But then again, why would she remember, with people coming and going as if this were a bus station? I ask her if my boss, Dave, is in. She says maybe tomorrow; his street isn't plowed.

She remembers that Dave left an envelope for me. I open it to find a one-way ticket to Split, Croatia. Attached to it is a Post-it saying someone will call me at my hotel to tell me how to get the rest of the way to Tuzla.

"That's all?" I ask.

"All what?"

"The commo plan is I fly to Split, and wait for a call?"

"Yeah, I thought it was funny too."

I stick my head in a couple of offices, but they're empty, and I go back to the hotel to pack.

◆

I arrive in Split on Friday evening, catch up on my sleep, and the next morning tour the old town, which is built on the ruins of the Roman Emperor Diocletian's palace. It's fantastic, with its limestone streets polished by a thousand years of people walking them. I think how the Romans must have turned a corner, the beauty of the Adriatic catching them by surprise too. By Monday morning I've seen all there is of Split to see, and there's still no call. I pick up the phone to make sure it still works. I go downstairs and ask the clerk to check my room's pigeonhole for messages. Still nothing.

In the afternoon I walk back down to town, buy a map of old Yugoslavia, and sit on the terrace of the Bellevue Hotel to study it. Two roads go to Tuzla from here, both passing through Sarajevo. I can't imagine anyone escorting us through Croatian, Serb, and Muslim lines—the three sides of Bosnia's civil war. But who knows.

Jacob comes in that afternoon. Like me, he's only been told to wait for a call. To kill time, we rent a car and drive around. The next morning we come out of the hotel to find that the car's been broken into, the glove compartment rifled. We spend the afternoon in the police station doing our best to be friendly with the station cops. Frankly, if it had been our car, we wouldn't even have reported it. It's prudent never to point yourself out to the authorities unless you have to. But with a rental we don't have a choice.

The next morning at six thirty the telephone rings. I look at it, wondering if I'm dreaming.

"Go to the airport tomorrow at two," a woman says. She's American, but that's all I can tell. "Wait at the kiosk."

"Should I look for someone?"

"They'll find you."

Jacob and I share a taxi to the airport and drop our bags next to the only kiosk there is in the small terminal. We don't want to risk going to look for coffee, so we stand there and watch an old woman swab the floor with a tin bucket and a mop.

At twenty past two, a guy in Levi's and a parka comes out of nowhere. He knows our first names and motions for us to follow him. He doesn't offer us his name, and without saying a word, he takes us through a door he has the code for, down a long corridor, and out onto the tarmac, where a single-engine plane waits. He points to the cargo door and tells us to climb in. Jacob and I find places on the floor between some crates. The pilot turns to take a look at us. "Welcome to our flying Winnebago," he says. I'm not sure I know what he means. Does he live on this plane? The way he's dressed, in a Hawaiian shirt over long underwear, it's possible.

When he finishes his preflight checks, he half turns in his seat to look at us. "You guys got earplugs? It's gonna get loud back there." He offers us some beef jerky. We both take a piece.

"We'll fly low to avoid radar. And we're not turning the engine off when we land in Tuzla. So hustle yourselves out the back."

I look out the window and see clouds close in on the hills around Split. We'll be flying into a storm, I think. Jacob sticks his earphones in and fiddles with his MP3 player. He closes his eyes as if he's about to take a nap. I'm happy it's Jacob with me on this one; his calmness is catching.

The engine pops a couple of times, then catches, and the plane moves forward. As we taxi, a wind pulls at the tail, causing the plane to sway back and forth. It comes to the end of the runway, the engine whines, and we take off in a steep ascent. Almost immediately it levels off, at about a thousand feet. We're so low I can see telephone wires and cows in the snow-patched fields.

I lose sight of the ground when the rain turns to snow, and then lose interest in looking out the window when the plane starts bucking. I close my eyes and think about the last time I was in a small plane in a storm. It was when my dad flew the family to Baja. I was sixteen. A thunderstorm came out of nowhere, forcing my father to take the plane under a thousand feet. The first airstrip we came to was flooded. The storm worsened, and my dad had to drop lower and lower. By now my mother was panicking, yelling for him to put the plane down on the ground. My father kept his cool, not rattled at all. Just as we ran out of sky, he spotted a deserted airstrip near a beach. As soon as the plane came to a stop, he turned off the engine. "Cheated death again!" he said, his signature sign-off to any close call.

It wasn't that my father was reckless; he just loved his thrills. He was already forty when he started to study at night for a private pilot's license, and with friends bought the small plane in which we flew to Mexico. Winters, he would fly my mother, my brother, me, and our dog on ski trips up into the Sierras, our skis stacked between us down the middle of the fuselage. Summers, there were trips to the Colorado River, where he'd find a dirt strip to land on. I'll never forget the time my mother and I watched as my dad and brother took off in a blustery wind, a wingtip scraping the ground, the plane nearly cartwheeling. My father righted the plane only at the last moment. I suppose that's why I'm not all that nervous; I've been here before.

It's dusk when I feel the plane start to descend. Lights are coming on in the houses. I sense that the plane is about to touch down, but there are no runway lights, and it's impossible to see where we're landing. It's a long, dead minute before the plane bounces hard on the runway. The pilot taxis to the end and spins the plane around, bringing it to a sharp stop. He keeps the engine running.

If there's a terminal, I can't see it—only camouflaged tents and a few soldiers standing in front of them watching us. The pilot turns around and motions for us to open the cargo door and get out. The look on his face says, *Move fast or else*. Three olive-colored Suburbans, their lights off, pull up alongside the plane, and a couple of guys get out to help us unload. As soon as the last crate is out, the plane wheels around and speeds down the runway and takes off like an angry wasp. Our driver tells us to get on the floor of the backseat; he doesn't want the Bosnian sentries at the airport gate to see our faces.

They let us off in front of the Hotel Tuzla. The lobby's a refrigerator, and I can see my breath. A young woman and a young man in faded but tidy uniforms stand behind the desk, looking surprised to see guests. We show them our passports, but all they're interested in is our cash. The rooms are Communist-spare, the windows cross-taped against shelling. There's no toilet paper, and just a thin blanket on the bed. I go and knock on Jacob's door to tell him to meet me in ten minutes down in the lobby. We'll go out and see the town.

Jacob and I walk the few blocks from the hotel to Tuzla's center. We stop at a bakery with a blazing brick oven and buy two loaves of fresh, warm bread. We walk to a small grocery store across the street to buy butter and jam. Then sit on a bench in front and make ourselves dinner.

At the square they call Kapija, teenagers standing in clumps eye us warily, lowering their voices as we get closer. A face blooms orange from a cigarette lighter.

"I have to teach you to smoke," Jacob says, pulling out a pack of cigarettes.

Jacob shows me how to hold a cigarette like someone who has nothing better to do than stand around and smoke. I put my back against a tree, pretending to inhale. Jacob smokes, shifting back and forth on his feet. The teenagers ignore us now and get back to talking in loud voices.

The next day Jacob buys a new Russian Lada from a car dealer we're surprised to find open, and I shop for clothes that make me look like a local: hand-knit sweaters and a cheap wool overcoat. I find a local purse for my 9-mm pistol. The one I've brought with me, a custom-made embossed crocodile with a concealed cavity, doesn't exactly fit in here. Jacob's fine with the Eurotrash leather fanny pack for his Glock.

In the afternoon I shop for food to supplement the Hotel Tuzla's breakfast, which is hard bread and soft-boiled eggs. I manage to find some fresh cheese and green apples. On the way back to the hotel, I pass a hardware store where there's a handmade sled in the window. I've seen people hauling their groceries around on them. I can't resist.

Jacob watches as I haul the sled up a hill behind the hotel. I pick the steepest part and let go. When I get to the bottom, there's an old man and woman watching me. I wave at them, and they smile back.

When we get back to the hotel there's a little black puppy in front. It runs up to me to play. I scoop it up in my arms, looking at Jacob. "Think what good cover it would be," I say. He gives me a look that says, *No way*. I put it down, and it runs off to try to play with a woman walking by.

As consolation, Jacob takes me out in the new Lada to look for a pizza place the desk clerk's told us about. Just outside Tuzla, we're stopped at a roadblock, a funnel of two old Soviet jeeps blocking traffic both ways.

A young boy with a Kalashnikov in his hand walks up to Jacob's window. "Papers," he says.

Jacob hands him his Virginia driver's license. An older man walks over with a clipboard and takes the driver's license. As he starts to write something, I watch Jacob crane his neck to see what it is.

As soon as we pull away, Jacob starts laughing.

"What?" I say.

"They're on to us."

"No, come on, what?"

"He wrote for my first name 'Drivers,' and for my last name 'License.'"

SIXTEEN

Kazakhs are famous for their friendliness and hospitality. When greeting a guest, the host gives him both hands to show that he is unarmed.

—www.independent.ie/unsorted/features/kazakhstan-the-unlikely-tourist-hot-spot-441205.html

Almaty, Kazakhstan: **BOB**

My boss, Garth, is already downstairs in the lobby—in a suit and a cashmere overcoat. He takes one look at my Levi's and old orange Gore-Tex parka and shakes his head no. As I head back upstairs two steps at a time to change, I think how he's probably right. Our host is the Kazakh Minister of Defense. We represent the United States. We may not be diplomats. But even faux diplomats wear suits.

When I come back down, Garth's talking with the minister, Tok, who's in a fleece-lined parka and snow boots, over some weird jumpsuit. He looks as if he's going out to chop wood. But it's too late to go back up to my room and change back. I remember my mother telling me it's always better to be overdressed than underdressed.

We follow Tok outside to a new black Suburban with a rack of squad-car lights on the top. Garth climbs in the front next to Tok, while I sit in the back.

"We see our beautiful capital now," Tok says. He turns on the roof lights and gooses the siren to move the car in front of us.

I've been to Almaty enough over the last couple years to know there isn't much to see. It's a little frontier town, at one time a Soviet listening post on China. Legend has it that the first apple tree grew here, in Neolithic times. Silk Route caravans passing through Almaty spread the trees, apple seeds apparently passing undamaged through the alimentary canals of horses and pack animals.

Even Tok gets bored driving around Almaty. "Good, no?" he says. "Now we have lunch." Although it's only ten thirty and we've just finished breakfast, neither Garth nor I say anything.

Frankly, an early lunch sounds good. It's been a long week. It all started at Dulles Airport's private jet terminal where we boarded the Director's ultra-tricked-out Falcon 7X. It quickly turned into a liquor-smeared blur: Guinness most of the night in Prestwick, Scotland; endless vodka toasts in Baku, Azerbaijan; vodka for breakfast in Ashgabat, Turkmenistan; and bottles and bottles of cognac in Tashkent, Uzbekistan; countless lunches, dinners, receptions. I started pouring my glasses into the potted plants as I'd seen Tajikistan's president do, but now I have a pretty good idea what it's like to go on a bender.

We're traveling the region, discussing how we can improve relations with our counterparts in the Caucasus and Central Asia, which usually means writing checks for one thing or another. We're supposed to get intelligence in return, but more often than not the money drops down a black hole. We're also on a farewell trip for Garth, who's going to retire in two months. As for me, I'm along for the ride—anything to escape Langley.

Tok drives up into the mountains, every once and a while turning on the siren to bully cars out of our way. For a while I think he's taking us on a long drive far out of Almaty, and my mood blackens. Then I hear Tok tell Garth we're going to Chimbulak, a ski resort above Almaty, and I feel better again. Maybe's there's a good restaurant there.

We're almost there when Tok abruptly yanks the wheel hard right, plowing the Suburban into a snowfield. The momentum carries the Suburban about five feet before it sinks to its windows. Tok gasses it, but the wheels only spin. A dozen soldiers appear out of nowhere, tumbling over the snow, swarming the Suburban, putting their shoulders in it to try to get us unstuck, but it doesn't budge. "No matter," Tok says. "We walk."

The soldiers dig out the doors so we can open them, and then stomp down the snow, making a path to a banquet table in the middle of the field. It's piled high with liquor bottles and platters of food. My shoes are instantly soaked, my feet freezing. I'm resigned to another very long day.

Tok barks something in Kazakh, and a soldier runs to the table, going down face-first in the snow a couple of times. He comes back with three glasses and a bottle of brandy. Tok fills up our glasses. "Oh, why the hell not," Garth says, finishing his brandy in one gulp. I follow suit, hoping it will take the bite off the cold.

Tok looks over my shoulder. "Now, sportsmen, we have fun." I turn around to see a soldier with an armful of skis, boots, and poles.

Garth sees what's happening. "You know, Tok, I think I would rather stay here with you," he says. "We have a lot to talk about."

I look at the banquet table, the dozen or more brandy and vodka bottles waiting there, and grab a pair of boots from the soldier. "I'd love to ski," I say.

Two of Tok's soldiers try to keep up with me by running under the lift. But the snow is too soft, and they fall behind. I'm halfway up before I notice my skis are different lengths. If anyone notices I'm skiing in a suit, they're too polite to say anything.

By the second run, my feet are killing me. I ski to the bottom and trek across the field to the banquet table. Tok meets me with a tumbler of something brownish. "The President's own cognac," he says, handing me a glass. "A toast to you, a great American ski champion," Tok says. He downs his. I take a sip. Tok frowns, and I throw back the tumbler.

I take the skis off and look for something to eat, knowing that the only way to get through the rest of the doomed day is on a full stomach. I find a plateful of pieces of something white, greasy, and pulpy. I ask Garth what it is. "Raw horse mane," he says. "It's exquisite, try some." I put it down and pick up another plate of something. "Oh that's delightful too," Garth says. "Sun-dried horse rectum." He giggles. Garth is already drunk. I grab a handful of radishes.

It's getting very cold, which at least keeps me sober—or maybe not, because I seem to have missed the fact that everyone else is heading back to the Suburban, which has been miraculously turned around. When I finally catch up, I ask Garth where we're going. "Do you know how to skate too?" he asks.

At Almaty's gigantic skating rink, we follow Tok down a set of stairs into a lighted corridor. Tok opens a door to reveal a stump of a woman with arms of steel. She's holding a bundle of birch sticks. "Now we take bath," Tok says. Tok doesn't mind when Garth and I say no. He tells the woman to bring us a bottle of vodka and glasses instead, and when she comes back, we toast eternal Kazakh-American friendship.

By now I'm on my way to being good and drunk. We follow Tok farther into the guts of the rink, down a dark maze of corridors and offices. I'm completely disoriented. People come out and shake Tok's hand. Everyone seems to know him.

At last we end up in a gloomy, windowless, private dining room with gaudily painted Styrofoam rocks attached to the walls. I think it's supposed to look like a grotto. One of the tables is set with a dozen vodka bottles. Tok opens one and pours us shots. A couple of men wander in, Russians and Kazakhs. Tok pours them vodkas too.

A woman appears with a giant platter of broiled carp ringed by potatoes. Everyone wolfs the food down, stopping only long enough to make toasts. Tok drinks along with the rest of us. So far

I haven't caught him emptying his glass under the table, but he's stone-cold sober as far as I can tell.

When we're finished, Tok takes the free chair next to Garth and throws an arm around him. "Mr. Garth," he says, "it is time that we enjoy ourselves as men."

"What?" Garth says, his eyes alert now. It's probably my imagination, but I think Garth is willing himself sober.

"Ladies. Beautiful ladies."

On cue, two very attractive girls in their twenties come floating in, accompanied by a recording of Tony Bennett and Frank Sinatra singing "New York, New York."

Garth looks as if he's going to throw up, but then roars with laughter. He stands up and puts his arm around Tok and pulls him in for a hug. "God, I love you Tok. Thirty-five years in the CIA, and no one has ever offered me a girl. I'll have to say no, but it truly is a wonderful offer."

The next morning, as we board the Falcon for London, I tell Garth that we should have invited the girls to come along. I sort of like the idea of getting thrown out of the CIA for ferrying two hookers on the Director's plane, if nothing else than to see the expressions on the faces of Her Majesty's immigrations at Heathrow airport.

In fact, how to get out of the CIA occupies more and more of my mental energy these days, and Garth knows it. It's part of why he has invited me along on his farewell tour. It's not only that we're pals, or that I've done time in many of the places we have been visiting, or that I can generally be counted on to do stupid things like barreling down a slope in mismatched skis and my meet-the-president suit. He wants to see how I handle myself in polite company, see if when I resign from the CIA, maybe we can work together.

Garth and I both know there's a big, endlessly fascinating world outside the precincts of the CIA, a place with lots of possibilities. It's a world we've convinced ourselves we could get along in very well, looking up old friends like Tok. We might even be able to make a good living at it.

Here's what I need to do before I pull the plug though: get the FBI off my back, divorce, and take one last bite of the cherry.

SEVENTEEN

U.S. Department of Justice
Criminal Division
Office of the Deputy Assistant Attorney General
Washington, D.C. 20530

Mr. Jeffrey Smith
General Counsel
Central Intelligence Agency
Washington, D.C. 20505

Re: NSA Serial Z/EG/00/60-95

Dear Mr. Smith:

  The Criminal Division of the Department of Justice has received from the Federal Bureau of Investigation a report of investigation involving the above-cited report. After carefully reviewing the FBI's report, we have reached a determination that the Department will decline prosecution of the matter.

  Thank you for your cooperation in connection with this investigation.

Sincerely,
Mark M. Richard
Deputy Assistant Attorney General

EIGHTEEN

> NATO commanders said they may have prevented terrorist attacks on NATO troops when they arrested 11 men at the home, which a NATO official described as a "terrorist training school." But the Bosnian government said it never posed a threat to the Implementation Force.
>
> No shots were fired in the raid and no one was hurt.
>
> Pentagon sources said three Iranians and eight Bosnian Muslims were taken into custody. Two of the Iranians were said to hold diplomatic passports or papers.
>
> The house is in Bosnian government territory near the town of Fojnica.
>
> NATO said it contained an "extensive armory" of handguns, explosives and rocket launchers. Pictures taken during the raid show ammunition and weapons stores and explosives hidden in children's toys.
>
> Also found were diagrams of buildings in Sarajevo, and training manuals written in Farsi, according to sources.
>
> —www.cnn.com/WORLD/Bosnia/updates/9602/16/

Sarajevo: **BOB**

I sit on the bed, listening to the landlady move around in the kitchen. I start to get up, but then decide I don't want to see her. Our impromptu Serbo-Croatian lessons are going nowhere, she bustling around the kitchen, pointing at things, giving them names, and me repeating after her like a parrot with a bad accent.

I keep reminding myself it's okay not to mingle with the Bosnians or learn their language. I came to Sarajevo for only one reason—to take my Parthian shot at the Iranians and their proxies Hizballah, my last hurrah before I leave the Company. And to do that I need anonymity. Mixing with the locals can only end up "eroding my cover"—CIA speak for the enemy smelling a rat. And, if I know Hizballah, they'll be a lot faster to smell one than the Bosnians.

Hizballah operatives and their Iranian backers are great spies and saboteurs, some of the best. They have been ever since they launched their undeclared war on the United States during Khomeini's revolution in 1979. I watched from the front lines as the Iranians won every skirmish we ever fought with them. They got away cleanly with taking our diplomats in Tehran in 1979, turned a rescue mission into a fiasco, blew up our embassies in Beirut and Kuwait, and kidnapped and killed our chief of station in Beirut. In Kuwait, they shot one of my best Hizballah informants point-blank in the face. In all of it, they never left a fingerprint behind.

And it's definitely not going to help that in Sarajevo the Bosnian Muslim government is a client of Iran. The Bosnians haven't forgotten that it was Iran that came to their aid when the Serbs had them under siege, sending money, food, and arms while the West turned a blind eye to the slaughter. If it's a choice between the CIA and the Iranians, they'll take the Iranians any day.

Finally, there's the added problem that Sarajevo is just plain small. It took me one day of walking around to realize that there's nowhere to go—no place to kill time or blend in with the locals. The only important landmark, the old National Library, is a burned-out husk. There's the Holiday Inn, where you can get a drink in the lobby bar, but it's almost always empty and gloomy. Operating in this place is going to be like swimming in a straitjacket.

I've picked this apartment with the chatty landlady because it's off the grid and out of Hizballah's sights. I didn't have to sign a lease or show an ID or a reference. The alternative was the Holiday Inn, where most foreigners stay. But it's a spy's trap because the desk clerks, maids, and everyone else report to Bosnian intelligence. And all the rooms are bugged too. If I stayed there it would be a matter of days before my presence filtered up to Hizballah.

As soon as I hear the landlady leave, I get up, dress, make my way through the chickens in the backyard, and let myself out the gate. I take a back alley behind a mosque and make my way into town.

The café I stop at is empty except for two men out front playing chess on a gouged board, painted stones standing in for the missing pieces. Neither is much interested in the game. They have to remind each other to make a move.

I pull out a book and try to read. But I'm too distracted to concentrate. I don't know if it's because of too much sleep or too much sitting around waiting. I order another coffee and go back to watching the chess players, checking my watch every couple of minutes.

At 9:55 I pay and walk to the synagogue off Vladislava Skarica. My inside officer, Dan, is already there, waiting for me behind the wheel of a new teal Jeep Cherokee. When I get into the passenger's seat, he pulls away, not saying a word. All that I know about Dan is that he's only been in the Company five years, he's the son of an FBI agent, he's recently divorced, and he gets up early in the morning to work out.

Dan keeps one eye fixed on the rearview mirror to make sure we haven't picked up a tail. We drive up into the mountains until we come to a restaurant that has a deck with a good view over Sarajevo. I get out to see if the place is open. I shout into the darkness of the restaurant, asking if anyone's there. A man comes out of the kitchen in a stained apron. I tilt my thumb at my mouth to let him know we want something to drink.

Dan and I sit at a table on the deck, Sarajevo at our feet. I have no idea why, but I say we should order a bottle of wine. Dan just as stupidly says yeah. The cook understands *vino*, and goes back in to find us a bottle.

I prod Dan for news. He tells me the boss has told him that we should start using different car pickups. He thought I should walk down a road where Dan's parked on the shoulder, the hood up as if he has engine problems, and we meet by chance.

"He even told me what you should say," Dan says.

"Let me guess: 'May I help you?'"

"Europe. What do you expect."

Operatives in Europe have a reputation for leisurely lunches and duty-free BMWs more than they do a spy's craft.

"What about my Land Rovers?" I ask.

At our last meeting I asked for a couple of armored Land Rovers, camouflaged to look like the British army's. They're everywhere in Sarajevo, like yellow cabs in Manhattan. They don't have license plates, and with their tinted glass, you can't see into them—perfect for parking and keeping an eye on Hizballah—static surveillance, as it's called. Or just moving around Sarajevo anonymously.

"They think you're an idiot."

"So I'm supposed to drive those fucking cars with advertisements down the side?"

At our last meeting I told Dan about the drive in with the girl who calls herself Riley, who as much as said she wasn't going to get back in one. Dan looks at me and doesn't say anything, swishing wine around in his mouth.

"I could see Riley in the turret of a Land Rover," I say, "manning the thirty-cal. She's got that certain gleam in her eye. I wonder what her real name is."

Dan doesn't answer. He's been in the Company long enough to have gotten used to false names, how an operative will be known to each of his informants by a different name (an alias), a nom de plume he uses to sign off cables (a pseudonym), and a made-up name for his informants (a cryptonym). In the CIA, there are even made-up names that stand in for countries, political leaders, and geographic locations. It's some bizarre nominalism, but it works.

But I'm not going to let the cars go. "Do they want us to ride around on bicycles?"

Dan doesn't say anything. We've run out of things to talk about, and drink in silence. The wine is warm, but I don't care. All I know right now is that I don't want to go back to my hovel even if it means drinking all day. What I've decided about Sarajevo is that it's a city radiant with sorrow. Everyone has slipped into a dull acceptance of violence, indifferent to what's left of their lives. And the one way to combat it is spend your time outside—and drink.

It could be a month before Langley gets the stuff I need here on an airplane. And in the meantime I've got people coming to work for me. I dread sitting everyone down and telling them they have to stay in Split until we get our act together. Their enthusiasm is going to fade as fast as mine.

Neither of us realizes how intense the sun is. We're surprised when we come to the bottom of the bottle. When the cook comes out to check on us, we order another one.

"At least I don't have a butcher's bill to pay," I say.

"What does that mean?" Dan gets up to go look for the bathroom.

I try again to remember what else Dan is supposed to do for me. I pat my pockets to look for a pen, but I don't have one. Dan comes back, turns his chair away from me to look down at Sarajevo.

"Where's my satphone?" I ask.

"Have another drink, you drunk." He half turns in his seat and tops up my glass.

"I need communications."

"Tomorrow, the next day. I don't know. Do you have a weapon?"

"When's the next resupply flight?"

"That's what I thought."

I make a circular motion in the air imitating a propeller. "The airplane. The airplane." I decide I'm drunk.

I think more about how we're going to have to fly by the seat of our pants, improvise, and keep our fingers crossed that we don't do something really stupid.

I slide my chair around so Dan has to look at me. "This is god-damned bureaucratic terrorism. We don't have cars. We don't have a place to live, and on top of it I don't have a clue where we're going to put this damn ray gun."

In fact it's not a ray gun. It's a kind of parabolic microphone that sucks conversations out of the air at a long distance, even through the walls of buildings. My plan is to find an apartment with a line-of-sight view of a Hizballah safe house, position the mic in the apartment's window so it can't be seen, and wait for the Hizballah operatives to blurt out something they shouldn't—a name, an address, or a telephone number. Whatever it is, we run it to ground. For instance, if we were to get the plate number of a Hizballah operative's car, we would then try to put an owner's name to it.

I'd like to put blanket coverage even on the Iranians—watch their offices, residences, and cars around the clock. But there's just no way to do it. First, we don't have enough people. Second, in a place like Sarajevo the Iranians would spot us in a second and re-taliate. Which makes the parabolic mic the silver bullet in this circus. However, with a little luck on our side, in six months we'll be able to hand European forces a dossier on Hizballah, one they'll use to unstitch the whole apparatus in a coup de main. That's my dream at least.

"I would have waited in Split if I were you." Dan points vaguely in the direction of Split. "There are better bars there."

I flip him off.

"You moron," he says.

"Who the fuck are they, sending me out here?" I have a headache. I empty my glass over the rail.

Dan pays, and I go out to the parking lot and get behind the wheel of the Cherokee. But I'm still sober enough to realize I'm too drunk to drive. I climb over the gearshift onto the passenger's seat.

"How far is Pale?" I ask when Dan comes out to the car.

Pale, a village in the mountains above Sarajevo, is where a handful of notorious Serbian war criminals are holed up. It's where the winter Olympics were held in 1984. No one will raid it for fear of reigniting the war. We've been warned never to set foot in the place.

I don't say it, but what I have in mind is seeing if Pale's a good place for Dan and me to meet, somewhere I know the Iranians, Hizballah, and even Muslim Bosnians would never dare set foot in.

"Let's do it," Dan says.

"Let's first go get Cheryl."

Cheryl is a contractor for the Agency for International Development. A big, ungainly, sunburnt girl, she's cut from that fabric of expatriates who happily go from one international disaster to the next. Dragging her along—an American official who can truthfully say what she does—is good protective covering.

The few people we pass in Pale stop and stare at our Cherokee with French diplomatic plates, narrowing their eyes in suspicion and hate. You definitely feel it when you're on the wrong side of a conflict.

We pick an empty café and sit outside. It crosses my mind they might not serve us. But a tiny woman in a bloodred apron comes out to take our order. There's not even the hint of a smile, though. No one wants to drink, but in solidarity with the Serbs we order their favorite drink, plum brandy.

A couple minutes later a lady in her seventies walks up to the café's terrace, and takes a seat at a table. She looks at the ground, avoiding eye contact. I notice her hands are trembling. She sits two tables away from us, facing the street. When she finally does look over, she's crying, daubing her eyes with a cotton handkerchief. Cheryl gets up and walks over to sit with her.

Dan and I drink as Cheryl talks to the lady in broken Serbo-Croatian. The waitress stands in the door of the café, watching. I notice that across the street a couple have pulled the curtains open in their house, looking at us.

Cheryl takes the old lady by the arm and helps her up to walk over to our table. Cheryl says the lady wants to go to Sarajevo with us in our car. The lady looks from me to Dan, her blue eyes pleading. I think she's going to start crying again.

Cheryl explains that the woman's son lives in Sarajevo. She hasn't seen him since the beginning of the war in 1992. She was always too scared to cross the confrontation lines, convinced the Bosnian Muslims would arrest her because she's a Serb. She would risk crossing it in a diplomatic-plated car, though.

Dan shakes his head no. I'm his senior, though, and say okay.

We've broken every other rule in the book today, so why not one more? And now the day has a purpose.

Headquarters has a problem with my tactics—living and working out of private houses, constantly switching cars, meeting in places like Pale. They haven't quite accepted that in Sarajevo we have no choice but to operate like light cavalry—mobile, fast, elusive. And I'm not sure anything like this has ever been done before. The CIA has forever worked from fortresses from which operatives sally forth, steal secrets, and then gallop headlong back in, pulling up the drawbridge behind them.

After my first trip to Sarajevo, when I was back at Langley, I explained to the Bosnian branch chief what I was planning. She looked at me in total confusion, as if I were speaking in tongues. When I told her the entire operation would be run from a house I'd rented in Butmir, a suburb near the airport, she asked if it would be secure. There's nothing to secure, I said. We'll be paper-less. Her confusion deepened when I told her that I intended to keep the parabolic mic in an ordinary apartment, rotating teams in and out to man it. And that the military support team, an Arabic translator and a communicator, would be in yet another house. When I said I would walk the tapes from the parabolic mic up to the support team's house every day to translate them and cable them back to Washington, she looked at me as if I were making fun of her.

The branch chief was a small woman with granny glasses and tendrils of auburn hair running down the sides of her head. She reminded me of my second-grade teacher. She'd never worked in the field. I would have gone on, but I just didn't think that she'd get the anonymity part. The thing is, you can't do things by the book in Sarajevo. I just knew instinctively that all the shuffling around, dressing like the locals, paying in cash, never talking on a phone or a radio, was the only way to escape the attention of Hiz-ballah. At the same time I knew it was unorthodox and risky. But I didn't see another way.

"What makes you think this is going to work?" she asked as I started to walk out the door to go back to Sarajevo.

"Watching Hizballah in Beirut."

She shrugged her shoulders. I was the chief of this lash-up, and she could only stand back and watch.

In the meantime, I'd settle for an apartment with a line-of-sight view of the Hizballah safe house.

NINETEEN

I cannot forget that picture of the little girl who, after the grenade fell on the marketplace in Sarajevo in August, turned to her mother and asked where her hands went, only to find out she had also lost her father.

—Carl Bildt, High Representative for Bosnia and Herzegovina

Sarajevo: DAYNA

In the second week of June, Charlie, the ex-Marine jet pilot, and I come down to Sarajevo from Tuzla to help Bob find an apartment for the parabolic mic. But by day three we sit in our usual café in the old city, talking about the same thing we talk about every morning: we're getting absolutely nowhere finding one. It shouldn't be this hard. There are hundreds and hundreds of empty apartments, most abandoned from the beginning of the war. You can walk by and look in the windows, the places untouched, unlooted, the dusty furniture still there, just waiting for nice, polite renters like us. The problem is finding the owners.

There are no real estate agents in Sarajevo. No one hangs out "for rent" signs. If there are listings in the newspapers, we can't understand them. Other foreigners like the press corps and international aid workers live in the Holiday Inn. And when they do decide to move into an apartment, they have "fixers" find them, local Bosnians with fat Rolodexes. We don't have that luxury. Fixers report to the local police.

We are on our second cup of cappuccino when the café starts to fill up with men of all ages, probably all out of work. They smoke one cigarette after another, staring at Charlie and me, the only two foreigners in the place. The windows steam up from the espresso maker. This is going to be another long day, I think. There's no way we're going to find an apartment before the parabolic mic arrives.

We're nursing the coffee along when Charlie sits up as if called. He smiles and says he has an idea. I wait for him to clue me in, but instead he tells me to stay put. He gets up and pushes out the door. I watch him out the window as he half trots down the street. God knows what he's up to now. I pull out an old *Herald Tribune* and start reading an article I must have read three times already.

Last week, Charlie went out to take a look at the Saturday car market, which is held in a field outside town. He came back after an hour with a banged-up white Ford Taurus with Sarajevo plates. Charlie said he didn't have to show his passport or anything when he bought it. I asked him if he thought it was stolen. He said it probably was, but no one was going to care.

When Charlie comes back, he's got a big smile on his face, fanning a stack of three-by-five cards. He sits down and drops them in front of me. There's something in Serbo-Croatian typed on them.

"I give up. What are they?" Charlie's pleased that he's made me ask.

"The girl who typed them for me was very sweet," he says. "A doll, in fact." Charlie won't wipe the grin off his face.

"Forget it, Charlie. I'm not playing." I push the cards back in front of him.

"I knew you'd be pissed it was me who figured out how to do this and not you. It says, 'American couple looking for an apartment to rent.'"

"What's this?" I ask, pointing at a telephone number at the bottom of a card.

"It's the girl's number. She's agreed to take messages for me."

I think this plan comes with a whole host of problems. One is that anyone we enlist to help us has to have his name checked with headquarters. Second, there's no way they'd allow some random girl to take messages for us. (And I don't even want to know what Charlie told this girl we're doing here.) On the other hand, Charlie's an operative with a couple of tours behind him, and I have to defer to him. Besides, the way Bob's running things, there's no choice but to innovate. We pay our check and go out to look together.

Couples seem a lot more innocent than people on their own, especially when they make it look like they're nesting. Bob's told us that as soon as we find an apartment, Charlie and I will move in, posing as a couple. We'll do this for two weeks, alternating operating the parabolic mic. We'll be replaced by Brad and Lara, the same couple I worked with in Los Angeles. If this thing really takes off, Bob will ask headquarters for other couples to spot us.

Charlie and I walk along the Miljacka River, noting buildings with a line of sight to the Hizballah safe house. A dozen different places would work. I see a woman coming out of one, and run across the street to catch the door before it closes. Charlie follows me in. The vestibule light switch is only a hole with dangling wires, but the place is clean and smells of cheap soap. I wonder if the building might not be completely abandoned when I hear a kitten's meow from an upstairs apartment.

I knock on the first apartment door with windows facing the river while Charlie stands off to the side. A strange girl standing in a door is less threatening than a strange man. I hear something moving in the back of the apartment and knock again. We wait some more, but the apartment is quiet. I put a card under the door, and we walk up to the second floor, footsteps echoing up and down the stairwell.

The second-floor apartment facing the river is boarded shut. From the dust in front of the door, it's obvious no one's been in the place for a long time. I put a card under the door anyway.

On the third floor we hear the kitten again. It's coming from the door of the riverside apartment. I can see the tip of its tiny paw under the door. I knock and bend down to play with the kitten's paw. Just as I am about to slip the paper under the door, the door opens a crack.

"Can I help you?" a man's voice asks in English. He leans over to pick up the kitten before it runs out.

Charlie steps out of the shadow and tells him we'd like to rent an apartment. A gaunt man in his early thirties opens the door wide, looks at us for a beat, and invites us in. "This isn't what you want," he says. "But please come in."

I walk to the window of the bedroom facing the river. It has an unobstructed view of the Hizballah safe house. The glass is cross-taped to limit shattering, but the tape will come off easily. There's a smell of moldy carpet. A dark spot in the corner looks like old blood, but maybe that's just my imagination.

There is no living room or dining room in the apartment. It was probably subdivided from a larger one. The kitchen and the entrance are the only common areas. Family photos dot the tables and the wall. The man notices me looking at one of a handsome woman in her thirties, wearing a wool coat with a brooch on it. "That was my mother," he says. I want to ask what happened to her but don't. It's a question you never ask in Sarajevo.

I go back to the bedroom and imagine Serb snipers in the mountains above Sarajevo looking through their scopes at this window. Did they see this man's mother moving in the window and shoot her?

A pot of tea starts to whistle on the stove, and our host asks if we'd like a cup. He invites us to sit down on the small couch in the entryway.

He's tall and good-looking in a Slavic way, but there's a sadness in his eyes, a hesitation in his step. His knit sweater is frayed, his pants shiny with wear.

"I lived here with my parents," he says. "But it's only me and my cat now."

I play with the kitten while Charlie tells him we'd be interested in the apartment. We would rent it for six months, maybe longer. And we could easily pay the entire rent up front.

"I am very sorry for my apartment. It is nothing." Given the way he speaks English, his deliberate enunciation, I wonder if he didn't once teach it. But I guess that since he's home in the middle of the day, he doesn't have a job now. And two Americans offering to rent his apartment has to be a temptation he cannot turn away from.

"I will live with my sister," he says, more to himself than us.

I still want to ask how his mother died, but instead I play with the kitten on my lap. I think about telling him we'll watch his kitten for him, but it may be all he has left.

Two days later Charlie and I come back to pick up the keys and pay the rent. The man takes the envelope without looking in it, picks up a small scuffed suitcase, and shakes our hands good-bye. He picks up the kitten, nestling it in the crook of his arm.

As soon as I hear the front door close, I run down the stairs and watch him walk down the street and disappear around a corner. I never see him again.

TWENTY

Sarajevo: **BOB**

The landlord of the house where I intend to put my military communicator and Arabic translator comes over and stands behind me to see what I'm looking at. I bend down to examine the basement bedroom floor where it's been cemented over, waxed, and polished, covering up some sort of a hole. I don't know why I didn't see it when I first rented the place.

"No problem, no problem," the landlord says.

I bend down to take a better look. I look up and notice a similar hole in the ceiling, plastered and painted over.

The landlord motions me aside. "No problem. Look." He stomps on the hole. "No problem."

"It was an artillery shell, wasn't it?" I ask. "It must have scared you to dig it out."

He stamps his foot down on the hole. "See! See!"

I now realize that the round is still buried in the ground. The concrete and the paint are cosmetic.

The landlord is afraid I'm about to demand my money back.

"Is there another one?" I ask.

"This is the only one. I promise."

I know about promises, but I've spent a lot of time trying to keep this place clean, and don't intend to give it up lightly.

"Don't worry," I say. "We'll be fine here."

After I rented the house two weeks ago, I made a point of never driving here if I didn't have to. I didn't want anyone to start connecting the house to my car. Instead, I walked. I had it timed almost exactly: one hour and ten minutes from the National Library to the house, which sits high up on a ridge above Sarajevo. The route started with a steep run of steps, a traverse through a narrow alley, and a path above a dozen old stone houses cut into the rock. From there, it crossed a field and passed through a grove of birches, which led me to a narrow path through a village. The last leg wound up the mountain on a one-lane road. Anyone following me would have had to be on foot like me, and I couldn't miss him.

Only rarely did a car pass me, or did anyone walk the route with me. Sometimes I'd pass children kicking a soccer ball in the road, but they'd ignore me. After the first week of this, I found a way to refine the route, cutting through a cemetery and a pine forest. I was absolutely sure anyone following me would have had to stay glued to my back in order not to lose me.

On the few occasions when I absolutely had to drive to the house to deliver supplies, I'd drive around for an hour to make sure I didn't have a tail, taking a new route each time. Halfway up the mountain, I'd take off the license plates. Even if the neighbors noticed me, they could identify the car only by year and model. In other words, this house was as free from scrutiny as they come.

This may all sound like a lot of hocus-pocus, but as much as cell phones and the automobile enable adultery, they are the Achilles' heel of spies. Keep your eye on an operative's car (or tap his phone) and the chances are good you can compromise his sources.

◆

When I get to the airport, the communicator and Arabic translator are already off the C-130, standing on the tarmac's edge with their equipment. One's short, the other tall. They're both in North Face Gore-tex jackets, cargo pants, and new fawn-colored desert boots—with fourteen enormous hard plastic cases stacked next to them. We can't fit them all in the car, and have to lash half to the roof.

On the ride up to the house, neither man says a word. I wonder if they've ever worked in the field before. When I stop to take off the plates, they stay in the Toyota.

Three little girls are playing inside the fence when we pull up to the house.

"Isn't that insecure?" asks Ron, the communicator.

"I don't know—maybe people will think we're running a kindergarten," I say. "It's better than the truth."

"We're going to have to lock that gate," he says.

I take them downstairs into the bedroom and point at the floor where the unexploded shell is. "I think it's inert. Are you OK with that?"

They look at me to make sure I'm not joking, then move to a corner to talk so that I can't hear them.

"There's always the Holiday Inn," I yell over.

They talk some more and walk back.

Ron looks anxiously at the Arabic translator, Curtis, whose pencil mustache makes him look like a cat, and asks if we can get it dug out. I say no. They look at each other as if they're considering running for it.

For the next fifteen minutes they silently poke around the house, opening closets, looking under beds, opening windows. In the kitchen they look for a moment at the fifteen cases of bottled water I drove up here the week before.

"Where is the rest?" Ron asks.

"The deployment order says there have to be twenty-eight cases of water," Curtis says.

I tell them I'll take care of it tomorrow. Of course, I hadn't read the deployment order—it must have been fifty pages long. I also don't ask my guests why they think they'll need so much drinking water. Maybe they think the Serbs are about to put Sarajevo back under siege?

Ron shakes his head in disbelief, as if their mission depends on the exact number of bottles of water they have. Curtis takes a bottle out of a box and examines the label. Not his brand, perhaps? But he holds back.

I hand them Cokes from the fridge as a peace offering. They drink them quietly as they take equipment out of the cases. I have no idea what most of it is.

That evening I drive back to the house with ten more cases of water, a case of beer, and a bottle of bubble bath. Someone's closed the fence, and I have to unlatch it to get in. No one answers the door, and I go around the back.

The two are standing on the lawn in front of what looks like a giant amber parasol. It's at least fifteen feet across. I know it's a transmitter antenna, but why is it so big? It could never be mistaken for the type of antenna you see relief groups here using.

Back at the apartment Charlie and Riley are sharing, we took great pains to keep the parabolic mic hidden, but this communication antenna might as well be a giant neon arrow pointing at the house I took so much pain to keep clean.

"Nothing smaller?" I ask.

"It's broadband to send back voice."

Ron bends down to make a last adjustment to the quadrupod the antenna sits on.

I never considered that they'd have to send back voice. What I imagined was my walking up here from the apartment with a cassette tape, the linguist translating and transcribing it into a text message, and the communicator then sending it to Washington via a tacset—an instrument the size of a briefcase.

It looks as though all my plans for invisibility are out the window. The neighbors have got to notice the antenna, which means it's only a matter of time before someone whispers something to Bosnian intelligence. We haven't even started and we're already running against the clock.

TWENTY-ONE

Ninja rocks are small bits of the ceramic from spark plugs, used by crackheads and jerkoffs to break any of the tempered glass on a car (anything except the windshield). Usually the door glass.

It has to do with hardness. Glass is actually "harder" than iron on the Mohs scale, and spark plug ceramic (technically called "aluminium oxide ceramic") is much harder than glass. Aluminium oxide ceramic actually rates a 9 on the Mohs scale; diamonds are 10, glass is 6.5, and iron is 4.5. That's the key to the whole thing, and why it's surprisingly hard to break a window with a hammer and surprisingly easy to break it with a small, light little shard of innocent white spark plug ceramic.

—www.ridelust.com/obscure-burglary-tools-of-the-trade-ninja-rocks

Sarajevo: **DAYNA**

Charlie and I have learned to live with the parabolic mic, the two of us camping where we can. Life is at its most basic, but Brad and Lara are on their way to relieve us. The only variable is that Bob moves our meetings farther and farther away from Sarajevo, deeper into the Croat areas where Bosnian intelligence won't go.

I notice that Bob's even more cautious these days because the parabolic mic has started to turn up a lot of good leads—for example, the names of Hizballah operatives and even a couple of telephone numbers. There have even been a couple of great intelligence reports. It's much better than anyone expected. Separately, with a telephoto lens we've been able to get plate numbers for their cars.

The problem now is what to do with it all. If it's a residential address we've picked up, how do we find out which Hizballah operatives live there? Or what their phone number is? The same goes with license plate numbers. We need to know who a car is registered to, and the address that goes along with it.

In the last couple of meetings Bob has been talking about getting into police records—recruiting a local cop. One day I finally raise my hand, saying I think I know how to meet one. He doesn't ask how, and only says, "Go do it."

I have to admit I'm a lot more comfortable working with Bob. There's a method to his nuttiness. All the moving people around at first looked like a circus without a ringmaster, but it's now coming together nicely. I still haven't accepted the idea of driving cars with advertisements down the side, but, who knows, maybe one day I will.

The next day I go to the Holiday Inn to rent a car. The one they pull around front is a fairly new Fiat with local plates and no dents. It's a car a tourist would rent—if there were any tourists here.

I spend the next couple of hours driving around to make sure I'm not followed. To avoid tying the car to the apartment, I park it behind the National Library. I spend the rest of the afternoon walking the streets to make sure I'm clean. At dark I stop at a kiosk that sells car parts and buy a set of spark plugs. Back in the apartment, I wrap them in a towel, put it on the floor, and smash it with the heel of my boot. I pick out the crushed ceramic pieces and put them in a handkerchief.

The next morning I go back to the National Library to pick up the Fiat. I drive it to the Bistrik police station. A cop is standing out front, talking to another man, but neither of them looks at me as I park. Before I get out of the car, I make sure the old carry-on suitcase is closed. I don't want anyone to notice it's empty. I lock all the doors.

At a little after midnight I stand watch on the street above the police station. Jacob and Charlie walk up and down on the block in front of it, smoking. When a man comes by, they stop and talk. As soon as the man is out of sight, they turn around and start walking again. As they pass my Fiat, I see Jacob's hand come out of his jacket pocket. I know he has a fistful of crushed ceramic in it. He barely brushes his hand against the Fiat's rear passenger-side window, and then there's shattered glass sparkling like diamonds on the pavement. Charlie and Jacob both keep walking, talking. I watch the police station for another ten minutes. No one comes out.

The next morning I push through the front door of the police station. The cop behind a bulletproof glass window glances up at me, but then goes back to reading. I pause, making it look like I can't make up my mind about what I want to do. He looks back up at me, quizzically this time. I look around as if I'm lost and then, with great hesitation, walk up to his window. "My car was broken into last night," I say. He doesn't understand English. I pantomime someone hitting something. I ramble on for a few minutes before asking if someone at the station speaks English.

He pushes himself up and goes into the back. He comes back with a young Bosnian military officer, a lieutenant.

"Can I help you?" the lieutenant asks. He's young, maybe twenty-two or twenty-three, unsure of himself.

"My car was broken into, right outside here," I say, pointing out the front door of the station and toward the street.

He walks around, comes out a side door, and follows me out to the car. The glass is still on the sidewalk from last night, the suitcase in the backseat. He asks me what was in it. I tell him books and a camera. He shakes his head in sympathy, saying, "We need to file a report."

He's obviously embarrassed this happened right in front of a police station, and I'm hoping he'll go out of his way to help me.

I drop by the station every day for three days to see if the lieutenant has any news about the car. I have a new question each time, from how much he thinks I should pay to fix the window to whether I should offer a reward in the newspaper for the return of my things. He offers to find the name of a good repair shop. On the third day I let it drop that his English is so good he should think about working for an international organization. "I have a friend looking for some help."

He nods his head, listening.

"It would be interesting work. And you could do it in your free time."

He's about to say something, and I interrupt. "You should just meet him, my friend."

"Why not?"

I pretend I'm thinking about it, and then I mention a café where we could all meet.

"What's this friend's name?" he asks.

"Harold," I tell him, and he writes it in his notebook.

TWENTY-TWO

Sometimes paranoia is just having all the facts.

—William S. Burroughs

Sarajevo: **BOB**

'm now living alone here in the Butmir house, our safe house near the airport. The days seem to grind on more and more slowly, and I kill time trying to fix the place up a little, and even do some gardening.

Riley's not due to come by for another three hours, so I go outside to survey the jungle around the house. The wild myrtle's almost suffocated the rhododendron by the front door. In the garage I find a pair of clippers, but when I come out there are two children standing in the driveway staring at me. I smile and wave at them. They turn and run away, frightened. I can only conclude that I'm the subject of conversation in the village. Their parents no doubt told the kids that I'm a foreigner, and they need to be wary of me.

It doesn't surprise me. This place may be off the beaten path, but that doesn't mean it's invisible, nor are the team members who visit me. There never was any way we could have gone totally unnoticed in a place like Sarajevo. I decide it's time to close this house down and find another one. In the meantime I have to decide whether the interest in the Butmir house goes beyond mere curiosity.

I go back in the house, find a book, and pull up a chair in the dark doorway that gives me a good view of the road. I read, waiting for someone to pass. The first to stroll by are two elderly ladies, scarves covering their heads. They walk by the house without giving it a glance. I get up and walk through the rooms to watch them from a window on the other side. They still don't show any interest in the house, so I go back to my chair and start reading again.

Twenty minutes later an old Volkswagen stops just beyond the house. Two men are in it. They sit with the car idling. Neither looks at the house, but still it seems strange. Why would they stop at that exact place? I take down the plate number. It's a couple of minutes before the car moves again.

I can't get the VW out of my mind. The road here is lightly traveled; only a couple of dozen cars a day pass along it. At my next meeting with the lieutenant, I'll give him the plate number and see what he comes up with.

I liked Riley's lieutenant. He was young and earnest. He didn't balk when I told him I was investigating organized crime, agreeing with me that it's a big problem for Bosnia. He seemed happy with the five hundred dollars I pushed across the table in an envelope, the first of his monthly payments. He didn't count the money—a good omen—and he didn't show up in his uniform, either, or ask why I didn't have an office, or a landline telephone number he could call. I wish all recruitments could go so easily.

A horsecart comes by now, and the driver, like the old women, doesn't look at the house. Right behind, though, two men walk by and give it a hard stare. At first I'm suspicious, but why wouldn't they? Butmir is a village. Curiosity comes with the terrain. By the time I give up watching the street, I'm trying hard to convince myself this is dumb paranoia. I've been here too long, and I'm seeing ghosts.

The next morning the doubts are back again, and I put on a pair of shorts and running shoes, my Interpol badge around my neck. I jog down 13 Juni, the road west of Butmir that leads toward the old Serbian lines. On either side of the road are signs with skulls and crossbones, landmine warnings. At the last house in Butmir I break into a run, not fast, but faster than I've been going. I run by the village of Donji Kotorac, where half the houses are shot up, empty, the doors wide open. Fifty yards down the road I come to the first Serb positions, which are abandoned. A French armored personnel carrier comes down the road, the gunner on top following me with his gaze. I make a left into Gornji Kotorac, which gives me a clear view of the road behind me. There's no one on it, not a car or a person. If anyone was on me, they didn't think it worth following me on my run.

I go back, change quickly, and head out again in the old Toyota. Normally, at this time of day I drive out of town on the Mostar road, into the Croat areas. Today, though, I head directly into Sarajevo down the main highway. I turn right on to Ante Babica, take the street that runs parallel to the main road I've just come off of, and then turn left back to the main highway. I drive in larger and larger squares until I'm in the center of Sarajevo.

When I turn around and head back to Butmir, I put on the gas, weaving through traffic, passing on the right. When I get to the straightaway on the main highway, I'm doing over sixty. A driver I cut off shakes his fist at me out the window. I pull away from a pack of cars and check my rearview window. No one's behind me.

TWENTY-THREE

> There's nothing like eavesdropping to show you that the world
> outside your head is different from the world inside your head.
>
> —*The Matchmaker*, Thornton Wilder

Sarajevo: DAYNA

I f I hadn't been standing in the window, I wouldn't have seen
the guy standing by the river, taking pictures of our apartment
building. Instinctively I take a step back and to the side, into the
dimness of the apartment.

It can't be a coincidence, I think. There's no reason anyone
would take a picture of our apartment. I peek around the curtain
for a second look. He's still there, his camera pointed directly up at
our building. I turn around to look at the parabolic mic. It's back
away from the window, and behind a cloth hanging from the ceiling. Even if he were level with our window, he couldn't see it.

I try to imagine what the man sees through his lens other than
the façade of a shabby apartment building. And why. He's the
only person along the river. There are no tourists, and the locals
don't go around taking pictures of their own city. Even a tourist
wouldn't take a picture of our building. There's nothing distinc-
tive about it.

I watch for the few seconds it takes him to click off another
half dozen photos or so. Maybe the man we rented the apartment
from turned us into the police. Okay, he didn't ask a single question about us—it was enough for him that we were Americans, the
people who could relieve his city from the Serbs' siege. But maybe
he had second thoughts and got scared and went to the authori-

ties. Still, wouldn't the police have just knocked on the door to see what was going on inside?

I find Charlie in the kitchen. "We have to go," I whisper. He's washing dishes and doesn't hear me. I move to his side. "We have to go," I whisper again, this time right in his ear. "What?" he says. I make a circular motion at the ceiling and then point at my ear—a spy's hand signal that the place might be bugged. (I have to assume that if, in fact, someone's watching us, the chances are good that the inside of the apartment's been compromised too, bugged.)

Charlie looks at me as if I've lost my mind. I point to the door. Outside on the landing, I whisper that someone's taking pictures of our building from across the river. "I'm sure of it." Convinced, he goes back in to quickly put away the parabolic mic in its concealment device. We both know that if the Bosnians catch us with it, we'll be arrested.

On the street Charlie and I lock arms, a couple out for a walk. Neither of us turns around to look at where I last saw the photographer. At the corner intersection we cross the river on the Cobanija bridge. On the middle of the span, I turn to him so we'll look like we're deep in conversation.

Charlie is facing me so I can look over his shoulder, in the direction of our apartment. He's gone. I tell Charlie I don't see him, and Charlie turns to look for himself. There's no one on the opposite bank at all.

We walk back across the bridge and circle behind our building so we don't come back in the way we left. As we round the corner to the sidewalk on the riverbank, I stop dead. He's standing right in front of our building, taking photos in the direction of the Hizballah safe house. It's as if he's marking what we would see from our apartment. Charlie sees him too, and I can feel him stiffen with panic. His expression tells me he knows we're into something we don't understand. It's all so blatant I wonder if someone is warning us that they know what we're up to. But that makes no sense, either.

The guy calmly puts his camera in his shoulder bag and starts back toward old town. Charlie points two fingers at his eyes to let me know we need to follow this guy. We wait until he's a block away and then follow from a distance along the river, linking arms again and sauntering along behind. As I walk I imprint in my mind the man's striped shirt, rust-colored hair, and thick-soled shoes, and his shape.

He gives no sign of noticing us, and we follow him all the way to the cobbled streets of the old city. His pace is deliberate, and he holds on tightly to the strap of his camera bag. Then suddenly he stops dead in his tracks, turns around, and heads directly toward us. "Oh shit," I hear Charlie say under his breath. But both of us stick to script and keep walking, arm in arm, directly past the guy without making eye contact. Charlie steers me into the closest building—a post office. Inside, he walks to the window, trying to see what direction the man's taken. That doesn't work, so he sends me out alone to see if I can catch up while he makes sure the apartment is safe.

I leave the post office and start back toward where we crossed paths with our photographer. I'm almost running at first, but then I slow down. It's the first thing they taught us: Never, ever run. And here I am panicking as though I've never worked a street. In this case, though, it doesn't seem to matter. We've lost him. When I get back to the apartment, all I can do is look at Charlie and shrug my shoulders—I don't have a clue what happened to the guy.

Oddly, when headquarters hears the story, they aren't particularly concerned. It makes us wonder if it was someone from headquarters or another agency taking the photos—and no one is going to cop to it.

At first Bob makes a joke out of it, but then quickly turns

serious, telling us it's best that we go ahead and rotate people in and out, as well as remove the parabolic mic as a precaution. Brad and Lara will move into the apartment, replacing Charlie and me. They will limit themselves to taking pictures of people coming out of the Hizballah safe house with a telephoto lens. They'll also try to determine whether the apartment is still being watched. If it is, the parabolic mic isn't coming back. Everyone agrees it's a risk leaving Brad and Lara here, but it's one that headquarters and Bob are willing to take until we know more.

To put my time to good use, Bob wants me to go to Frankfurt to pick up a new armored SUV that's been waiting there for us. It comes with British military plates, which, with all the European troops arriving in Sarajevo, will give us an added measure of anonymity. Bob will leave the city briefly too, since he needs to return his rental car in Geneva. I'll catch a ride with him as far as Geneva, and from there a train to Frankfurt.

In training they used to drill into our heads the wisdom of backing off the moment you think you're about to be "burned"— caught red-handed. *Listen to your paranoia, live to fight another day.* But this guy taking pictures of the apartment isn't a figment of my imagination. Someone knows we're here and is playing with us. It spooks me that I don't know who.

TWENTY-FOUR

A sunny place for shady people.

—W. Somerset Maugham

Sarajevo to Frankfurt: DAYNA

few miles after we cross the border into Croatia, Bob pulls over to the side of the road and noses the car into a clump of trees where it's not so conspicuous. He asks me if I mind if he makes a call.

I watch as he pulls out our Inmarsat satellite phone, opens the hood, and attaches the phone to the car battery. He finds a number in a black notebook and dials.

"*Kif halik?*" I hear him say, Arabic for "How are you?" He talks for the next five minutes in rapid Arabic, none of which I understand.

A step van slows down as it passes to take a look at us, but then speeds up. I turn to see if any cars are coming, but none is.

When Bob finishes, he unhooks the Inmarsat, puts it back it in the rear seat, and gets back in the car.

"Mind if I stop in Nice to see a friend?"

"OK with me," I answer.

"It's for dinner. But I'm not sure you would want to come."

I don't ask who the friend is. I just assume that it has something to do with work. Probably he's an informant. And truthfully I don't mind. He can stop anywhere he likes. I'm just happy to have a break from Sarajevo.

We're just north of Split, driving along the Adriatic. It's becoming warm when we both notice how the water in the inlets is crystal clear, right to the white, sandy bottom. Without warning, Bob abruptly crosses the lane and drives down a path to the water. "How about a quick swim?" he asks.

He rummages in the back of the car, looking for a bathing suit. This is really nuts, I think, but the water is inviting. Bob goes behind some trees to change. I slip into a bathing suit in the car.

I float on my back while Bob swims out from shore. There's no one in sight, and Sarajevo is instantly airbrushed from my mind. I want to stay here all day, but then Bob is standing on the shore, holding a towel for me. "Let's see if we can make Nice by tomorrow afternoon."

I put my clothes back on over my bathing suit. We stop for a quick beer and a sandwich at the next village, and then get back on the road.

Bob tells stories, and when he's tired of talking, we listen to music on the radio.

I'm barely awake by the time we start up the Julian Alps, the mountains that separate Slovenia from northern Italy. At the Italian border, Bob fumbles with two passports before he picks one to show to the guard. Walking around with documents in two different names is completely transgressive, but right now I'm too tired to care.

By the time we get to Trieste, I'm pinching myself to stay awake. Bob is lost, but I just stare straight ahead, praying there's a hotel open this late. Miraculously, he finds one. He checks us in and comes down to the car to hand me my key.

We're off early the next morning and gobbling up the miles until, halfway across Italy, the car starts coughing. Bob stops at a service station. The mechanic looks at the engine, but only scratches his head. By the time we finally drive up to Avis rental at Nice Airport, it's belching smoke. I'm afraid it's going to explode and jump out, backing away from it, as Bob runs inside to find the manager. I can't imagine what Avis is going to say.

A week or so ago, when we thought that our cars were starting to get noticed, Bob called Avis from the satellite phone at the Butmir house to see if he could return it in Zagreb, Croatia, and get something different. The Avis lady was under the impression he was still in Switzerland, where he rented the car, and reminded Bob in no uncertain terms that he could not take the car out of Europe. I'm wondering how much trouble he will get into if they figure out he's had the car in a war zone.

He's back in five minutes, dangling a set of keys. "They gave us a bigger car, gratis."

"What did you tell them?"

"I told them their damn rent-a-wreck ruined our vacation. They're embarrassed."

He loads up the new Renault luxury sedan. I don't know if he thinks I disapprove or what, but he says, "Well, I did have the car for six weeks at full rate."

A mile before we come to the village of St-Paul-de-Vence, Bob turns off on a narrow road and then up a long driveway lined with pines. We round two tennis courts and pull up in front of the Mas d'Artigny, a dazzling hotel with lots of glass, polished white marble floors, antique Provençal furniture, and a swimming pool that runs into the hotel itself. All of the rooms have unblocked views of the Mediterranean.

A haute-bourgeois couple on a divan shoot us a disapproving look as we stand at the front desk. I'm instantly conscious of my jeans, dirty boots, and T-shirt. The bellman ambushes me, grabbing my duffel bag. Normally I'd hold on to it, but this isn't a place where you schlep your own anything.

I find Bob at the concierge desk. "We can't stay here," I whisper. "They'll kill me if this place appears on my alias credit card. What is it, five hundred dollars a night?"

The desk clerk turns up from her computer and hands Bob one room key. He looks a little chagrined and then says something to her in French. She nods and hands him the telephone. He talks to someone in Arabic. She takes back the phone, listens, and says, "*Oui, monsieur. D'accord.*" She produces a second room key, which Bob hands to me.

We stand at the elevator, the bellboy behind us. "Don't worry about it," Bob says. "The room's taken care of."

"I can't let you pay."

"I'm not. Made up your mind about dinner tonight? You're certainly welcome." I tell him I'll be just fine on my own, and he hands me the car keys. "Take a drive along the Riviera."

The bellman takes me to my room, a suite. It's as elegant as the lobby. Brocade curtains and bedspread, a walk-in closet, a huge marble bathroom with a tub and an enormous shower featuring two showerheads the size of dinner plates and a heated bench. The soap is hand-milled.

I open the duffel to see if I can find something that doesn't make me look like a refugee. The best I can do is a pair of black ankle pants, gray ballet flats, and a lightweight ivory cashmere pullover. I won't exactly fit in here, but maybe the other guests will stop staring at me.

Bob has already left for dinner by the time I come down, and I drive to St-Paul, a walled medieval town with cobblestone streets. I find a bakery and have pastries and a glass of cold milk for dinner.

The next morning I find Bob in the lobby, checking out.

"We're invited to lunch," he says.

"Thanks, but I'll wait for you here."

I'm still not exactly sure whom Bob's meeting, but I guess an informant. Driving across Europe with an operative to dump a car is one thing, but meeting an operative's informant without clearing it with Washington is crossing one of those bright, shining red lines.

"They're expecting you. You can't say no."

Before I can say anything, a handsome young man with curly raven hair and brown eyes comes across the lobby toward us. He's wearing a linen shirt, pressed slacks, and soft leather loafers without socks. He hugs Bob, then turns to me and shakes my hand. He says his father and mother will be delighted to meet me. There's nothing I can do now.

Outside, a teal Bentley with white leather seats stands softly idling. The young man holds the door for me to get in the back, while Bob climbs in the front. We drive up a steep hill lined with great sprawling houses enclosed in walled compounds with security cameras and guardhouses. We slow down in front of one, and a ten-foot gate opens into the courtyard of a house that wraps around the contour of the mountain.

I follow Bob and the young man into the house and out onto a stone terrace that overlooks a tiled infinity pool. There's a jet of water at one end, a young girl in a bikini swimming. Two other young men come up to me to shake my hand. The girl climbs out of the pool and runs up the ten steps to introduce herself to me.

A man with a shock of gray hair walks across the terrace toward us. He's in a blue blazer, a pair of white pants, and white shoes with gold buckles.

"Riley?" he says. "I'm delighted. My name is Ali. I hope Bob has made your trip here comfortable."

Ali has a strong Middle Eastern accent, but I can't place it. His quiet but forceful tone is somehow calming.

"Would you like an arak?" he asks. Arak is the Arab version of Greek ouzo. I tell him water. One of the boys comes back with an ice water. Bob takes an arak. Another son comes over with a box of Cuban cigars. Ali picks out one, squeezes it to make sure it's fresh, and cuts it. He hands it to Bob. He picks one for himself. They light their cigars, and the three of us stand at the railing, looking at the azure sea.

Out of the corner of my eye, I notice the cook shuttling back and forth from the kitchen with platters of fresh raw vegetables, grilled chicken, lamb, fatoush, tabouleh, freshly made yogurt, baskets of pita bread, and two bottles of white wine chilled on ice. I catch Bob's eye and look at my watch. Is there any way we're going to make it to Geneva?

Through lunch the conversation is lively, Ali making sure all the children participate. His wife, a conservatively dressed woman, doesn't speak English, but one of the boys translates for her. She asks me questions about where I'm from and what I do.

"So, Riley, do you know Robert, Charlotte, and Justine?" the son who drove us here turns to me and asks.

I have no idea whom he's talking about, and only say no.

After lunch, as soon as we are out of the driveway I ask Bob, "Did Ali pay for our rooms?"

"It would have been impossible for us to pay. He would have reversed the charges on our credit cards. He considers the Mas d'Artigny his private guesthouse. What can I say, Arab hospitality."

As we drive down the hill to catch the freeway to Geneva, I reflect that I'd normally dread spending all these days in a car, but it's actually been fun.

It comes out of my mouth before I can stop myself. "Are you married?"

"Yes, but she's like a French wife."

I'm not going to touch that one, but I can't help asking if he has children.

Bob looks over at me. "Three."

"What ages?"

When he tells me, I realize that's who Justine, Robert, and Charlotte are. I look out my window, not wanting him to see me deflate.

Before we get on the freeway to Geneva, a 200-mile drive north, I ask Bob if it's okay to send Ali and his wife a thank-you note. Bob pulls over at a stationery store, and I go in and buy a card. When I come out, Bob hands me a piece of paper with a phone number on it. It's for his house in France. He's going there after he drops me off in Geneva. He says to call in case of an emergency.

At that moment it dawns on me that Ali and his family must think I'm Bob's mistress. It explains the one key at the hotel. I can't decide whether I'm embarrassed or not. But I do smile inwardly at what is maybe the wildest thing about the whole trip. It's not that we've gone from hell to heaven in a little over two days. Rather it's that no one I've met, including Bob, even knows my real name.

TWENTY-FIVE

Corgoloin, France: **BOB**

When we finally get on the freeway, it's too late to make it to Geneva for Riley to catch a train to Frankfurt. She doesn't mind, and I tell her I know a couple places to stay along the way.

We're just outside Annecy in France when I pull into a gasoline station to take a look at the map. I put it between us, my thumb under Gsteig, a little Swiss village in the mountains above Gstaad. "Let's go skiing," I say. "I want you to see one of my favorite places in the world." Her first look says, *Should we really be doing this?*

It takes me only five minutes of convincing, my case helped by the fact that the next day is Saturday, and the office in Frankfurt is closed. "No one will know," I say. Riley smiles and her eyes dance as if we're pulling off the perfect prank.

We stay at the Hotel Bären, a chalet in the middle of a verdant pasture. There are red geraniums in the windows, the only sound a waterfall that breaks above the village, and the occasional cowbell. Dinner is cheese fondue.

In the morning we take the cable car up to the top of the Col du Pillon, where we rent ski equipment from an old woman with tight, weather-worn skin. She tells us that she raced for the Swiss Olympic team in the fifties.

It is warm enough to ski in shirtsleeves. I let Riley go down first. She's a good skier, telling me that she's skied all her life. After a couple of runs we stop for lunch at the little restaurant at the bottom of the glacier. We have enough cash between us for only a carafe of wine and French fries. (We aren't about to use our alias credit cards here.)

I don't know what it is. The stillness, the beauty of the spot, but I tell her that I often dream about running away to live on the side of a Swiss Alp.

She laughs. "Doesn't everyone?"

It occurs to me, sitting here looking across the Alps, that I brought Riley to lunch at Ali's because I wanted to show her off. Beautiful, collected, quick with a laugh, someone you know right away won't settle, she strikes me as the perfect confederate.

That afternoon, after dropping Riley off in Geneva, I drive to the French house to see how the kids are doing and fix a few things around the house. Ever the procrastinator, I still haven't managed to consummate my divorce. If my wife had it her way, we never would; she's comfortable with the idea of marriage, if not the practice of it. She's brought the children here to escape Washington's heat.

When I first bought the French house, I was certain that I'd own it forever, even retire here. Right away I started naming rooms, imagining the purpose they'd serve after the house was fixed up. The little room at the northeast corner of the house's front, with its commanding view over the vines, the Saône, and Alsace-Lorraine beyond, I called the breakfast room. But since no one ever eats breakfast there, I now think of it as the castle keep. With the way the grapevines drop off so steeply in front of the house, it does give you the sense of being in a tower. If I lived here by myself I'd turn it into my study.

In the winter, after a good, hard rain and a strong wind, you can sometimes see Mount Blanc from this room, a little white nipple poking out of the rust fields. In the summer, I open the room's windows to let in the breeze off the vines, freshening the house. I often sit here imagining what it would be like living in the house year-round.

I don't mind at all the house's cramped spaces, the rooms without windows, the rough pitch-pine floors. Someone in the village told me the house should have been five rooms, but the vintner who built it sixty years ago chopped it up into ten. The municipal water doesn't run up to the house; instead, there are three cisterns. They freeze in winter, and you need a pole to break up the ice. There's no central heating, either. Mornings you have to run down the stairs to light the cast-iron stoves—*poeles*, as the French call them. The nearest house is in the village, more than a half mile down the hill.

For a while the house was a working vineyard. There's still a press in the garage, and two great oak vats. But now the vintner above us takes care of the vines and harvests them. In the spring he drives down the hill in his little old Deux Chevaux—a small, boxy station wagon that reminds me of a sardine can—with twenty boxes of wine for us. Every couple of years the wine gets a gold medal from the Ministry of Agriculture.

When we first moved here—I was in Tajikistan—the kids went to school in the village. Their French soon was better than their English. I laughed when they'd call a fly a *mouche*. I wanted to keep them in school here, and afterward college. I pictured them coming home on breaks and vacations and even weekends. It all seemed idyllic. But back then I was under the illusion that a family can be built around a house.

The next morning the sun is shining, and I find the children playing in the orchard. I ask them if they want to help paint. They say no and run through the vines into the forest on the side of the house. I find a paint bucket and a brush in the garage.

My goal is to paint four shutters, the worst ones. When I bought the house, there were no shutters at all on the windows, and the wind made the curtains dance. But that spring I found a carpenter in a nearby village. When he came to measure the windows, he shook his head. This wasn't going to be easy because all of the windows were different sizes. It took him two months to make the shutters. But they turned out beautifully, and he put them up with good strong hardware. I still enjoy waking up in the mornings and opening them to see the sun rising over the Saône.

I know it sounds odd, but the forest-green shutters really do make the house, offsetting the dirty rose. The shutters need to be touched up every year because the wind in winter strips off the paint like coarse sandpaper. The French call the wind *la bise*. If I could spend the entire year here, it would be easy to keep up the shutters—one a month. That fits the rhythm of Burgundy.

I tell myself that when I have more money I'll add a bathroom on the second floor. It won't be fancy—toilet, sink, and shower. The kind of work I do is called *bricolage* in French. Do-it-yourself. The hard stuff, such as the plumbing, I'll save for the village plumber, although it will take him months. After an hour or two of work he'll ask if it's not time to open a bottle of wine.

I love the farmhouse, and Burgundy. I was the one who bought it, worked on it, saved money for it, and talked about resigning and living here. But my wife and children came to look at it as purgatory. They always seem to want to be somewhere else. But no one ever says anything, especially the children. Children know instinctively not to question a parent's dream. I'm sure they'll sell it as soon as they can.

The phone in the breakfast room rings at a little after nine. My wife puts the phone in the open window for me to answer. Who could that be? The children stand at the phones, sure it's their grandmother. My mother calls every weekend when we're here.

"Hi." It's Riley. "Is it OK to call?" I can tell by her voice that something is wrong, a little catch.

The children look at me with disappointment when they realize it's a work call, and run back upstairs to play.

"They have pictures," Riley says.

"Pictures of what?" I ask.

At first I think Riley is talking about someone taking pictures of the apartment again. But that makes less sense than it did the first time.

"They said it's serious," Riley says.

"What do you mean?"

Riley is being elliptical because I told her on the drive across Italy that the French tap my telephone.

"It's OK," I say. "Just tell me. No one here cares about what we're doing there." In fact, we and the French are on the same side in the Bosnian conflict.

Riley pauses for another beat and then says that in Frankfurt the boss pulled her into an office and asked, "Who in the hell is Harold, and why do the Bosnians have pictures of him?"

It has to be the lieutenant, I think.

"Apparently he got cold feet," Riley says, reading my thoughts.

I understand what's happened. The lieutenant reported my meeting with him. The pictures must be of the lieutenant and me sitting at the outdoor café. It's the only thing that makes sense.

I reassure myself that I didn't say anything to the lieutenant to let on that I was CIA, and there's no reason the Bosnians should doubt my cover story that I'm in Bosnia investigating organized crime.

"Go ahead and drive back to Split and leave the car there," I finally say. "There's absolutely nothing to worry about."

"Are you sure?"

"Have a good trip."

But after we hang up, it all starts to nag at me—the man photographing the apartment, the people looking at the Butmir house, and now the Bosnians knowing about the lieutenant. I don't know whether they're connected or not, but if they are, we'll have to close down the operation and bring everyone home. Or more likely it will be headquarters that will come to that conclusion. It won't be long.

Tuesday morning the Bosnian desk chief at Langley calls. "We need to talk to you about something," she says. Her voice is mechanical, like she's telling me I'm late on my accounting again. I tell her that I'm due to come back to Washington in a week. She says "they" need to see me tomorrow. I start to ask her what it's about, but I know it's the lieutenant. It crosses my mind that she'd like to rub my nose in it, remind me how she'd told me my grand plan wasn't going to work.

One convenient thing about the Burgundy house is that it's a ten-minute drive to Beaune, where I can catch a fast train to Charles de Gaulle airport. In fourteen hours I can make it from my front door to Washington, in time to rent a car and be at headquarters before everyone goes home at the end of the day.

The next morning the taxi comes before anyone is awake. As I get in, I admire the three shutters I did manage to paint.

TWENTY-SIX

Life is being on the wire, everything else is just waiting.

—Karl Wallenda

Sarajevo: DAYNA

There's no food in the apartment, so Lara and Brad decide to go out for pizza. Because Bob has cautioned us to spend as little time as possible out and about Sarajevo, they drive to Mostar, an ethnic Croatian town thirty minutes away. It's a little after ten when they finish and start back for Sarajevo.

They've gone only a couple of miles when Brad looks in the mirror and sees a car coming up on them very fast. He moves over to give it room to pass on the left, but instead, the car moves to cut them off on the right. That's when Lara spots the pistol in the driver's hand and yells, "Go! Now!" There's a flash and a sharp crack—a gunshot.

Brad hits the brakes hard, just as he was taught. The car skids to a stop, as the other car flies past them. Brad keeps the car in first, the engine revving, ready to ram the car if it stops in front of him. But it keeps going. Brad looks over at Lara and sees her holding her stomach, blood pumping out between her fingers. He puts his hand over the bullet hole to stanch the flow and takes off, driving with his free hand. All he can think about is that he has no idea where the hospital in Sarajevo is. If he loses precious minutes looking for it, Lara is going to die.

There's not a car on the road, and Brad drives as fast as the old Taurus will go. But it feels like he's dragging a ball and chain behind him. On Sarajevo's edge he sees a light in front of him. As he draws closer, he sees it's a wheeled armored personnel carrier with French tricolors painted on the sides. Brad squeezes the last power out of the car, passes the carrier, and jams the brakes on so the car skids sideways in the road. The carrier stops only inches from the car. Brad grabs an American flag and jumps out of the car, waving it. Lara's blood is all over him.

The French help Brad get Lara out of the car and into the carrier. It takes ten minutes for them to get to the French field hospital, where medics wheel Lara into an operating room. Shaking, Brad runs up to the young French soldier on guard duty. Later he remembers grabbing the guy's lapels, putting his face in his.

"I'm American. I need you to call the American embassy in Sarajevo right now."

After delivering the SUV to Split, I'm on leave in Washington when the phone rings at a little after seven in the morning. A call that early can't be good news. I recognize the voice, a guy from my office. "Lara's been shot," he says. At first it doesn't register because he's said it so calmly, as if Lara has caught a cold. "Turn on the news," he says. Before he hangs up, he tells me I need to go back to Sarajevo on the first flight I can. I'm booking the flight when ABC reports there was a random attack on unnamed Americans in Sarajevo.

A lot goes through my head. How could this happen? Did the person taking the pictures of our apartment have anything to do with it? I remember that day when Brad came to take over the apartment. I went through the pantry with him, pointing out things I'd found in the market, instant Nescafé, Cheerios, a funky pair of local coffee cups. Brad knew Lara was a clean freak, and laughed at the bottle of Mr. Clean I'd managed to find. She would appreciate that, he said. I said I was sorry I couldn't do more to spruce up the place.

When I drove down from Frankfurt with the new SUV, I thought how it would help Lara and Brad to blend in with European military forces who drove SUVs just like this one. It would also be a lot safer than the Taurus Charlie bought. But as these things happen, it was taken by Tuzla, and never made it to Brad and Lara. The SUV's armor would have stopped the bullet that hit Lara.

When I get into the office, nothing is any clearer. All they tell me is that Bob is en route to Sarajevo, and that I'm to meet him there. The two of us will clear Lara and Brad's stuff out of the apartment. The reason it falls on Bob and me is that no one wants to expose someone new to the apartment. If it wasn't compromised before the shooting, it is now.

It's dark, just after ten, and Bob stands outside keeping watch while I pack up Brad and Lara's things. I wonder what the owner will think about our leaving like this, with six months' rent paid up, not even calling to say good-bye. Maybe he'll move back in with his kitten, which must be a full-grown cat now.

They agree to meet us the next day on a deserted road with straight reaches in both directions so you can see anyone approaching. The young officer who pulls up alongside is nervous, swiveling his neck around. We put the box of Lara and Brad's stuff in the trunk, and he drives away without looking back. It's obvious the operation has gone bad in more ways than one. No one wants to be seen with us. We're radioactive, and it could be catching.

I take Bob to his car. "See you at the next war," he says.

I wave as he drives away. As I get into my car, I think that the CIA is big and sprawling and it's possible I may never see him again.

The French surgeons save Lara's life, but we never find out for sure who shot her. I doubt we ever will. The simplest explanation is the most likely: the Taurus had a Sarajevo plate, it was driving through a Croat area, and the shooters mistook Brad and Lara for Bosnian Muslims. More stupid sectarian bloodletting. It was a mistake not to have sold the Taurus, or at least changed the plates. Or maybe we just shouldn't have been going out after dark.

But I can't help wondering if there was something more sinister behind it. Maybe we hadn't been that good—the man who photographed the apartment was part of some setup for an ambush. They followed Brad and Lara from the apartment that night when they went out for pizza and waited for them to come back, and if it had been Charlie and me going for pizza, they would have followed us, too. Luck of the draw.

With twenty-twenty hindsight, a shooting like this always suggests recklessness, an underestimation of danger. I find myself resisting the idea, and I think it has more to do with a self-defensive psychological mechanism one picks up serving on the ragged edges of the world. You simply can't interpret every little anomaly in the fabric of your day as a warning sign that must be heeded and acted on. It would lead to panic and paranoia. Soldiers in combat no doubt understand the phenomenon a lot better than CIA agents do.

Another thing I think most people would be surprised about is that in espionage, few mysteries are ever solved. The CIA is simply too small to comb endlessly through cases that can't easily be untangled, and whose resolution serves no purpose other than the satisfaction of closure. One just has to let things go. Obsessions end up in paralysis.

Still, this is a hard one to get over. Lara and I shared a common history. She'd been plucked from the drudgery of Los Angeles, just as I was. Our paths had crisscrossed at any number of unlikely spots, and we had plenty of tales to swap about endless hours on the L.A. freeways. All that counted, but here's why I think I had so much trouble getting this near miss out of my mind: we predated operational rules, so I knew Lara's real name.

TWENTY-SEVEN

> Were you ever out in the Great Alone, when the moon was awful
> clear, And the icy mountains hemmed you in with a silence you
> most could hear; With only the howl of a timber wolf, and you
> camped there in the cold, A half-dead thing in a stark, dead
> world, clean mad for the muck called gold; While high overhead,
> green, yellow, and red, the North Lights swept in bars?—Then
> you've a hunch what the music meant . . . hunger and night and
> the stars.
>
> —Robert Service

Washington, D.C.: **DAYNA**

In the last week of October I'm walking down a hall at Langley
when I hear a voice call out, "Riley!" I turn around, and there's
Bob.

"It's Dayna," I say. No point in keeping up aliases now that
we're back at headquarters.

We chat for a while, and then, out of the blue, Bob invites me
to dinner. He says we should catch up on Sarajevo, talk about how
we were exonerated over the lieutenant, how Lara is doing. It's as
spontaneous as that. We agree to meet at an Italian restaurant near
Tyson's Corner that night.

Halfway through dinner, Bob tells me he's going to Europe to
work on his French house and afterward hike in the Alps. Do I
want to go hiking with him? I laugh, certain he's kidding. I tell
him it's a trip he'll have to make on his own. But at the end of dinner he asks me again, saying he's absolutely serious.

I accept, knowing just how wildly impulsive it is. But the truth
is, I can be as spontaneous as anyone. If I wasn't born that way,

then these last years I'd spent picking up and flying to the other side of the world at a phone call made me so. When we played hooky and went skiing in Switzerland, it didn't take all that much convincing on Bob's part.

And of course if I hadn't been in some way attracted to Bob, I never would have said yes. And I guess deep inside I was hoping he felt the same way, or he never would have invited me. Would he?

Two weeks later, though, as I drive down from Paris, none of this stops me from wondering if I'm a complete idiot. The more I think about it, the more I realize I barely know the guy. What can you know about someone after spending two days in a car with him? It then occurs to me that Bob might just want a hiking companion, nothing more.

We spend the next four days in Zermatt, hiking from one mountain hut to another. It's at the end of the season, and there are only a couple of other hikers on the trails. Those three days are like a forced march. My boots are too small and I lose a toenail. Dinners in the huts are basic: a bowl of soup and fresh brown bread. There are no showers or baths. The people who run the huts assume we're a couple, and must think it strange when Bob asks for two rooms. Still, at night I lie in bed looking forward to the next day.

One night over dinner, Bob tells me a story about how a friend of his used to take a long, hard trip in a small car with a prospective girlfriend before deciding if they were compatible or not. He'd know before the first thousand miles. I don't say anything, but I think he's talking about us.

The last morning it's drizzling, and we buy ponchos. The ground is slippery, but the Swiss, in their meticulousness, have spread sharp crushed rock on the trails. By midday the drizzle turns into a steady, icy black rain, and we turn back for Zermatt. I want to stay inside and get dry, but Bob talks me into a tram ride to the bottom of the Little Matterhorn.

We walk out of the tram station to be met by a driving blizzard. A few hardcore skiers ride up a little T-bar nearby. Bob says we should take a quick hike to the top of the Little Matterhorn. It isn't all that far, he says, and he's brought his ice ax. We start out, but when I look back and can't see the station, I tell him he's out of his mind. He cheerfully agrees, and we go back. As a compromise, we walk back to Zermatt and stop for beers at the first place on the way down.

As much as you can know about these things, I realize on that walk down that I've fallen in love. The two of us will never have much money or even a lot of stability, but right now neither seems to matter. All I can think of is that Bob has a way of throwing open the windows and doors of my life. With him, things will never be predictable or boring. And not being bored counts a lot with me.

When we come back to Washington, we move in together at the Wolf Trap Motel in Vienna, Virginia. We buy two bicycles, chaining them to the balcony outside our room. On dry days we ride them to work. Two months later we upgrade, renting a one-bedroom apartment a block off Connecticut Avenue in Washington. We take the Metro to work.

I beg my boss not to deploy me, and can't thank him enough when he finds me a desk job. I laugh at myself, thinking how there was a time I kept a suitcase packed in my closet and would go anywhere at a moment's notice. You need me in Kingston tomorrow? No problem. But now, for the first time in all these years, I no longer want to get on an airplane to go anywhere.

In the summer I'm offered a slot in the operations course at the Farm—the CIA's secret training facility in rural Virginia. It's the first step to becoming an operative, something I've dreamed about for a long time. Not only will a lot more jobs open up to me, but I'd be qualified to run informants, and even learn a hard language. I'd accept on the spot if it weren't for Bob.

Normally the two of us could probably take a "tandem" assignment, a posting to the same place. But the reality is that finding two jobs in the same overseas station is nearly impossible. There's the added complication that Bob eventually received a citation and a medal for his work in Iraq, and if he sticks to the straight and narrow, he'll land another station where he'll be chief. But the way the rules are written, a wife or husband can't work for a spouse. We'd be lucky to work in adjoining countries. Meanwhile, the pressure would be on me to take an overseas assignment apart from Bob.

I know the way these things go. After the Farm I could drag my feet for a while, turning down one posting after another. Inevitably, though, the day would come when I'd have to say yes. At first it would be something like a three-month assignment, and then six months, and eventually a full two-year tour. Soon enough, Bob and I would be leading separate lives.

Also making me hesitate to go down that path is that I can't see myself doing this forever and risk ending up like Cheri, my friend in the shooting course. I don't want to become some Flying Dutchman, driven around the world by whatever random wind that comes along. And it pretty much would stay that way until I retired. I know that one day I'll want to settle down, in a place where, I don't know, a kitten can grow old. Maybe not right now, but one day.

For Bob, the solution is for the two of us to resign and make a life together on the outside. He wants to reboot in Beirut, a city he fell in love with when he worked there in the 1980s. I like the idea of Beirut too, but frankly I dread giving up something very important in my life. Bob's had a full, fascinating career in the CIA, and he saw a lot more of the world than I did. I've only put a handful of years, and my star now is on the rise. So, in the end, I hedge my bets and take a leave of absence.

After he nails down a consulting contract with an Argentine oil company through his friend Garth, Bob resigns from the Agency on December 4, 1997. Two days later we're packed, everything not movable sold, and waiting in front of our apartment for a taxi to the airport. We have two small suitcases between us.

Somewhere I read that love is a push out from shore and a belief the ice will hold. Boarding the airplane to Beirut with Bob is certainly pushing away, but I'm still not certain the ice is thick enough to support us both.

TWENTY-EIGHT

> **HONOLULU, July 30, 1997—Secretary of State Madeleine K. Albright announced today that she was lifting the 10-year ban on travel by Americans to Lebanon. But she said Lebanon remained very dangerous and urged United States citizens not to go there.**
>
> **It has been illegal for American citizens to travel on American passports to Lebanon since 1987, during a period Westerners were being taken hostage by pro-Iranian militants.**
>
> —*The New York Times,* July 31, 1997

Beirut, Lebanon: **DAYNA**

I spend my days walking around Beirut. Although it's been six years since the end of the civil war, parts of the city look like the fighting was yesterday. The buildings along the Green Line—the battle front between Christian East Beirut and Muslim West Beirut—are in ruins, like sand castles hit by a wave. The Holiday Inn on the water is still charred on one side, all the windows blown out. The Lebanese government nominally runs the country, but in fact Hizballah, the radical Shia militia, is the strongest force in Lebanon. Syrian troops occupy half of the country.

I may be out of the CIA now, but it doesn't really feel like it. I catch myself memorizing the location of pay phones that work, and being suspicious of cars and people I see more than once. In a café I always sit facing the entrance. I even catch myself looking for surveillance. I know it's dumb instinct. Still, it's going to be a while before it sinks in that no one is interested in following me anymore.

I eat lunch and dinner at the place we found when we first got here, Abu Khudur's. It's a little hole-in-the-wall. But it's on the same street as our hotel, and it's open day and night. They know me here now.

"Chicken with no pickle, madam, yes?" Ahmed says in Arabic as he makes my *schwarma*—the Lebanese version of a wrap sandwich. Ahmed thinks it's funny that I always order the same thing. He likes to tease me by offering me calf's brains and intestines.

"When is *zowj* coming?" Ahmed asks, as he carves chicken off the spit.

Zowj is "husband" in Arabic. Bob and I are not married, but it's simpler to let people here think we are. Ahmed doesn't wait for my answer. He's warming pita bread on the grill. *"Za'tar?"* he asks. Thyme?

I've managed to learn a few words of Arabic and like to practice them when I can. *"Zowj fi Paris."* My husband is in Paris. I take a Sprite out of the refrigerator. *"Bukra, inshallah."* Tomorrow, God willing. I'm happy that next week I start studying Arabic with a tutor.

I stand at the window, watching the street. Almost none of Beirut's streets are marked by signs. Even our hotel only lists its address as Hamra—Beirut's old commercial center. Like the Lebanese, I've started to learn my way around by walking the streets, remembering landmarks and the bigger stores.

"Where's Hasan?" I ask.

Ahmed hands me my *schwarma* wrapped in paper. "In the south."

The first day we came here, we figured out that Ahmed and Hasan are Hizballah reservists. When the fighting against the Israelis in the south flares up, they're called up to join their units. Ahmed still has a bandage on his arm from a wound he got in a fight a month ago.

Ahmed comes around and stands by my table, looking out the window at the stalled traffic. It sounds as if everyone is honking at the same time. Ahmed shakes his head.

The gridlock is worse today, but Hamra is always a circus. Old Mercedes taxis tap their horns to solicit fares. Hawkers and store owners stack their wares on the sidewalks. There's nowhere to walk except in the street, dodging cars.

A boy on a motor scooter comes racing down the sidewalk, swerving to miss a lady with her shopping bags. "The idiot," Ahmed says.

"Ahmed, we're looking for an apartment." I ask it on a whim, but who knows.

He motions for me to put down my sandwich. I follow him out into the street.

"See that?" he points up at a sagging banner in Arabic over Abu Khudur's neon sign. "It says 'apartment for rent.'" Ahmed points directly at the sixth floor above us. I can just see the wall of a tiny apartment on the roof.

As Ahmed writes down the telephone number from the banner, I bolt my sandwich, then run back to the hotel to call from our room, where it's quieter.

The man who answers the phone speaks fluent English. He says he's Dr. Hajj.

"It's new and has a new couch and some other nice furniture," Hajj says. "It's perfect for an American." It reassures me that he recognizes my accent. Alone in a strange place, the familiar feels good.

Hajj and I ride up together in the apartment's elevator, a wobbly, rusted cage. The building's electrical and telephone wires run down the elevator shaft, and as we pass the third floor, the cage snags a wire and makes it spark. Hajj pretends he doesn't see.

I follow Hajj as he lets himself into the apartment with a key, through another door, and out onto the terrace. I know why he brings me here first—the view is breathtaking: the American University of Beirut framed by the Mediterranean. In the east there's the snowcapped Shuf, the mountain range that separates the coast from the Biqa' Valley.

I watch a man on a terrace across the street whistling to pigeons that wheel in the air above him, flying higher and higher until they're just black specks against the sky. The man whistles three times. They pause. He whistles sharply, and they come back, putting down on the terrace around him. He speaks to them softly, enticing them back into their cages.

We go back inside. The living room is cramped and dark, but it's freshly painted and clean. There's a small cutout for a galley kitchen, a bedroom that just fits a queen-sized bed, and a bathroom with a drain in the corner for a shower. The floor is those hexagonal brick tiles you find in French provincial houses. The place is tiny, but who's going to visit us? We'll probably spend our time on the terrace anyway. Maybe I could find a kitten to sun itself here.

"Did you just come from the States?" Hajj asks as he follows me around the apartment.

Hajj must be in his early sixties. His tweed jacket and starched blue oxford shirt with button-down collar are distinctly American. He hands me his card. He's an engineer and a professor at the American University of Beirut.

"Do you like it?" he asks.

I think he is asking about Beirut, and I don't know what to say.

"The apartment," he says.

"It's great. I'll take it."

"And Beirut?"

He doesn't say anything when I don't answer. I'm glad he doesn't press me, or ask why we came here. I'm no longer quite sure myself.

I never do get through to Bob while he's in Paris to tell him about the apartment. I wonder if my phone is broken. But I know he'll love it, and I call Hajj to confirm. The same day I walk up to

Hamra's main street to buy some move-in items, everything from sheets and pillows to dishes. On the way back I walk past Abu Khudur's, so I can tell Ahmed we're neighbors.

I leave the packages at the hotel and go back out to look for a portable washing machine, the kind you attach to the sink faucet. I find one in a small shop off Hamra, put down a deposit, and tell the shopkeeper that my *zowj* will be back in a taxi to pick it up.

With time on my hands, I stop at a general store with racks of brooms, mops, and cleaning brushes. On a shelf outside, a black and white baby rabbit sits in a small cage. The shopkeeper notices me playing with it through the mesh wire and comes outside.

"Is it a pet?" I ask. He nods, but I'm not sure he understands.

"Yes, you buy." He says something in Arabic, but I only catch *hayawan*. Animal.

"Where did you get her?" I ask. I can picture the rabbit running around the terrace of our new apartment.

"In field," he says, stroking the side of the cage. "If you want, you say."

"I'd love to have a rabbit, but right now I'm living in a hotel," I say as slowly as I can. "And I have to ask my *zowj*."

"Ask *zowj*."

I promise myself that I'll bring Bob back to buy it as soon as he's home. The rabbit can be his present to me—Christmas is only a week away.

TWENTY-NINE

Nov. 4, 1997. Argentinean Bridas has said it was close to signing an agreement with Afghanistan's Taleban to build a gas pipeline between Turkmenistan and Pakistan, crossing through Afghanistan. "The state of negotiations is well advanced, we are in the final stages," Sebastian Otero Asp, the head of Bridas' Afghan operations, said. Bridas has a rival in a consortium led by Unocal to build the pipeline. Unocal announced the creation of its consortium to build a $1.9-billion pipeline in the Turkmen capital Ashgabat at the end of October. But the president of Unocal, John Imle, said in Islamabad last week that it had held no negotiations with any of the factions in wartorn Afghanistan and would wait until there was a government to deal with. Otero said Bridas was holding negotiations with the Taleban authorities. "Now we are discussing with the acting Minister of Mines and Industry," he said. Otero said Bridas would start building the pipeline as soon as the deal was signed, despite the country being divided and the anti-Taleban opposition alliance being recognized as the legitimate government by most of the outside world. "As soon as we sign, we will start building. Bridas doesn't want to get involved in politics at all. Our main interest is to make business—there is a market in Pakistan and there is gas in Turkmenistan," he said.

—Alexander's Gas and Oil Connections, www.gasandoil.com/goc/company/cnc75004.htm

Paris, France: **BOB**

don't pay attention to where the short Argentine oilman with a silver mane of hair is taking me until we're inside the restaurant, a hamburger place packed with tourists and the odd French businessmen slumming it. I wait while Carlos walks up and down, searching the booths for the man we're having lunch with. Carlos finds him, and summons me to join them.

Sitting in a dark booth is a man dressed in a pair of khaki slacks and a checkered wool shirt. "Howyudoin," he says, standing up to shake my hand. His American accent is nearly flawless. "My name's Ahmed Badeeb."

I don't know why Carlos didn't tell me we were having lunch with Badeeb—he's a legend in my old circles. During the Soviet Union's war in Afghanistan, he was the bagman for the Mujahidin. He would show up in Peshawar with suitcases filled with tens of millions of dollars, all in neat, cellophane-wrapped bricks of hundred-dollar bills, and hand them out to the Afghans like candy. The Mujahidin used the money to buy the arms that brought down the Soviet Union and ended the Cold War—not a bad item to have on your résumé. Badeeb is now chief of staff of Saudi intelligence.

He asks me something I can't hear because of a little girl shouting and crawling under the table next to ours. I lean in closer.

"How's your Dari?" he repeats.

"So-so," I say.

"You'll learn it fast."

I'll wait to figure out what he means by that.

Badeeb stops a passing waiter and looks at Carlos and me. "Cheeseburgers?"

He doesn't wait for our answer. "Your very best meat, sir," he tells the waiter, "and medium rare."

While we wait for our lunch, Badeeb and Carlos talk about a meeting next week in Riyadh. It's to discuss raising money for Carlos's Turkmenistan-to-Pakistan gas pipeline.

I stay out of it, but I'm curious to see how this unfolds, and I'm fascinated by the venue. I always imagined power lunches like this taking place in a cloud of cigar smoke in some baroque drawing room, over a port, and not a cheeseburger.

The burgers come. Badeeb pours ketchup and mustard on his, carefully holding the lettuce and tomato in place, and we eat in silence for a few minutes.

"When will you be able to leave for Afghanistan?" Badeeb asks, looking up from his hamburger.

Carlos looks at me with an expression that says there is only one answer to this question, and I'd better know what it is.

"Oh, almost anytime," I say.

For the last two months I've been consulting on the Middle East for Carlos. He runs his company, Bridas, like his personal fiefdom, hopping around the world in his private jet. He likes it that I've set up in Beirut because it's a convenient hub for the places he does business. Kabul is a new twist, but I can't say I'm not interested. I'll run it by Dayna if and when it gets serious.

"What about the Russians?" I ask. "They couldn't be happy about it."

It's pretty much a given that the Russians want all Central Asian pipelines to go through Russia rather than Afghanistan. They want an economic stranglehold on these countries.

Badeeb waves his hand in the air as if he's swatting away a fly. "The Russians are bluffing. They wouldn't dare try to stop this pipeline."

Badeeb and Carlos go back to talking about financing, calculating that construction will start next year.

After lunch Carlos walks out with me onto the Champs-Élysées. It's starting to rain. Carlos doesn't have an umbrella, and I offer him mine. He looks at it for moment, but doesn't take it. Instead, he asks me to spend another night in Paris so I can meet one of his bankers tomorrow for lunch.

"I have a flight in three hours," I say.

"But this is a very important lunch."

I start to tell him that Dayna is in Beirut, expecting me home, but then decide Carlos won't care. I know enough about his world to realize that while there's nothing more important than family, family never gets in the way of business.

"I'll be there," I say. "But I absolutely must go back to Beirut tomorrow afternoon."

I walk up the Champs-Élysées to call Dayna from a phone booth. Her cell rings once and then turns off. I feel panic setting in. It's two days before Christmas, and I was only supposed to be gone for two nights.

I should have told Carlos no and just gone back to Beirut. And the more I think about it, the crazier the idea of our moving to Kabul to work with the Taliban seems. Why would the Taliban ever accept me, an ex-CIA operative? But I can't turn down the proposal out of hand. Garth introduced me to Carlos, and I can't embarrass him.

The next day, when I show up to the Plaza Athénée, one of Paris's great Beaux Arts hotels, Carlos and the banker are already in the restaurant, two Kir Royales on the table in front of them. Carlos sees me, and signals to the waiter that I need one too.

After Carlos introduces me to the banker, they ignore me and talk about interest-rate spreads. Every time the banker makes a point, he shoots his sleeve, exposing his dime-thin, gold Patek Philippe watch, and gives his neck a quarter turn as if his collar were too tight.

I look at my own watch. I have exactly three hours and twenty minutes until my plane takes off for Beirut. I pick up a menu, catching Carlos's eye. I ask him if he's ever had the sole here. He looks over at me, doesn't answer, and goes back to talking to the banker.

"What kind of wine do you like?" I interrupt again, pushing the wine list in his direction.

Irritated, Carlos picks it up. He doesn't like the choices, and catches the steward's attention. He orders a bottle each of white and red, wines I've never heard of. But from their names they sound expensive.

As Carlos and the banker leave off interest rates to discuss a Swiss investor they don't like, I continue worrying about my flight. I can't disappoint Dayna and miss it. I push my chair back and say I have to make a call. Carlos waves me away in the direction of the door.

All the phone booths around the Place de l'Alma are occupied, but after maybe fifteen minutes of waiting, one frees up and I try our cell that Dayna has. It's busy. Who could she be talking to? I try a second time, but it's still busy. On the third try, a canned voice tells me in Arabic that the phone number is no longer in service. It feels like feral cats are eating the inside of my stomach.

Carlos doesn't even look my way when I sit back down. The waiter pours me a glass of white wine. I don't touch it, and instead glance at my watch. I now have two hours and twenty minutes before the plane takes off. I try to remember what Paris traffic is like on Thursday afternoons, another wasted thought. The only thing predictable about Paris traffic is that there's always a snarl on the way to the airport. The *premier plat* hasn't even arrived.

When the banker starts to talk about his summer house in Provence, my frayed nerves turn white-hot with fury. I consider ripping his Patek Philippe off his wrist and dropping it in the flower vase. Carlos glances over at me, probably wondering if I've lost my mind.

There was a time not long ago when I would have moved heaven and earth to sit at a meeting like this, listening to two players in the Great Game redraw the map of Central Asia. But right now I can only think about getting home for Christmas with Dayna. In the chaos that is my life, she's the only certainty I have. There's no way I'm going to let this relationship become a throw-away like so many before.

I push my chair back again. "I have to leave."

"Is something wrong?" Carlos asks.

"A family emergency."

Carlos looks at me in disbelief. I turn and walk out, and then half run across the lobby.

I make the plane, and the next morning Dayna takes me to see a little rabbit she's found. She can't locate the shop right away, and we walk the neighborhood in a grid. The store's closed, but she sees the cage just inside the front door. We peer into the window. The cage is empty. Too bad, she says. He must have sold it.

Just to make sure, she looks in another window. I hear a little startled sob. I follow her gaze, and there, hanging from a pole, is a small black and white rabbit skin. Dayna turns and begins running, fast enough that I have trouble catching up to console her.

I half knew that working for Carlos wasn't going to work, and Paris fully convinced me. If I'd stayed through lunch, there would have been dinner, and then another meeting the next day. And then, likely as not, Carlos would have invited me on his jet to Riyadh, and, who knows, from there to Kabul. This is exactly what I promised Dayna we wouldn't do, live separate lives.

And, as it turned out, Carlos's Afghan pipeline never was to be anyway. On August 7, 1998, al Qaeda bombed the American embassies in Kenya and Tanzania. The attacks were orchestrated by Osama bin Laden from Afghanistan, under the umbrella of the Taliban. An embargo on Afghanistan followed, putting an end to Carlos's business there.

THIRTY

Just opposite the ruins, the Palmyra is one of the most wonderful colonial-era relics dotting the Middle East, its guest book an impressive testament to how glamorous travel in the region once was. Having said that, you'll either love it or find it hair-raising: "faded grandeur" is putting it mildly, and on winter nights it's cold, draughty and downright spooky. . . .

—The Lonely Planet

Balabakk, Lebanon: **DAYNA**

T hinking it might be good to get out of town for a few days, Bob suggests a drive to Balabakk, the site of an ancient Phoenician city and possibly the best ruins in the world.

As we're sitting in the car rental office waiting for our vehicle, I ask Bob if Balabakk is safe. It is where Hizballah first organized in the early eighties, and it sits in the middle of Lebanon's lawless Biqa' Valley.

"These days Balabakk's safer than New York City," he says.

As soon as we cross over the Shuf mountains, we fall behind a convoy of tanks and armored personnel carriers. Strangely, they're running on their treads, rather than carried on transporters, tearing up the asphalt. Shtawrah, the biggest town between Beirut and Balabakk, is eerily quiet. Most of the stores are closed and there are few cars on the street.

"Is it a holiday?" I ask Bob.

"It feels like it."

Halfway to Balabakk, we come to a Lebanese army checkpoint. In the fields on either side are tanks, their crews digging defensive berms. Bob says it must be some sort of military exercise.

When our turn comes at the checkpoint, a soldier walks up to Bob's window, notices we're foreigners, and asks where we're going. When Bob says Balabakk, the soldier doesn't say anything. Bob asks if there's a problem. Instead of answering, the soldier tells Bob to open the trunk so he can inspect it. Another soldier gets down on his knees to study the undercarriage. Finally they wave us on our way.

Balabakk, normally a place where people live life in the street, is deserted. We rack our brains wondering what could be going on. Laughing, we joke that we'll certainly have the ruins to ourselves.

The Palmyra Hotel, one of the most storied hotels in the Middle East—a place where Agatha Christie, Charles de Gaulle, and Jacques Cousteau once stayed—is tonight as deserted as the rest of Balabakk. In fact, we're the only guests. A bent old man, well into his seventies, comes out to take our suitcases. To spare him, we carry them ourselves. On the way up to our room Bob asks him what's going on. "*Alhamdillah, fi huduh,*" he says. Thank God, it's all quiet.

He shows us into the "best room in the Palmyra," as he puts it. Suspicious, I turn the tap on in the sink. The water's cold. I turn around, and the old man's standing there looking at me. "Would madam like a bath?"

Ten minutes later a relay of two young boys brings up buckets of steaming water from the kitchen. Just as they're filling up the bath, the electricity goes off. One of the boys comes back with a bag of candles that he lights and places around the room, giving the place the feel of a Gothic cathedral.

By the time we come downstairs for dinner, the hotel lobby is arctic cold. The only light in the dining room is from the fireplace, where there's a great blazing fire. Dinner is a simple Lebanese *mezze* with roasted chicken and a bottle of local wine, a Kasara.

Just as the old man walks in with a platter of chicken, we hear a boom and then two more. The man stops and listens. It's quiet again, and he puts down the platter.

"Is there some problem?" Bob asks before he can get away.

"Thanks be to God, all is quiet."

We go back to our dinners, and then there's a rapid series of explosions, followed by exchanges of machine-gun fire. The fighting is in the distance, but we quickly finish dinner and go back upstairs. Artillery booms last half the night.

Not until morning, listening to the radio, do we learn that there has been a battle outside Balabakk between the Lebanese army and a breakaway faction of Hizballah.

Thanks be to God, I think, that the hotel is still standing. And us too.

THIRTY-ONE

> Sheikh Hamad bin Jassem bin Hamad al-Thani has been on the
> run from his government for over three years and could face
> execution following his imminent trial. The government alleges
> that the former minister of economy and ex-police chief was
> paid $100 million to carry out a coup to put the previous emir
> back on the throne. Qatar's current ruler, Sheikh Hamad bin
> Khalifa al-Thani, overthrew his father in a bloodless coup in
> 1995.
>
> —BBC News

Beirut, Lebanon: **BOB**

Sheikh Hamad bin Jasim bin Hamad Al Thani, a prince of the
Qatari royal family, now will meet me at only one place, a little restaurant in the mountains above Beirut. It's always quiet
during the day, the sheikh knowing he'll be left alone to smoke his
sheesha. A waterpipe.

As usual, the sheikh's late and flies down the steps to the terrace, almost tripping over his *dishdash*—a cloud-white cotton robe
that goes down to the ankles. He looks like a square-rigger in a
stiff wind. His driver, holding the sheikh's briefcase, follows in his
wake.

As soon as the sheikh gets his tea and the waiter starts his *sheesha,* enveloping him in smoke, he sighs and tells me he's discovered that he has a problem he has no idea how to solve.

"I've lost a piece of property in the United States," he says.

"What do you mean, lost it?"

"I paid more than ten million for it."

The sheikh takes a deep puff from the *sheesha,* sending a cloud of smoke drifting across the silvery topaz sea behind him. "I will visit the United States after I solve my main problem and then fix it."

Like everyone else in the Middle East, I know what the sheikh's "main problem" is. He's a wanted man, tried and convicted for trying to overthrow his cousin the emir of Qatar in February 1996. He was Qatar's chief of police at the time. When the coup fizzled, the sheikh fled to Damascus, certain that Syria would refuse to extradite him back to Qatar. He's able to visit Lebanon because Syria has the final say when it comes to Lebanon's foreign policy, including who's extradited and who's not.

The sheikh works the lock of his briefcase like he's trying to open it, but then gives up. "I can't remember whether my land's in Maine or Colorado. I was very, very busy in those days, and I never had the chance to see it. The deed's in Doha. Heaven knows where. Do you think you can help?"

"You should have someone search the property records in both states."

He wiggles his tea glass in the air without looking back at the waiter. "I don't know whose name the property's in. My property manager bought it, and now I can't find him."

I wonder how the sheikh ever managed to organize a coup, even in an Arab Gulf sheikhdom as small as Qatar.

The more I get to know the sheikh, the more I'm interested in whether he's thinking about another coup. I haven't lost my fascination for political upheaval, and anyhow it would be an invaluable piece of information. A successful coup in Qatar—unlikely as it is—could have serious consequences for the Gulf, even ripple across the Middle East. The knowledge might even put me back in the good graces of Carlos.

But it's not a question I can just come out and ask the sheikh.

At our next meeting I steer the conversation, in a very general way, to the Qatari royal family. Most people like to talk about their families.

The sheikh throws up his hands. "It's all the fault of my sonof-abitch cousin."

I know who he's talking about—not Qatar's emir, but rather its powerful foreign minister, another Qatari prince. Many Qataris consider the foreign minister the de facto leader of their country. The foreign minister is the man behind Al Jazeera, the influential Arab TV network, as well as much of the political reform in Qatar. Because the foreign minister opened informal relations with Israel, he's the darling of the Clinton White House.

"He's from the shit part of my family," the sheikh says. "We allowed that snake in the royal nursery although he had no right to be there. We understood how he was worming his way into the emir's affections only after the emir cut us out, all of us.

"Mind you, I was blind like the rest. Even when we were boys, I did not understand what it meant when this evil man flattered my cousin, became his intimate. And then he put the worm in his ear, against me and anyone else with good sense. If only my country would be rid of that evil man."

This is an unforeseen opening I can't pass up. "Didn't you try?"

"A few troops, and it's easily done. I know how to do it."

"What do you need?"

"Landing craft."

That night I call a friend who has a line to surplus Ukrainian military landing craft. He faxes me some paper on them.

The next evening the sheikh only glances at the faxes and pushes them aside. "It's that bastard the foreign minister. If he were only gone, the emir would see the light."

"But what do the generals think about the foreign minister? I'd imagine they're unhappy with him just as you are."

The sheikh doesn't answer. He points down at the coast, at

Junieh, an old port north of Beirut. It's dusk now, and the lights are just coming on.

"You won't believe what happened to me there. I went to a nightclub in Junieh the other night. I danced with a half-dozen girls, but met one I particularly liked. She was lovely, twenty maybe. We danced until two, and then I took her to an apartment I have in Beirut. Just before dawn she woke me up and asked if I'd drive her home. She didn't say where she lived, but I agreed.

"It alarmed me when we went past Cocadil and into Bir Hasan (the Shia southern suburbs controlled by Hizballah). She pointed to a street off the airport road. I realized too late we were in Bir al-Abid. When I turned to say something to her, she was slipping on an *abaya* (a black head covering and ankle-length robe worn by conservative Iranian women). I dropped her off in front of an apartment with Hizballah banners flying over it and paid her a hundred dollars. I'll tell you, that sobered me up—sharing my bed with Hizballah."

Hizballah is out of the kidnapping business, but their reputation lives on.

I wait until our next meeting to bring up the generals again, but the sheikh ignores me and starts telling a story about the minister of religious affairs. At first I don't pay any attention. So many of the sheikh's stories drive off a cliff that they're not worth following to the end. But when he starts telling me how he tapped the telephone of the minister of religious affairs, who kept calling a man named Khalid Sheikh Hamad, I listen.

At first I don't know exactly who the sheikh's talking about. But as he goes on I realize it's Khalid Sheikh Muhammad, or KSM, an al Qaeda field commander. Two years before, the Department of Justice had issued an arrest warrant for KSM indicting him for planning to blow up twelve civilian airliners. The FBI sent agents to Doha to arrest him, but he disappeared by the time they got there.

I mention the vanishing act to the sheikh.

"Yes, the minister of religious affairs protected him so he wouldn't fall into the hands of the FBI."

"What do you mean?"

"He hid him in the minister's beach chalet until the FBI went away. The foreign minister told him to."

"How do you know this?"

"The foreign minister knows everything. I told you. He is the one who protected Khalid Sheikh Hamad."

"You can prove this?"

"I have the transcripts of the phone calls. They're with me in Damascus."

The truth is, I can't really trust the sheikh. He'd say anything to dirty the name of the foreign minister. But I agree to go to Damascus to take a look at the transcripts.

THIRTY-TWO

In the British investigation of the aborted El Al attack, Hindawi
told British police he was recruited by Haitham Said, an aide
to Major General al-Khuli, chief of Syrian Air Force intelligence.
According to the evidence presented at the trial, al-Khuli's
operatives: (1) supplied Hindawi, a Jordanian, with a Syrian
passport; (2) gave him $12,000 and promised him more money
when he completed his mission to plant a bomb aboard an El
Al civilian airliner; (3) provided him with the bomb which was
carried into London aboard the Syrian Arab Airlines, which
also gave him SAA crew member hotel accommodations; and
(4) trained him in the bomb's use.

Hindawi tried to use his pregnant girlfriend as the unwitting
carrier of the sophisticated bomb which was built into her
carry-on bag. If an alert security official had not spotted the
device after her bag cleared an earlier check, 375 innocent
persons, including some 230 Americans, would have perished.

—U.S. Department of State Bulletin, February 1987

Damascus, Syria: DAYNA

A s we pull up in front of Sheikh Hamad's mansion, I tilt my
head to get a better look. This can't be it, I think.

The house is a monstrosity, a prison blockhouse with a
wedding-cake façade. There are three stories of it, cracks everywhere, masonry crumbling off, pieces hanging in the dry bushes,
piles of dirt from digging the foundation but never hauled away.
There's not a tree or even a shrub to protect the house from the
steady, hard desert wind. The nearby houses are all new too, some
half built. Few look occupied.

Qasem, a businessman and the sheikh's friend, and Bob get out, leaving Qasem's wife, Leila, and me to wait in the car. Bob tries to push open the cast-iron front gate, but it's bolted closed and locked. There's no bell. Bob pounds on the gate, but the house is as still as a stone. Qasem and Bob walk around the side to see if there's another entry. It's then that I see someone moving in a window. I open the car window and call Bob and Qasem to come back around front. Another few minutes go by before a head pokes out the door, but it pulls back and closes. Finally a man in ironed Levi's, a plaid shirt, and cowboy boots comes out. His shirt mis-buttoned, he looks as if he's just woken up, even though it's eight in the evening. He shakes hands with Bob and Qasem through the gate while a servant slips around him and unlocks the latch.

The man turns and sees Leila and me in the backseat of the car and walks toward us, squinting as if he can't imagine who we are. I get out of the car to introduce myself. He shakes my hand. "Sheikh Hamad. You're very, very welcome to my home." He turns to go inside the house, and we all follow him. The servant relocks the gate behind us.

Inside the foyer, the sheikh stops abruptly as if to nail down a thought. "No, wait," he says. "First come out into the garden to see my new barbecue."

Outside on the terrace, he points to a giant barbecue with six separate grills, lighted by bare bulbs on a string hanging between two poles. A half-dozen marble tables with marble benches surround it. "Next time we will grill," the sheikh says. "When the house is finished and I can invite all my friends. A party."

I notice a man in an apron and chef's toque grilling at his own barbecue in the house next to the sheikh's. The sheikh nods at him, and the man waves back. "Do you know who that is?" the sheikh asks Bob, dropping his voice to a whisper. "It's General Khuli." Bob asks if it is "the same" General Khuli. The sheikh replies, "Yes, that's him."

In the eighties, General Khuli masterminded an attempt to

blow up an Israeli El Al plane flying from London to Tel Aviv. The explosive device was planted on an unwitting, pregnant Irishwoman.

"Shouldn't he be in hiding somewhere?" I whisper to Bob.

Before Bob can answer, the sheikh takes us back inside, into what he calls his *diwan*. The only furniture consists of two identical burgundy divans pushed up against midnight blue damask walls. Little stars woven into the fabric twinkle in the chandelier's light. A huge, hand-woven Persian silk carpet occupies the center of the room.

We sit in the corner, the four of us along one wall, the sheikh along the other.

"Problems, problems," the sheikh says. "I have more than I care to tell you. You won't believe what happened to me two days ago." He slumps in his seat, tousling his hair in an untamed tuft.

"The evening started so pleasantly. I wanted to be by myself, a night on the Golan Heights to think things over with a *sheesha*. A frigid wind picked up, and I told the driver to move the pipe into the van. Just as I settled down in the backseat, the van was suddenly engulfed in flames. This foolish man had carelessly let a spark escape. The van burned to its rims, everything ruined."

The story's funny, I suppose, but I find the sheikh a sad figure. How many friends could he have, living in exile like this? Bob told me there are a lot of people after his money, con men and corrupt Syrian officials. I'm sure he grotesquely overpaid in building this soulless house, and filling it with its mismatched furniture.

As the evening proceeds, the sheikh becomes more agitated, getting up every fifteen minutes, only to come back with his hair in spikes, his eyes redder.

At one point he leaves the room and comes back grinning, nearly ecstatic. "We must buy a bank together!" Bob plays along and asks how much capital we will need. The sheikh turns to Qasem, "How much do we need?" Qasem says a minimum of $20 million. "We'll find it!" the sheikh says.

It's a little after eleven before the sheikh finally leads us into dinner. I stop in the doorway, not knowing what to say. A twenty-foot banquet table sits covered with gold platters, towering mountains of lamb and saffron rice, at least twenty different bowls of things like quail eggs, caviar, and sweetmeats. The sheikh is delighted and claps his hands like a child.

THIRTY-THREE

> The Edge . . . there is no honest way to explain it because the only people who really know where it is are the ones who have gone over.
>
> —Hunter S. Thompson, *Hell's Angels*

Beirut, Lebanon: BOB

The taxi drops us off in front of the Albergo Hotel, a restored Ottoman mansion in the old Christian Beirut suburb of Ashrafiyah, and we run to the door with coats pulled up over our heads against sheets of frigid rain. The hip Italian restaurant inside is packed with young Lebanese out for a fun night. We don't see Qasem and Leila until they wave to us from a table. Qasem's in a suit, Leila all in cream, with a pair of large teardrop diamond earrings.

We've come to really like Qasem and Leila. He's earnest, but at the same time always ready with a genuine laugh. Leila, a professor, is charming, beautiful, and smart. After our dinner at the sheikh's house in Damascus, they invited us over for dinner, and tonight we're reciprocating.

As soon as we order drinks, Qasem looks to Dayna and Leila. "Do you two need to freshen up?" Leila takes the cue and gets up, but Dayna stays. Qasem waits a moment, then half turns in his seat to make sure Leila isn't on her way back. "There's this business plan I think we should mull over," he says. He stops again, obviously considering how he's going to put this.

"Look," he says, moving a bottle of wine out of his way. "We will borrow ten million from the sheikh, for the bank he wants."

"But we don't know anything about banking," I say.

"No, of course. That's not the point. We take the money from the sheikh"—Qasem stops again and looks around the restaurant to make sure no one is listening in—"and not pay it back."

"Why not the full twenty million while we're at it?" I ask, trying to pass it off as a joke.

"You don't understand." He pauses again, dropping his voice to a whisper. "We borrow the money and then have him taken care of."

I can't hear the rest of what Qasem says because of a ripple of laughter from the next table, and it's too dark to see Dayna's expression—but I can imagine it. Like me, she's probably thinking that the sheikh might be eccentric, but he certainly doesn't deserve what Qasem seems to have planned for him.

Qasem must see the expression on my face. "It's not my idea. It's Badar's. It's crazy, no?"

Badar is a Syrian-American we all know. He's always struck me as slippery. He was the one who sold us the cell phone that stopped working when I was in Paris meeting Carlos.

I catch sight of Leila coming back. "Don't pay any attention to Badar," I say. "He has a sick sense of humor."

On the ride home after dinner, neither Dayna nor I say anything until we're out on the terrace of our apartment. I pull two chairs together to talk.

"This doesn't exactly sound like a good business plan to me," she says.

I know what's going through her mind. While we never considered going into business with either the sheikh or Qasem, the very idea that anyone would think we'd be interested in murder for profit is unnerving. We may have spent our lives in a fairly rough trade, but we're not killers.

"This cannot end well," Dayna says. "We need to leave here."

She's right, of course.

◆

Two days later we do leave Beirut, abandoning our apartment, our furniture, and two months' rent. As soon as we land in Geneva, I call the sheikh. He seems already to know people are plotting his murder. His driver died when the brakes mysteriously failed on the sheikh's new van. Before I hang up, I tell him to be careful.

Like a lot of things in life, it will take time for us to see Beirut for what it's been. Both of our lives have turned so many times over the years that it's been hard to tell the major shifts from the minor ones. But later I'll see Beirut as the biggest of them. I went there looking for a raw look at the "real" Middle East, one outside the bubble of the CIA. I suppose I was even looking for adventure. But what I found was more trouble, the kind that convinced me I should leave the CIA. I, of all people, should have known that adventure and trouble go hand in hand. But, apparently, I would need one more lesson.

THIRTY-FOUR

Marathon Sparks Block 32 Feeding Frenzy—U.S. oil producer
Marathon Oil is selling a 20% stake in Angola's deepwater
Block 32 that could fetch almost $2 billion, attracting bids
from China's big three oil companies, India's Oil & Natural Gas
Corporation (ONGC) and Brazil's Petrobras, sources close to the
matter said.

—www.upstreamonline.com/live/article160847.ece

New York City: BOB

My son Robert has now been in the shower for twenty minutes, and we have to be out the door in five more or he'll be late for school. I knock. "Hey, Slick, we gotta get going."

Having Robert living with us—he's now twelve—has taken a bit of adjusting. He came to us when his boarding school in southern France called me shortly after we got to Geneva from Beirut. The school said it might not be the best fit for Robert; he'd fallen in with an Algerian gang. They put him on a train the next morning, and I met him at the station. With his beat-up suitcase and wrinkled blazer, he was a good match for his nomad father. Dayna, understandably feeling unmoored and in need of a real-world skill, was in the middle of applying to law school, and I took him under my wing. Better late to fatherhood than never.

Robert exits the bathroom in his towel, followed by a cloud of steam, and runs to his bedroom. He's back in a minute, fully dressed. I don't know how he does it. He looks at the bowl of cereal I put out for him and says he'll eat on the walk to school. Then he goes to the cupboard, reaches in the back until he finds a granola bar, and shoves it in his jacket pocket. He runs for the door.

"The rabbit?" I say.

He taps his forehead with the palm of his hand. "Who could ever forget the rabbit?"

When Robert first found out that a rabbit was part of his new family, he was speechless. His wonder only grew when I told him the story about the ill-starred rabbit in Beirut, and how Dayna had searched the city until she found this one in the bird market. Traveling with the creature presented certain challenges. For example, when we were all flying to New York, KLM wouldn't allow the rabbit to fly in the cabin, worried it might escape and attack the cockpit. Dayna had no choice but to fly separately on Air France, a company that allows rabbits in the cabin. But Robert has grown fond of the rabbit and doesn't mind that it's his responsibility now.

He runs into his bedroom, looks under the bed, then dashes into our room and gently coaxes the rabbit out from under our bed. As he puts it in the cage, I go to find my folder.

Out on Second Avenue, Robert asks, "The bus or walk?"

"Let's walk. It's your birthday."

"It's tomorrow."

He likes to walk, especially when I accompany him all the way to school.

"So what's for tomorrow?" he asks.

"Oh, I don't know, I was sorta thinking of the opera—or we could stay home and read."

"Come on."

"First we'll go up the Empire State building."

"And then dinner?"

"Wait until you see what Dayna has for you for your birthday."

"I already know."

By 42nd Street we're behind schedule and I pick up the pace.

"What is it again that you're doing today?" Robert asks, hurrying to keep up.

"A big, important business deal," I say, teasing him.

"Dressed like that?" I'm in jeans and an old slicker with a ripped pocket.

"They're friends."

After I drop off Robert at school, I cut over to Fifth Avenue to kill time window-shopping and browsing in Barnes & Noble. I'm looking at new fiction when my cell phone rings. I push through the doors and am back out on to Fifth Avenue.

"How's your schedule?" It's Chuck, the investment banker I'm meeting.

"Pretty clear."

"Look, I'm jammed up. Mind if we meet at eleven thirty?"

"That's good."

"And better yet, let's do it in front of McCormick and Schmick's, find a place to get a cup of coffee. I got a lunch date there later."

I get to McCormick & Schmick's early. At eleven thirty I stick my head in to make sure Chuck didn't somehow slip by me. He's not there. Everybody's late in New York, I think. I wait outside, checking my folder again to make sure I didn't forget any papers.

At five to twelve I pick out Chuck, a big man, borderline fat, his shoulder curved forward, negotiating the noontime crowd on Sixth Avenue. When he's up to me, he pulls a handkerchief from his coat pocket to wipe the sweat off of his face. "Jesus, I'm sorry." He takes a couple of deep breaths. "I had to batter my way out of a meeting."

Chuck looks up and down Sixth Avenue, obviously for his lunch date. "Lunch is at noon."

"I got everything here," I say, tapping the mauve folder.

Chuck looks at it, but doesn't say anything.

"Chuck, very quick. This is an offer for Angola's deepwater

Block 32. I mean ten percent of it. No middlemen—other than me, that is."

"I don't know what Block 32 is."

"A megafield, a new one. It's carried interest. Total puts down the capital and lifts it. I don't know, maybe a 120 thousand barrels a day."

I know that I'm out of my depth, trying to sell one of the biggest oil properties in the world. But, as much as I understand it, it seems pretty straightforward: the French major oil company Total drills the oil, pumps it, and markets it. Whoever buys the 10 percent I'm selling gets a percentage of the money flying through the door. It's just a matter of determining what 10 percent of the block is worth, which is why I called Chuck.

Chuck motions for me to give him the folder. He opens it and glances at the first fax.

"I know this sounds weird," I say, "but I have an exclusive on it for the next three months. It's a friend-of-a-friend sort of deal. You know the strange people I know."

Chuck closes the folder and puts it under his arm. "I'll see what I can do."

Chuck spots three men in suits coming toward us. "That's them. I'll call you." Chuck turns and walks away to meet his three lunch partners at the entrance of the restaurant.

I never do hear back from Chuck on Block 32, although it did seem to me like an interesting offer. But I have to admit I'm not all that surprised Chuck passed; I'm not much good at selling things.

THIRTY-FIVE

> This provincial capital Ramadi is the eastern terminus of a highway across the desert from the Mediterranean Sea. The town was founded in 1869 by the local rulers of the Ottoman Empire in order to control the nomadic Dulaym tribes of the region. The British won an important victory over the Turks there in 1917. Ramadi was established for political reasons, but proved vital as a stopover on the caravan routes between Baghdad and the cities of the Levant.
>
> —www.globalsecurity.org/military/world/Iraq/ramadiyah.htm

Washington, D.C.: DAYNA

The day I finish taking the bar exam I come home to find a message for Bob from ABC News on our answering machine. "Your contract's ready." It's a woman's voice I've never heard. "Can you leave for Iraq next week?"

Iraq? Going to Iraq isn't exactly a detail that someone you're living with should keep to himself. Especially when the United States is about to invade the country. I'm both pissed and hurt that he didn't tell me. I call him on his cell phone. It's off, so I leave a message: "Have a great time in Baghdad." Period.

It's just like Bob to make travel or work arrangements and then fill me in at the last minute. He didn't tell me until years later that he'd promised the crazy Argentine oil guy Carlos we'd go to Afghanistan, and even then he dropped it into a conversation purely for color: "Well, we *almost* went to work with the Taliban in Kabul." *We* almost did *what*? Now the same thing is happening. It especially hurts because we're just starting to put down roots.

We moved down from New York to Washington for me to go

to law school. We bought a tiny carriage house on Capitol Hill that we filled with two Labradors. Bob was trying to learn an entirely new profession, turning himself into a writer.

There was a setback to our little family when Robert's State Department–employed mother was assigned to Pakistan, and, given a choice, Robert went to live with her. We missed Robert a lot when he left. He and I both liked to bake, and we made elaborate frosted cakes together. Bob and Robert had boy-chats on the way to school. But I knew the decision was right for him, and frankly I was a little jealous that he was off on a grand adventure of his own. And now Bob is going on one too.

It's not that I blame Bob for wanting to see the war, to be there for Saddam's end. He was always fascinated by the man. But I need to make him pay for not checking with me first, so when he comes home that night, I pick a fight. Well, not a fight, more like an accounting.

"How could you make plans without even telling me?" I say.

"Well, I didn't think it was serious."

"But there's a contract."

"Well, I know . . . but these things rarely work out . . . and you know one thing leads to another."

He tells me that ABC's plan is to send him and a cameraman across the border to help film a documentary on the last days of Saddam. They'll stay with Bob's Iraqi friends at their compound near Ramadi, to capture their reaction to Saddam's fall.

Somewhat mollified, we go to Las Placitas around the corner on Eighth Street, where the margaritas put the day's problems far behind you. On the walk there, I admit to him that I'm not so much mad because he didn't tell me about the ABC deal as envious that he has this offer to film a war and I don't.

"I'd be envious too," he says.

But things have a way of working out. The next day ABC calls and tells Bob they can't find a single cameraman willing to go to Ramadi with him. He immediately volunteers me for the job, convincing ABC that in the CIA I'd become a whiz with small cameras—and it's only a small step to TV cameras. Buying it, ABC sets a date to train me in New York to operate the miniature camera that the reality television shows are using now.

Dropping into the middle of a war in the Middle East is not exactly the real world I thought I'd enter when I went to law school, but it does make me believe that maybe I did leave the CIA with a few transferable skills, after all.

THIRTY-SIX

The Iraqi tribal structure consists of a confederation, tribe, clan, lineage, and the extended family. A confederation is a group of tribes who are related to each other by shared geographic residence, historical ties, kinship, ethnicity, or some other factor. The tribal confederation is not based on kinship rights. A tribe is a group of clans which vary in size, anywhere from a few hundred to several thousand members. A tribe is usually named after a founding ancestor who in some cases may actually be a fictitious figure. A clan is a group of lineages related through a common ancestor. The lineage is the number of extended families related through a common male ancestor. Traditionally, extended families live within the same village, work on shared land, and act collectively as political and military units.

—First Lieutenant Jonathan M. Davis, Military Intelligence
Professional Bulletin

Washington, D.C.: **BOB**

'll tell Dayna later, but the truth is that getting into Iraq before our troops arrive comes down to the strength of my friendship with Marwan, the man I drove with Robert through a Washington blizzard to see. That night, after Dayna and I first talk about the Iraq trip, I try to fall asleep, but wind up lying awake, making an accounting of my own.

Marwan and I first met in Paris in September 1990, a month after the Iraqi invasion of Kuwait. He was staying at the Meurice, an elegant old-world hotel facing the Tuileries Gardens and the Seine River. Marwan had the penthouse suite, the only room on the seventh floor.

Marwan called down for a bottle of wine, and we went outside on the room's private terrace to enjoy the sunset and watch the tour boats and barges ply the Seine. Not five minutes later a waiter let himself out onto the terrace with the bottle of wine and two glasses, followed by a boy with two chairs and a table. As we watched them set the table with a white linen tablecloth, Marwan started to tell me about himself.

He first came to Paris in the sixties to work for a Texas oilman. He'd just graduated from Stanford with a degree in petroleum engineering. Marwan would stay with the boss at the Meurice. When the boss went out at night—he kept a mistress in Paris, a ballerina—and Marwan was on his own, he'd wonder where life would take him. Until then he'd never understood the wealth and power that comes with oil.

Since then, Marwan had spent his life in oil and construction, almost all of it in the Middle East, first in Saudi Arabia and later in Iraq, where he worked for a Sunni tribal chief from Iraq's Anbar Province. The chief, whose tribe belonged to the Dulaym confederation, was extremely influential in Iraqi politics. The chief was a member of the ruling Ba'ath Party.

Through Iraq's modern history, the Dulaym had been a mainstay of every ruling Sunni regime, providing about 25 percent of the noncommissioned officers and soldiers in the Iraqi army. Saddam Hussein, a Sunni like the tribal chief, looked at the Dulaym as a critical source of support. Saddam would push work in the tribal chief's direction, calculating that the chief's construction company would come to depend on government contracts.

After Marwan worked on several projects for the tribal chief, a close friendship developed between the two. Marwan soon was treated like a member of the chief's family, eventually taking over management of the family's money. "I'm closer with them than with my own family," Marwan said.

That first night in Paris, Marwan gave me a tutorial on Iraq that paralleled the one Ali gave me on Syria. As Marwan told me, Iraq's tribes, held together by tradition and blood loyalty, are a permanent fixture in Iraq. Their unbroken allegiances and ties go back thousands of years, before even Islam. While they've always stuck together, even during the worst times in Iraq, men like Saddam seize power for the moment, but they inevitably fall and are eventually forgotten. The tribes are what endure. "They're of the land and aren't going anywhere," Marwan said.

In marked contrast, without genuine tribal roots, Saddam and his family lack any sort of traditional social standing in Iraq, or respect. In fact, most Iraqis look at Saddam's family as little more than common criminals who stole power and held on to it through sheer brutality and cunning. Saddam pretended to have tribal roots and solicited the support of the tribes as a way of firming up his political base.

After dinner at the Meurice's restaurant, Marwan and I walked in the Tuileries. It was dark, and the park was nearly empty. We got all the way to the Louvre and walked back. We must have done this three times while Marwan talked on and I made mental notes. Finally we sat down on a hard stone bench to talk some more. It was only when we got up that we noticed the gates were locked—with us on the inside.

We walked to the Seine side of the park until I found a place where I thought we could get out. I climbed down the battered wall to the street and then helped Marwan down. He was surprisingly agile for a man over sixty and more than two hundred pounds.

It was past midnight when I walked home in a light drizzle. I passed the movie theater on the Champs-Élysées where my mother had taken me to see *Lawrence of Arabia*, starring Peter O'Toole, when I was ten years old. I remembered being completely mesmerized, making her sit through a second showing. It must have been six hours in all.

◆

That fall, during the run-up to the Gulf War, I would see a lot of Marwan. He'd fly into town and immediately call me for dinner. We'd usually eat at the Meurice's restaurant—seven courses with two bottles of wine, followed by a cognac and a cigar. It was Marwan who taught me about French wines. He'd never let me pay, to make sure our relationship couldn't be misunderstood.

Often, when I met Marwan for coffee, I'd bring along one of my kids. They called him uncle. When he'd phone, he'd chat with them for a long time. Marwan told me he relished spending time with them, having no children of his own.

Marwan would talk for hours on end about Saddam and his family, mentally walking me through Saddam's natal village, Al 'Awjah. When Saddam was born there in 1937, Al 'Awjah was a miserable little hardscrabble village with mud houses and mud streets. Almost everyone was poor, many of them servants to Tikrit's rich. Al 'Awjah also had its share of outcasts and thugs, and it was from them that Saddam learned about street fighting—lessons he'd carry into politics. When Saddam came to power in 1968, it was from Al 'Awjah that he drew his closest advisers. Roughly speaking, Al 'Awjah was to Saddam what Plains, Georgia, was to Jimmy Carter or what Midland, Texas, was to George W. Bush.

I didn't know the term then, but Al 'Awjah was home to Saddam's "charismatic clan." It was his refuge in times of trouble, and a source of strength for his extended family. Publicly, Saddam professed a commitment to Arab nationalism and Ba'ath socialism, but in fact he only cared about his family's survival and what Al 'Awjah symbolized for it.

I absorbed everything Marwan told me, fascinated by the idea of Al 'Awjah, how a close-knit clan, held together by blood loyalty, could so neatly trace its origins to a poor village. I couldn't help noticing the similarities to the Assad clan in Syria, and the small village they came from in the Alawite mountains, Qurdaha. I would later see the same phenomenon in Tajikistan's Kulyab Province. Families like these were so different from anything I knew.

The closer we got to the Gulf War, the more I pressed Marwan to tell me what he thought was going on in Saddam's head. Was Saddam really going to fight to hang on to Kuwait and lose his army? I could not comprehend how this would aid Saddam and his clan's vicious hold on power. Marwan would only say that his friend the Dulaym chief, who'd spent time in prison with Saddam, was confident that Saddam would only leave Kuwait if he was compelled to—by armed force.

I trusted Marwan, but I had a hard time understanding how a tribe such as the Dulaym could remain so well plugged in and influential in a modern state like Iraq. To check his story, I asked him if he could arrange for me to meet the Iraqi ambassador to Paris. This wasn't as easy as it sounds. The ambassador was Saddam's unofficial emissary to the West, very much in demand. Marwan told me to pick a night and a place. The ambassador showed up at the George V exactly at eight, without bodyguards. We had a pleasant dinner, although I can't say that I learned anything new from him. But the dinner did fortify my confidence in Marwan and his Dulaym chief.

A couple of days later I met Marwan for coffee. He told me that my meeting with the ambassador had gone over well in Baghdad. I didn't ask, but it made me wonder what exactly the Dulayms' relationship with the Iraqi government was. Or Marwan's, for that matter.

As we watched people run out of the Metro, unfurling umbrellas against a cold rain, Marwan signaled the waiter for another coffee. "Now you have to meet the family," he said.

"Is this some sort of a back channel to Baghdad? Because if it is, I can't do it."

"It's just a token of friendship."

I understood that with Marwan there would always be a certain degree of ambiguity in our relationship, and I agreed to meet the Dulaym chief's son Malik and the chief's brother when they got to Paris. Within the week, though, Marwan called to say French visas couldn't be arranged. Would I meet them in Rome?

At first I lied to Marwan, telling him I had commitments in Paris. The truth was, there wasn't enough time to get permission to travel to Rome. I couldn't do it on my own hook, either—traveling across international borders without Langley's permission was a no-no. If caught, I'd be brought home and reprimanded.

"They're coming here especially to see you," Marwan said. "They think of you as their only American friend."

"Can't this wait?"

"They're already in Amman."

I made a quick calculation. I could fly to Rome for dinner and be back the next morning at work before anyone knew. "OK," I told him. "I'll move my appointments around."

Two days later I left work early, took a taxi to Orly airport, and bought my ticket to Rome in cash. The plane was delayed, and traffic into Rome was at a near standstill. But Malik and his uncle were in the hotel lobby waiting for me.

We were all tired, and over dinner we talked about mostly small things: the empty plane, Rome, the price of the dollar. No one said a word about the war, which was all but inevitable now. So far, our dinner—my trip to Rome—was only a gauge of our mutual respect.

At the end, though, as we were getting up to leave, I hazarded the question still on my mind: Would Saddam withdraw from Kuwait at the last minute to avoid a war?

Malik noticed his napkin was still tucked into his trousers, pulled it out, and placed it on the table. "Saddam will never withdraw."

"But if he loses his army?"

"He will stand and fight."

"So will the United States," I replied.

The war that started on January 17, 1991 proved us both right. The Dulaym lost thousands in Kuwait fighting the American on-slaught. Their businesses were nearly ruined. Malik's father, the Dulaym tribal chief, would soon fall ill and die. He'd positioned Malik to replace him as tribal chief, but Malik wasn't immediately accepted by the tribal elders. But the Rome dinner launched a re-lationship with Malik, one that neither of us wanted to let die.

Malik and I kept in touch through Marwan. On his way back to Toronto from Iraq, Marwan would make a point of coming to see me in Paris with news of Malik and the Dulaym. When I was posted in Morocco, Marwan and I would meet in Casablanca and eat dinner at a fish restaurant on the harbor's mole, Marwan bringing fresh news of Malik and his family. When I was on leave in France from Dushanbe, I made a point of taking a train up to Paris to meet Marwan for lunch.

In 1994, after I came back from Tajikistan and was assigned to Iraqi operations at Langley, I had good reason to see Malik. Every month or so I'd fly to Jordan's capital, Amman, on business, and would make sure to fix in advance a time to see him, in between my CIA meetings. Usually it was the first night I arrived. Exhausted and jet-lagged, I'd go to the Dulaym's house right from the air-port. It was an austere place, a limestone house on top of a lime-stone hill. We'd sit for hours talking about Iraq and drinking tea. Family always played a big part in our meetings. Malik's children would come down and hug me before going to bed. Like Mar-wan, Malik knew the names of my children and would ask about them. Dinner wouldn't be served until ten, followed by more tea. I wouldn't get to my hotel until after midnight.

At first, conversations with Malik were difficult. Iraq's Anbar tribes speak a corrupted Arabic, peppered with Turkish and Farsi, even a few words of Aramaic. But with each meeting I understood a little more. Malik's confidence in me grew at the same pace. Every time we'd meet, he'd regale me with fresh stories about Saddam's sons and their dirty business deals, wild parties, and brutality. On one level it was amusing—Saddam the tyrant, unable to control his bratty children. On another, it gave me insight into how Saddam ruled. It was Malik who first told me in 1995 that Saddam's son-in-law was about to defect to Jordan, and Malik who later told me how Saddam intended to lure him back and murder him, which Saddam did. With each meeting, the confidence we had in each other grew.

In all these years serving in the Middle East, with maybe the exception of Ali, who instructed me on Syrian politics, I felt stuck in the shallows, never coming close to the inside of national power structures, or truly understanding these societies. With Malik, though, I felt I was finally starting to see down into the depths. It helped that our relationship was based on friendship alone, and had nothing to do with the CIA.

At a meeting in Amman in 1994, Malik offered to sneak me into Ramadi. I'd be safe in the family compound there. Who knows, he said, maybe Uday would drop by one evening, and I could judge his character for myself, see what Al 'Awjah produced. I couldn't go to Iraq then, but I promised Malik I would one day.

Now the day is here.

THIRTY-SEVEN

And it came to pass, that, as I made my journey, and was come nigh unto Damascus about noon, suddenly there shone from heaven a great light round about me.

—King James Bible, Acts 22:6

Damascus, Syria: DAYNA

As is true of many cities in the Middle East, Damascus's modernity is a thin veneer covering ancient civilizations. But a visit to old Damascus, which hasn't much changed since Saint Paul walked its streets, is enough to convince you there are parts of the city that don't even bother with the veneer.

Bob and I are at the door of the Chinese restaurant at the Cham Hotel waiting for a table, when Marwan and Malik come up behind us. I've known Marwan for several years now, although he still calls me Riley, as do most of Bob's friends from the Middle East. Marwan gives me a hug, and Malik shakes my hand.

Malik isn't anything like I'd expect an Iraqi tribal chief to be. Clean-shaven, he's in a dark, European-cut suit, a starched white shirt, and a conservative tie. He's young, maybe in his mid-thirties, handsome in a weatherbeaten way, and looks serious and self-assured. He sits with his back straight, hands folded over each other on the table, while Bob and Marwan talk about the coming war. Malik has a presence that's hard to describe. I'm fascinated by him.

Marwan speaks English for my benefit, but I tell him to go ahead and speak Arabic. I pick up words here and there—they're talking about family. Marwan asks about Bob's children and his mother, and Bob asks after Malik's children. As they move on to the Dulaym tribe and the war, they lower their voices. Syria is allied with the United States in this war, but still can't be trusted.

Toward the end of dinner they discuss plans for getting Bob and me across the border into Iraq, and Marwan translates for me.

"You'll be Malik's guests in the compound for as long as you like," Marwan says.

"But how do we get there?" I ask.

"You just drive across the desert and call Malik on a satellite phone. You give him your GPS coordinates, and someone from the tribe will come and get you."

Marwan sounds as if he's giving us directions to take the Metro from Capitol Hill to the mall at Pentagon City. He must see the look on my face and adds, "Don't worry. It's done all the time."

I don't like the sound of "it's done all the time," and Marwan hasn't exactly said what he means by "just drive across the desert." I let it go, though, and ask Marwan the more basic question I need answered. "Really, how safe is the compound?"

"Nobody cares about the place. It's way in the middle of the desert. There's no need to worry at all."

The next day we hire an old Range Rover and driver and head to the border to see for ourselves if it's as easy to cross as Marwan says. We're about sixty miles outside Damascus when the Range Rover starts to whine and lose power. The driver pulls over to the side of the road, gets out to open the hood, and is met by a cloud of smoke. As Bob and I get out to assess the damage, a truck with Iraqi plates stops. A balding, heavyset driver climbs down from his cab with a bottle of water in each hand, and runs over and douses the engine fire.

We're all standing there studying the charred engine block, when our driver turns to the Iraqi and tells him we're Americans. The Iraqi's face turns crimson with fury. He yells at us, "Why are you bombing us?" He stomps back to his truck, climbs in, rolls down the window, and shouts as he drives away, "We are poor Iraqis only trying to make a living."

Bob's trying to call for help on the cell phone, but there's no coverage. I'm the one who sees a lopsided, rose-colored bus coming down the road from the border. Bob steps out in the road to flag it down, and the driver agrees to take us to Damascus. As we climb in, Bob tells our driver we'll send help. The Iraqis on the bus smile at us and make room so we can sit together.

The next morning while Bob goes out to rent a car—this time without a driver—I buy a Syrian map from the gift shop at our hotel and sit down to study it. It shows what look like spur trails crisscrossing the desert, a few even cutting across the Iraqi border. These must be the routes Marwan's talking about. When I show Bob, he says that maybe it's like the border between France and Switzerland, porous, with no one caring who comes and goes. I'm thinking, *Yeah, right*, but agree to take another drive to find out.

After an hour and a half we catch sight of the border post from a rise in the road. Bob pulls over to see if we can spot any tracks in the desert. We're parked only a minute when a Bedouin with a tethered female camel and its baby come out of a *wadi* walking toward us. I ask Bob if we should ask if the Bedouin knows about the spur tracks, but when Bob opens the car door, the wind snatches up our map and sends it across the desert at a full gallop.

THIRTY-EIGHT

No one can confidently say that he will still be living tomorrow.

—Euripides

Amman, Jordan: BOB

There's this to be said for a professional lifetime spent in the company of eccentrics, rogues, and scoundrels: I have someone to call on for just about every occasion, and now, just when we need one, a prince of the Jordanian royal family. There are hundreds of them, but this one knows the back alleys of his country better than any. Inside the family he's nicknamed the Black Prince.

As soon as the Black Prince sees Dayna and me, he shouts from across the Hyatt's lobby, "To lunch, to lunch."

The Black Prince is a big, baggy man, with a big Hemming-way beard. In black fatigues and black combat boots, he looks the character he is. I first met him in the mid-nineties, and we've kept up ever since.

"I'm famished," he says. His accent is English public school.

The three of us file into the Hyatt's cavernous restaurant, where a sprawling buffet waits. Dozens of servers stand at the ready, but we're the only guests.

"It's fixed," the prince says, sitting down with a plate of pasta and a Pepsi. "Can you be ready in two nights?"

The plan is that the prince's driver will meet us in front of our hotel and drive us to al-Ruwayshid, a small town in the Jorda-nian desert. From there the Bedouin will take us north through the desert to a place where they regularly cross the border, about ten miles north of the Baghdad-Amman highway. They'll walk us across the border, and on the other side we'll be met by fellow Bedouin who'll drive us to Rutba, a town back on the Baghdad highway. Malik's people will meet us there.

"Why will they do this for us?" Dayna asks.

"I promised to pay them a hundred sheep," the prince answers.

I agree to the Black Prince's plan, but need a reality check. As soon as we're back at the InterContinental, I call another Jordanian prince, an adviser to the king. That night he sends his car to pick up Dayna and me for dinner.

This prince's house is outside Amman, in the royal compound in the middle of snow-covered hills and pine forests. On walls of the prince's house are paintings you find in art books with the notation that they belong to a private collection—no name offered.

After dinner the prince takes us into the glass-cased library. There are so many books that they're Dewey-decimal categorized. On one wall I notice a framed, glass-encased Kalashnikov. The action is gold-plated. The prince stands behind me, telling me Saddam gave it to him a couple of years ago.

We sit in a corner with soft leather chairs, and the prince offers us tea. Like his cousin the Black Prince, this prince speaks English with a public-school accent. He went to Sandhurst. But his sophistication comes as much from spending his life in such places as London, Paris, Monte Carlo, Biarritz, and Crans-Montana. I'm sure he's read and reread the thousands of books in his library, almost all classics. No wonder the Jordanian royal family is the West's window on the Middle East.

"So you want to see the war," the prince says. "And stay with our friends."

The prince has known Malik for years. Malik's father, the Dulaym chief, was a good friend of King Hassan.

"It's fine. But don't go in with the Bedouin," he says. "If you absolutely must be there before the American army arrives, it should be by helicopter."

The prince gives me the private number for the deputy chief of Jordan's General Intelligence Directorate, saying he'll call him in advance.

As we move to leave, the prince asks if we're sure we want to do this. When I say yes, he offers us a story. A couple of years ago he went to Baghdad to meet Saddam. After the meeting, Saddam's son Uday invited the prince to go hunting. The prince imagined standing on the bank of the Euphrates with a shotgun, waiting for a flock of ducks to fly over. Instead, Uday landed in front of the prince's guesthouse in an Mi-8 helicopter. There was no way to refuse.

As the helicopter approached Lake Thar Thar, Uday handed the prince a Kalashnikov, pointing to the ground where deer were scattering from the thump-thump of the rotors. The prince declined to join in the slaughter, but Uday emptied a magazine on the deer. Afterward the helicopter landed lakeside, where a small boat waited. Out on the lake, Uday pulled a stick of dynamite out of a pouch, lit it with his cigar, and threw it into the water. There was a muted explosion, and half a dozen dead fish rose to the surface. Uday took off his pouch and jumped overboard. When his head came up out of the water, he had a dead fish clutched in his teeth.

"You see why I don't want to put you in the hands of just any Iraqi," the prince says.

The next morning I call the GID deputy. He's polite enough, but says now that the bombing campaign has started, it's too dangerous to fly a helicopter to Ramadi. That puts us back to crossing the border with the Bedouin.

In the InterContinental business center we find a computer

terminal so we can read our e-mail. There's one from Marwan saying he needs to talk to me right away.

I go upstairs for the satellite phone and come back down so I can call from poolside. With no water in the pool, there's no one around to overhear me.

"There's someone who'd like to meet you at the compound," Marwan says.

Marwan starts talking about family obligation, friendship, how much Malik and the Dulaym are respected in Iraq. "It's at times like this that we all need to help each other," he says.

"What are you talking about?" I say, interrupting him. "Who is it you want me to meet?"

"It's someone important."

It's obvious he's not going to tell me on the phone who it is. I can only assume it's some Iraqi political figure.

"He understands I'd be meeting him for ABC News and not my former organization?" I ask.

Marwan says he does. But even as Marwan says it, I wonder if he still doesn't suffer from the once-in, always-in syndrome you come across in the Middle East: the belief that CIA operatives never leave the CIA, no matter what they say.

Back inside the lobby, a frenzy of journalists are getting ready to go into Iraq the moment Iraqi forces abandon their posts on the border. Everyone's got one eye glued to cable news as they talk on their cell phones.

Dayna and I find a quiet corner in the hotel's Mexican restaurant. Journalists are three deep at the bar, drinking, telling stories about other wars they've covered, the close calls they've had, how they've smelled enough cordite to last them a lifetime. I suspect it's not all bravado. Right now there are dozens of them in Baghdad, covering its impending fall. More are embedded with coalition forces.

That night, while waiting for the Black Prince's driver to show up, Dayna and I help the ABC News team pack up for Baghdad—they'll convoy in as soon as Baghdad falls. Looking at the mountain of camera cases, antennas, water, and food, you might get the impression that ABC itself is about to liberate the city. There's not a lot we can do, and Dayna and I go to our room to finish our own packing. The driver will call us from the lobby.

By midnight there's still no sign of the driver, and I can't get the Black Prince on the phone. The next morning we stick close to the hotel, constantly checking the front desk for messages. There's nothing, and the Black Prince's phone is still off.

On April 11, still no sign of the driver, we go down to the hotel's business center to read our e-mail. It's the usual junk, but there's one from Marwan, the subject one word, "Malik." The text isn't much longer. I read it twice before I comprehend what it says. I call Dayna over. She stands behind me and grabs my shoulder when she gets to where it reads, "Malik and family are no more. They were killed this morning in an air strike." Dayna slumps to the floor, her head in her hands.

I call Marwan. He's barely able to talk, but finally says Malik's house was hit early this morning with six American cruise missiles, killing sixteen family members. Malik, who was holding his two-year-old daughter, died instantly.

THIRTY-NINE

> The recollections of a young man named Fahal Abdul Hamid, a nephew of the dead sheik, made the events of a terrible night all too real: "It was 2:00 a.m. and the house was crowded—more than fifty people . . . most of the men were in another building watching the war on satellite TV. There was a blast of light and a fog of dust; it was hard to breathe. I went towards the big house but not much of it was left. More than half of the victims were kids under the age of nine. Malik's six-month-old daughter was never found; his mother, his wife, his sister, and four of his nieces died. I found my younger brother—dead.
>
> "We thought we'd be safe because . . . we believed the Americans had to know where Malik was. We have houses in Jordan, Syria, and Egypt. We could have gone anywhere, but we chose to stay because the sheik should be among his people when times are hard."
>
> —*Sydney* (Australia) *Morning Herald*, June 12, 2004,
> "Blown Away: How America Bombs Its Friends"

Baghdad, Iraq: **BOB**

On April 13, after the Amman-Baghdad road is taken by American forces, we make it into Iraq—in the ABC convoy.

On the twelve-hour drive in, I make friends with our Iraqi driver, an old habit that pays off when we get to Baghdad's Sheraton and find there's no running water. The driver arranges to have a dozen plastic containers of water brought up to our room on the seventeenth floor. A makeshift shower and a toilet that flushes make a world of difference.

We're exhausted, but we can't sleep. Dayna and I stand at the window and look at the dark city lit only by the orange glow of burning buildings. F-16s pass overhead on their way north on bombing raids. We have a sense we're watching history being made, but don't understand how.

Dayna calls her father on the satellite phone to tell him we made it here safely.

"We're fine, Dad," she says. "We're in a big hotel. There's lots of U.S. troops around us."

She listens for a while and tells him again not to worry. "The fighting is far away. We'll be careful." She hangs up.

"You didn't tell him about the house," I say.

"It would have been too much for him."

The next morning our driver takes us to Malik's compound near Ramadi, or Kilo-18 as it's called. I haven't called ahead, and I have no idea how we'll be received.

For thirteen years now, I've imagined Malik living in a desert encampment, with tethered camels, dun tents, and children chasing goats. But the compound we drive into is a sprawling truck depot, and heavy equipment is everywhere—front loaders, dump trucks, cranes. There are a dozen pits where trucks pull over to be repaired. No one is at the entry gate, and the driver keeps going until we come to a one-story cinderblock house. The sun is up in the middle of the sky, and the temperature is over a hundred degrees, a haze sitting over the Euphrates.

A man comes out of the house to see what we want. The driver asks where the main house is. The man looks in the car at Dayna and me, and asks who we want to see. I tell him we're friends of the family. He points at a cluster of trees. We can't see anything there, but drive across a rough open space until we come to the trees and behind them a large mound of rubble, about three feet high and the size of a tennis court. Although not a wall remains, you can tell it was a house. The rubble's charred, pieces still smoking. There's a pungent, burnt smell. We get out of the car.

"We've recovered the bodies," someone says in Arabic behind us.

It's Hamid, Malik's uncle who came to Rome with Malik the first time I met him. I hug Hamid. *"Allah yarhamuh,"* I say. May God protect them. He's crying. He shakes Dayna's hand, and she starts to cry too.

We walk in silence to a guesthouse that sits next to the Euphrates. The place is spare—no pictures, cheap terrazzo floors, and roughhewn wood furniture. Hamid shows us onto a narrow terrace, which sits over the water. A young boy brings a tray of cookies and sugared tea. Hamid tells us he was in another house when the missiles hit. Malik and his wife and children were gathered for the evening, as was their custom. They were all killed. Hamid helped pull out the bodies.

I have no idea what to say. I ask if there's anything we can do. Hamid thanks us and says, "May God preserve you."

After tea, Hamid drives us to Ramadi, where condolences by tribal leaders are being offered. We sit for three hours in a *diwan*, a large room with hard wooden benches pushed against the wall. A seemingly endless line of tribal elders files through, Hamid presiding, sitting in an overstuffed chair. We are the only foreigners, but no one seems to notice us.

The press would report that Barzan al-Tikriti, Saddam's half brother, was the target of the strike that hit Malik's house. Marwan would admit that it was Barzan who wanted to meet me. He said Barzan was desperate and thought that somehow an ex-CIA operative could save him from capture and execution. Barzan would have been killed along with Malik, but earlier that evening he'd left for Habbaniyah, a nearby air force base. Many more years later, Marwan would tell me that Saddam himself was in a guest-house on the compound. After the rockets hit, Saddam stood out-side and watched as they pulled burning bodies from the rubble. Marwan said that the sight of it had a deep effect on Saddam, and he wrote about it in his diary.

FORTY

I've wandered much further today than I should and I can't seem to find my way back to the wood.

—Kenny Loggins, "The House at Pooh Corner"

Al 'Awjah, Iraq: **BOB**

Before we leave Iraq, I close my last Iraqi chapter, a visit to Al 'Awjah, the small village on the Tigris where Saddam Hussein was born—the lion's lair. It was here in March 1995 that my Iraqi generals prepared to corner him and either arrest or kill him.

I'm the first one to see the small Al 'Awjah sign along the Samarra-Tikrit road. I tell the driver to turn. He looks over at me and says he thought we were going to Tikrit. He's shaking. As it is with every other Iraqi, Al 'Awjah is the seat of his worst nightmares.

Fifty yards down the narrow, paved road, before we get to the first houses, the driver slows down, hoping I've seen enough and don't mind if he turns around and goes back the way we came. *"Yallah,"* I say. Let's go.

He inches the Toyota along the narrow road, his head turning from side to side. Saddam's secret police don't exist anymore, but the dread of them does.

Just as we reach the first houses on Al 'Awjah's edge, we spot a knot of men standing at the side of the road. A couple hold two-by-fours; one has a shotgun. The driver stops when he comes up alongside of them. One in a tribal robe steps to the window and says something to the driver I can't hear. I lean across him and ask where the American troops are. He ignores me.

"Drive through them," I tell the driver, but before we can move, another man steps in front of the Toyota, swinging his two-by-four. The man at the driver's door shouts, "What do you want here?" He tries to open the car door, but it's locked. The driver looks at me, the blood drained from his face.

I lean across the driver again and, through the half-open window, tell the man in Arabic, "We're French. This is not our war." He's surprised to hear his own language. He pauses for a moment and then turns to the others. "It's OK. Let them pass."

Another half mile down the road, we come to a walled compound with a large house on top of a hill. I recognize it from satellite photography I'd seen when I was still in the CIA. It was here that the generals intended to corner Saddam, their tanks crashing through the gates. By the front gate you can see where there'd recently been some sort of tracked armored vehicle, probably a tank. But it's gone now, and the gate into the grounds is wide open.

We drive through it and up to the front of the house. The double door's opened a crack. None of us moves, though, half expecting someone to come out to see what we want. Finally we all get out, but still hesitate to go in. The driver looks at us nervously; I'm sure he's hoping we'll decide not to.

You can see why Saddam picked this site to build his palace, the way it sits on a bluff over the Tigris with a boundless view of the river and the palm plantations beyond. There's a steady breeze that makes the weather almost tolerable. Saddam must have climbed up this hill as a child, dreaming about one day building a house here.

We finally get up the nerve and let ourselves in. There's plaster, broken masonry, and brick everywhere. In the ceiling there's an enormous hole where a missile came through. Pigeons sit around the inside of the Palladian rotunda watching us. We walk through the darkened rooms silently, our hands behind our backs, not touching anything, as if it were a museum.

The house looks as if it hasn't been occupied in a while. Closets and drawers are empty—or maybe just looted. There's a layer of dust on everything. I imagine Saddam coming here only for a night or two, his entourage hurriedly packing up his things after he left.

In the library I pull a couple of books off the shelves, expecting to find rare ones, maybe even old manuscripts. But they're all cheap editions, some with broken spines. There are a lot of paperbacks. I open one book and find the traced hand of a small child in pencil on the flyleaf. Underneath is written "Qusay," no doubt Saddam's eldest son. Was it Saddam who traced Qusay's hand in a moment of tenderness?

We walk around Saddam's indoor pool. The water is clean, but it could be a community pool anywhere. In a room off to the side stands a treadmill and a Stairmaster. Stiff, white ordinary towels are stacked on a bench. I'm surprised there's no speaker system or television on the wall.

We walk around back to the servants' quarters and find a mammoth, rolled-up rug on the lawn. It looks as if someone dragged it out of the house to steal it, but then changed his mind. I bend over to take a closer look. It's synthetic, inexpensive, made in Belgium—cheap like everything else in the house. Saddam either had vulgar tastes or didn't care how he lived.

I watch Dayna as she picks through things on the burnt lawn in the back, stopping at a rusted swing set, sun-faded plastic toys scattered around it. She stops to listen to the F-16s passing overhead.

I used to joke with Dayna that I'd take her to the ends of the earth, but always tacking on, "What if there's only a red plush sofa there?" I was wrong about the details, but I think I had the sense of it.

FORTY-ONE

Kind faces will meet me, and welcome me in,
    and how they will greet me, my own friends and kin.
This night will be warmer, as old songs are sung.
    It's where my heart lies, in old Silverton.

—"These Are My Mountains" by Allan Copeland, lyrics adapted by
Dolores LaChapelle

Silverton, Colorado: **DAYNA**

It's not long after Bob and I come back from Iraq that we marry, and then drive out west to explore the Rocky Mountains. On our drive back to Washington, we stop in Silverton, Colorado, an old mining town deep in the San Juan Mountains.

On our last morning I happen to walk by a house for sale. Actually it's more of a spruced-up cabin. But Bob loves it, and, on a whim, we buy it—our little getaway from Washington's awful summer heat. We spend the next summer there fixing up the place and hiking. We promise each other we'll go back to Washington at the end of September. But when the aspens lose their leaves and the tourists decamp, the solitude takes hold of us, and we decide to stay on.

In the off-season, there are fewer than four hundred full-time residents in Silverton, including a stray wolf the locals call Wolfie. No one can tell us where Wolfie came from; he was just there one day and never went away. In the summer no one sees him because he retreats up into the mountains. He's waiting for the tourists to leave so he can go back to sunning himself in the middle of Silverton's streets.

There are no traffic lights, and only one paved road through town, Greene Street. Silverton has no pharmacy, no bakery, no doctor or dentist or vet or even mail delivery. You have to haul your trash to the dump. The ambulance and fire department are all volunteer.

Silverton is the capital of San Juan County, the highest administrative unit in North America. It sits at the lowest point in the county, and it's still at a nose-bleeding 9,318 feet. The county holds the American record for most snow in twenty-four hours: seven feet. The only way into the county is across a couple of 11,000-foot passes and a highway described as the most dangerous in America, or up the narrow-gauge Durango & Silverton Railroad, which only operates May through October. The locals like to impress tourists by telling them they have to drive downhill to ski.

Silverton makes up for remoteness with small-town friendliness. It's the kind of place where if you need something from the hardware store and it's not open, you call the owner, go over to his house, and get the keys. We discovered this the first week we moved here. Bob was standing in front of the house, trying to figure out how to haul away a pile of dead brush, when a local we know walked by and told Bob to borrow George's truck. The man pointed at an old navy blue Ford F-150 parked down the street. "The keys are in it," he said, adding that George wouldn't mind. Not long after, a tire went flat on our pickup and we left it for the next morning to fix. We woke up to find that someone had already changed it for us.

The phone rings one Thursday morning. It's rained for the last two days, but it's a washed, cloudless blue sky today. I listen as Bob talks, his voice getting louder.

"No, you can't land here." Bob looks over at me, frowning.

"Yes, I do believe you that it's on the charts, but . . ."

He stops to listen.

"No, they never built it," Bob says. "I'm telling you, it's not there. Tell your pilot that what he's looking at is a landing strip plotted out in 1947. They just never made new maps."

"Who was that?" I ask when he hangs up.

"Some guy named Patrick calling from his jet."

Patrick tracked down Bob through a journalist at *Newsweek*. There's something he wants to discuss with Bob that he can't put in writing or talk about over the phone.

All right, I knew Bob hadn't fallen off the edge of the earth in moving to Silverton, but a cold call from a stranger in a private jet trying to land on an imaginary airstrip is more than odd. And while we stopped being spies a long time ago, old habits die hard. I tell Bob he has to meet this guy in a public place, somewhere I can watch. I suggest Handlebars, a bar owned by a friend. It's a charmingly rustic place decorated with game trophies and other backcounty bricabrac, and it's crowded all day. A couple of times I volunteered there, and it will be a good place for me to go unnoticed, as if I were working there. If there's trouble, I'll call Mike McQueen, the undersheriff.

McQueen is not someone you want to mess with. A few months ago a guy in a ski mask fled a traffic stop in Ouray, a mining town across Red Mountain Pass. McQueen chased the man from the top of the pass, down the most dangerous highway in America, across two more 11,000-foot passes. The state patrol was waiting on the south side of the pass, and, knowing he was trapped, the driver headed off on a dirt road. McQueen followed him to the road's end. He'd alerted the police tactical squad in Durango, but now decided he could take care of this himself. As McQueen approached the car, he spotted the man putting on a flak jacket and taking a rifle out from behind the seat. When the man aimed his rifle at him, Mike drew his .45 and shot him in the forehead, killing him instantly. He was a hundred feet away. The Colorado

Bureau of Investigation said they'd never seen precision shooting like that.

I'm behind the bar when Bob comes through the door first, followed by a bear of a man dressed in a turtleneck and Levi's. Just behind him is a much smaller man with olive skin, a thick beard, and an old-fashioned hunter's cap with the flaps down but untied. He's definitely Middle Eastern.

Handlebars isn't too busy, and between making drinks and talking to Ken, the owner, I keep an eye on Bob's table. Whatever they're talking about has Bob engrossed. As I probably should have expected, the duo's odd arrival aside, nothing out of the ordinary happens.

When I get home, Bob shows me Patrick's business card. He's Patrick Byrne, CEO of Overstock.com. It's the company that has commercials with the catchy line, "It's all about the O." The man in the hunting cap is the son of a famous Lebanese politician.

"What did they want?" I ask.

"They told me the financial markets are going to collapse. Something to do with naked short trading, and corrupt Wall Street bankers ripping off widows and orphans. I understood about a tenth of it."

"You don't know anything about finance."

"I told them that. But they had this idea that somehow an ex-CIA operative could get to the bottom of it. Too many Hollywood movies, I guess. They wanted me to go home, pack, drive to Durango with them, and jump on their jet."

"You shoulda gone."

FORTY-TWO

Call it a clan, call it a network, call it a tribe, call it a family:
Whatever you call it, whoever you are, you need one.

—Jane Howard, *Families*

Silverton, Colorado: **BOB**

The last week in October there's already a good dusting of snow
on the peaks around Silverton. The aspens are bare, and the
shop owners are nailing up plywood over their windows against
snowdrifts soon to come. The only cars on Greene Street belong
to the last hunters of the season.

Our two Labs watch as I clean out the fireplace. I know what
they want: a hike in the mountains. They don't care what the season is. Cabin fever is cabin fever. Dayna is restlessly surfing the
Internet.

"What do you want to do today?" I ask.

Instead of answering, she turns her laptop so I can see the
screen. A woman in Grand Junction has a litter of Lab puppies up
for adoption.

The next day on the way to Grand Junction, we tell each other
we're just going to take a look. Do we really need three big dogs?
Can we fit three Labs in our station wagon? Another dog is a big
decision, and we should take time to think about it. But I've seen
the list Dayna has folded in her pocket: a puppy bed, a dish, tiny
rawhide bones—the whole starter kit.

Dayna is first out of the pickup and walks over to a lady standing behind a wire mesh fence. I stand back and watch, pretty certain how this is going to end. As soon as Dayna lets herself into

the enclosure, a little yellow puppy breaks from the litter and runs up to her. She picks it up in both arms and turns to me with a very happy smile. I know we're not leaving without it. Dogs adopt Dayna, not the other way around.

As soon as we get back home, Dayna makes a bed for the puppy next to ours, on her side. That night she gets up at least five times, clutching the tiny Lab tightly as she descends the steep stairs from our loft. She stands out in the cold to let it pee. In the morning, she makes a bed out of old blankets for the puppy so it can sit at her feet while she's on the computer.

In December we drive to Corona del Mar to spend Christmas with Dayna's parents, taking our three dogs with us.

On Christmas Eve, Dayna's mother asks her husband to make a fire. He's now eighty-two. He gets up without saying a word and disappears into the garage that connects with the house. Five minutes later he's back, unsteadily crossing the living room with a lighted blowtorch in one hand.

At the end of dinner, right after dessert, Dayna's father stands up and announces matter-of-factly that he's going to go see "his other daughter." I see Dayna's head whip around like a barn owl. He finds his jacket and walks out the door.

Dayna and I look at each other. *Other daughter?* There's only Dayna and her brother. But I know who he's talking about: his accountant, a woman Dayna's age. The summer before, Dayna's father and the accountant raced to Hawaii on a sailboat they'd bought together. But calling her his daughter? The woman has a father of her own. All along, Dayna's mother keeps loading the dishwasher, as if it were the most normal thing in the world. Dayna has to hold back her tears.

◆

Two days after we're back in Silverton, we agree to meet a couple in Ouray for dinner. The sky is dry when we leave the house, but as we wind our way up Red Mountain pass it starts to snow. And by the time we get to the top of the pass, it's a whiteout. I can't see the side of the road, and stop and turn off the engine. No other cars are moving, either, so it's okay. We watch the snow in silence for a while.

"You know running a dog kennel isn't going to do it for you," I tell her. "Or for us." Neither of us confuses dogs with people.

We go back to looking straight ahead at the snow. We're not going to make it to Ouray for dinner. I try my cell phone to call the couple we're supposed to have dinner with. But there's no signal.

I finally ask the question that's been on my mind for a long time. "Hey, what do you think about adopting?"

"Don't joke about this."

"I'm not."

"This is serious stuff."

Dayna's surprised, but in a way we've been edging toward this moment ever since we first moved in together. While we talked around the subject of having a child for a long time, we never could come to a decision, mainly because our lives kept slipping moorage: Beirut, Geneva, New York, Washington, now Colorado. It's been on my mind because my family has been drifting away.

My three children now all live abroad. My two daughters are in school, one in Paris and the other in Cairo. Having grown up with their mother, they spend their vacations with her. Robert is living in the French house, and I rarely see him. Phone calls and e-mails are infrequent. It's all even harder to take because it's only now that I understand how thin is the thread our relationship hangs from. It's impossible to know what will happen to us, being apart for so long.

I've been estranged from my mother since 1997, when I stupidly wandered into the Democratic Party's campaign-finance scandal.

It happened when one of my informants told me he was giving money to the Democratic Party in return for White House favors. I reported everything to my bosses, sending memo after memo. No one said anything, but when the scandal broke in the press, I somehow was dragged into it. When I had to hire a lawyer to represent me for a grand jury hearing, I told my mother. I'd thought she'd be merely curious, but she assumed the worst. "You wouldn't be so nervous if you hadn't done something wrong," she wrote. When I asked to come to Los Angeles to explain that I'd only done my duty, she said no. "I don't feel like cleaning my house." There were a few more calls, but they all ended acrimoniously.

Silverton has been a wonderful way station and refuge, the Alp I dreamed about living on with Dayna. But we both realize that we can't stay here forever, on our own like this, only thinking about taking care of ourselves. If nothing else, it's too remote. So last spring we found a two-bedroom Craftsman house in Berkeley, California, on a blocked-off street, a place where you don't worry about kids and cars. A school sits catty-corner, a grocery store four blocks away. BART is another block away, and from there it's a twenty-minute hop into San Francisco—suburbia and city lights in the same package. Dayna's the one who picked out the neighborhood, and I have this inkling it's with a child in mind. But, biologically, the clock has already raced past where it needs to be.

The snow is thinning out now, and I start the pickup.

"Are you sure you really want another child?" Dayna asks.

"I'm sure."

FORTY-THREE

Edhi established his first welfare centre and then the Bilqis Edhi Trust with a mere Rs. 5,000. What started as a one-man show operating from a single room in Karachi is now the Edhi Foundation, the largest welfare organization in Pakistan. The foundation has over 300 centers across the country, in big cities, small towns and remote rural areas, providing medical aid, family planning and emergency assistance. They own air ambulances, providing quick access to far-flung areas. In Karachi alone, the Edhi Foundation runs eight hospitals providing free medical care, eye hospitals, diabetic centers, surgical units, a four-bed cancer hospital and mobile dispensaries. In addition to these the Foundation also manages two blood banks in Karachi.

Edhi is to Karachi what Mother Teresa was to the poor of Calcutta. Edhi and [his] wife Bilquees have spent a lifetime working for people, and their welfare work to date remains unparalleled in Pakistan. They are both very private people who shun publicity. They have had little formal education, and are totally committed to the cause of helping the poor and needy.

—www.edhifoundation.com

Berkeley, California: **DAYNA**

ob and I decide early on that we want to do an international adoption, preferably from a country we will return to as the child grows up. We also want to do the adoption ourselves—no international adoption agency, no middlemen or facilitators, no agencies that contract out to orphanages. It's not the cost involved—we're prepared to make a large donation. Rather, we're determined to be very hands-on about this. Unlike a lot of couples who start down this same road, we have unusual resources in far-flung places. Surely, we think, two operatives with nearly thirty years of experience between them can figure out how to do this on their own.

Chechnya is Bob's idea—a war-torn country without organized international adoptions but with several large refugee camps. What could be a better fit? He gets on the phone to a KGB officer in the Caucasus, an old friend. I can hear only Bob's end of the conversation.

"An OR-PH-AN," he says, repeating himself for the third time. Bob listens and then gives me the thumbs-up to let me know the guy's going to help. But when he gets off the phone, he's laughing, a bit nervously.

"You won't believe this one," Bob says. "He told me that if we don't find a Chechen orphan, he'll make one for us."

It's a dumb joke, of course, but soon enough we find out Chechen adoptions are not doable. Chechens are a close-knit Muslim society where orphans are taken in and cared for by extended families. Bob hits the same wall with his other contacts. The countries he knows best are Muslim, and adoptions are rare. I find it ironic that Bob's friends can put their hands on a stolen Russian fighter, but can't find us an abandoned child to take in.

I'm the one who decides to look into adopting from Pakistan. It's one of my favorite places, especially Peshawar, the dusty frontier outpost at the bottom of the Khyber Pass. I'd driven there the first time on the old Grand Trunk Road, barely surviving a terrifying game of chicken with big, colorful buses that pulled into the oncoming lane without looking. I was entranced by Peshawar's old city, the houses and narrow streets, and the women in their colorful, head-to-toe abayas, with intricate cutouts to cover their eyes. It was all wildly exotic, a place I'd go back to in a second, given the chance.

Scouring Pakistani law to see whether adoption is possible, I come across a Muslim welfare organization called the Edhi Foundation. It's the vision of a husband-and-wife team, Abdul Sattar

Edhi and Bilqis Edhi, who began by rescuing baby girls left in the street, taking care of them, and offering them up for adoption. Their foundation eventually turned into the largest relief organization in Pakistan, running a morgue, air ambulances, a cancer hospital, blood banks, aid for refugees, prisoner welfare services, and even an animal shelter. It also provides burials for unclaimed bodies.

Bob, I know, is going to be impressed by the fact that the Edhi Foundation took care of the remains of Danny Pearl, the *Wall Street Journal* reporter who was beheaded in Karachi in February 2002. Bob had spoken to Danny just days before the reporter left for Karachi. Maybe, I think, there's some kind of karma going on here—a life for a death, a new beginning for a brutal murder. Weirder things have happened.

The more I read about Edhi, the more I see what it's managed to accomplish in a country not known for its public service, the more fascinated I am. It won't accept government funds, relying instead completely on donations. It also won't accept donations from adoptive parents, to make absolutely certain that it won't be dragged down into the muck of the international adoption business. Instead, it operates a "crèche" system in which parents who can't afford to keep their babies leave them, Mrs. Edhi personally taking charge of placing them. Most end up with families outside of Pakistan, where they stand a better chance in life.

In so many ways, this is just what Bob and I have been looking for. But I soon learn from my research that there's a serious obstacle: in Pakistan a foundling is automatically considered a Muslim. And since Christians cannot adopt a Muslim child, the chances Edhi can help us are close to zero. We send in an application anyway, but it's beginning to look as if the most likely way for us to adopt in Pakistan is to locate a child under the care of a Christian church.

Pakistan's population is 2 percent Christian, nearly 3 million people. They live mostly in slums in the larger urban areas, and are frequently persecuted by Islamic fundamentalists. In the upside-down way I've come to think about these things, that's an attraction: yes, I'd be taking our baby away from its community, but life in the United States would offer a child a way out of a grim future.

Over the course of a week, we call everyone we know in Pakistan and make a long list of likely places that would know about orphans, from aid organizations to churches. I find a nun in Lahore who cares for abandoned Christian babies. I call every other day. She soon recognizes my voice, and after "hello," she says, "No babies, no babies today." After a few weeks of this, I start to realize how difficult it is not to go through an agency. And then, as so often happens with adoptions, the weeks turn into months, and the months add up to more than a year.

When we settle into our new house in Berkeley—we've already picked out a room for our child-to-be—I'm still nowhere with the adoption. Everyone promises to write back. Some do, most don't. I've started looking at other countries when one morning I open an e-mail from one of my new correspondents, a woman whose husband works for the United Nations. Attached is a picture of a little baby girl on a *charpoy*, a reed bed that sits on four short wooden legs. I can't take my eyes off her. She's adorable, a little pixie with dark eyes and curly black hair. She's wearing ragged rose-and-cream pajamas. She stares at the camera as if she knows her picture's being taken.

"You better come look at this," I say to Bob.

He doesn't have to say a word. One look and we both just know.

❖

Baby X is ten months old, her parents Christian. Her mother died two months after she was born from complications of childbirth. Her father, who already has seven children and earns only thirty dollars a month, had to abandon her at a Catholic parish in Faisalabad. I write back saying that if it's legally possible, we'd love to adopt her.

By now I've learned that while Pakistan doesn't recognize adoption, it does permit guardianship, which would allow us to take Baby X out of Pakistan. Formal adoption would then take place in the United States. We hire a lawyer, Munir, who has an office in Pakistan's capital, Islamabad. He agrees to prepare the documents for the court and for a U.S. visa: the mother's death certificate, the child's birth certificate, a passport, and an affidavit from the father abandoning all rights to her. The parish is now caring for Baby X along with several older orphaned boys, but Munir thinks a nanny—an *ayah*, as they're known in Pakistan—would be better for her.

One morning Munir calls to ask what name we intend to give her. He needs it because he is preparing the guardianship papers.

Why haven't we thought about this?

That night Bob and I bat names back and forth. She was baptized as Miriam, but we both think she needs something special. Or maybe we just need it. The next morning we call Munir back with a name: Ryli—inspired by my Sarajevo alias.

As it turns out, though, the name doesn't translate into Urdu, and on her Pakistani passport she is now Reela.

FORTY-FOUR

As the standoff at the Lal Masjid, or Red Mosque, between government forces and the radical Taliban-supporting followers of Maulana Abdul Aziz and Ghazi Abdul Rasheed continues, one of the leaders of the mosque has been captured while attempting to escape, according to the BBC. Maulana Abdul Aziz was captured wearing a woman's burka. His arrest was confirmed by the Chief Commissioner of Islamabad. "He was the last in a group of seven women all wearing the same clothes. He was wearing a burqa that also covered his eyes," a security official told AFP.

—www.longwarjurnal.org/archives/2007/07/abdul-aziz-red-mosqu-print.php

Islamabad, Pakistan: BOB

One habit I haven't lost since leaving the CIA is combining pleasure with work. In March, I'm on the East Coast, finishing up a documentary on car bombs for British TV, while Dayna is in Corona del Mar staying with her mother. Her father is on another sailing trip with his "other daughter." It's the perfect time, then, for me to go to Pakistan to get a feel for how the adoption is going to work.

I haven't been in Pakistan in almost thirty years, but it doesn't seem that a lot has changed—at least inside Islamabad's airport. The Pakistani customs officials, in their same starched uniforms, haven't lost their British efficiency and politeness. The sweepers, as they have always done, mop up the floor with rags on the ends of brooms and buckets of soapy water.

As always, the order comes to a quick end when I exit the terminal. A sea of people swarm the metal barriers just outside: children racing around, extended families, old people who should be home, hawkers selling cigarettes and flowers, shoeshine boys. Taxi drivers shove people out of the way, trying to get to me first. They call out prices, and reach to grab my sleeve.

A short man in a starched pale yellow shirt and ironed slacks is in the middle of them, timidly waving at me. "Mr. Bob?" he says. He introduces himself. It's Rafiq, the man who's been working with our lawyer, Munir, on the guardianship. Dayna has been exchanging e-mails with him for the last three months.

"Come see your daughter," he says, taking my suitcase.

I follow his pale yellow shirt as he runs interference through the mob. In the parking lot just at the side of the terminal, there's a woman in a sari, her pomaded black hair pulled back like a dancer's. She smiles at me, and I notice she's holding something in her arms, a bundle a little bigger than a football. She turns it around, and I see a little face with two little brown eyes staring back at me, as if deciding whether she can trust me or not.

Not until this moment do I truly start to understand the new turn my life is about to take. My days of trying to defy gravity are definitely over and done with. Just as Dayna knew she wasn't leaving Grand Junction without that puppy last fall, I know I'm not leaving Islamabad without this little girl.

I ask the ayah how she's doing. She smiles again and only says, "Reela," making me realize she only speaks Urdu. She pulls the blanket back so I can see Reela better.

In the back of the car, the ayah offers to let me hold Reela, but I say no. I don't want to risk scaring her, making her cry. I like it that she's so quiet, especially since it must be way past her bedtime. I put my index finger in her tiny hand, and she tightens her fingers around it.

No one says anything as we drive through Islamabad, a city on the brink. There are army and police checkpoints everywhere. Concrete barriers and army checkpoints ring the parliament building. Islamabad's five-star hotel, the Serena, with its security fences and sodium lights, looks more like a penitentiary than a hotel.

That night I sit out on the terrace of the bungalow I've rented two rooms in, listening to the ayah sing the little girl to sleep. The city is still alive with late shoppers and traffic. I can see car lights ascending the road to the top of Daman-e-Koh, the mountain behind Islamabad where open-air restaurants let the locals escape the heat of the plain.

The ayah stops singing, and I hear the television go on, a program in Urdu. I'm still not tired, and go back into my bedroom to get a book. I come back out and read in the cooling night, moths mobbing the terrace light.

At about midnight the ayah turns off the television, and it's very quiet until there's gunfire in the distance. We're far away from Peshawar and the tribal areas where there's fighting between the army and the Islamic militants, so I figure it's just a Pakistani soldier clearing his weapon.

The next morning I start a routine I soon settle into, one I'll keep up until Dayna arrives in ten days. As soon as Reela is fed and bathed, the ayah brings her to my room to play on the floor. She can't sit up or even crawl forward, but she gets her exercise backing around the room. The ayah stays for a while to be sure things are going well, and then leaves us alone. Reela seems pretty independent and doesn't mind exploring on her own. In the other room I can hear the ayah talking to her sister, reassured the two are ready to come to my aid at a moment's notice. After lunch I leave Reela with the ayah and walk to Munir's house.

Munir is a gentleman: polite, British-educated, attentive, and sensible. He's well read too. He lives modestly to save money to send his kids abroad to college. When I come over, he offers me fresh-squeezed orange juice, which he makes himself. It's followed by green tea.

Every day Munir shows me a new document he's prepared—an affidavit from the father; a petition to the court for guardianship; an advertisement to put in the newspaper, which is required by the court. Munir offers to have the advertisement translated from the Urdu for me. But I tell him it's OK; our fate is in his hands. When I'm ready to leave, I always ask how he thinks it's going to go.

"It will be fine. The judge will see that you are good, honorable parents."

One night Munir and his wife and their children take me up to Damam-e Koh for dinner. It's just starting to cool down, but it's still in the eighties. The terrace is full, but Munir has made a reservation for us.

Munir finally lets down his reserve when I tell him I'm thinking about taking Dayna, Reela, and the ayah up into the Hindu Kush, while we wait for a court date.

"Aha!" Munir says. "That is where the gods are!"

Munir tells me that when he was a young man, he walked Pakistan's mountains almost every summer. The stone villages hanging on cliffs in those mountains haven't changed since Alexander the Great, and neither have the odd languages they speak there. As he talks, I realize that Munir is a genuine traveler. He's been to the United States many times, and understands Americans.

On the drive back to Islamabad, I ask Munir's wife about Pakistan's Christians. If Pakistan were to slide off the edge, succumb to Islamic militants, what are their chances?

Munir answers for her. "It's a difficult question. You need to understand *their* mentality. For a while I represented the leader of the Red Mosque, Maulana Abdul Aziz."

I can't ignore this. The fight that occurred at the Red Mosque in July 2007 was a dark omen for Pakistan's drift into Islamic militancy. Not only had Abdul Aziz been close to Osama bin Ladin, he made no secret of his desire to turn Pakistan into an Islamic republic governed by a Taliban-like regime. When the mosque armed itself, it left the government no choice. On July 3, Pakistani paramilitaries assaulted the Red Mosque, finally taking it on July 11, killing scores of people, including women and children. Abdul Aziz was arrested trying to escape dressed as a woman. He's now in government custody, but his wife is free. Munir says he'll arrange for me to meet her.

A taxi drops me off on a quiet, tree-lined street in front of a two-story house. There are no guards or any other sign that this is an Islamic center advocating the government's overthrow. The man who answers the door shows me into a room with cheap wall-to-wall carpeting. The only light comes from two overhead phosphorescent tubes. I take off my shoes and sit on the carpet against a wall.

A half hour later a beefy man in a lime shirt, Dacron pants, and a cardboard belt comes to collect me, leading me to another room with more cheap carpet, more tube lighting, and more bare walls. Almost as soon as we sit down on the floor, Maulana Abdul Aziz's wife enters, and I jump back up again. She's dressed in a black robe, her face behind a thick black veil that betrays none of her features. She has black silk gloves on, so not the smallest part of her skin shows. I can't say why, but I have a sense that this petite vision in black is a fierce woman.

She sits down, but rather than face me, she turns to the wall. It's an act of Islamic propriety I've never seen in all the years I've been in the Middle East. A young boy comes in with a bag of cookies, and I take one. It's crusty, but I eat it anyhow. Abdul Aziz's wife takes one, but doesn't eat it. The boy comes back with a glass of berry juice for me.

After I thank Mrs. Abdul Aziz for receiving me, I ask her about the future of the Taliban. The man with the cardboard belt translates between English and Urdu.

"We are losing because there's no unity," she says. "Divided people in history are doomed to lose, subjecting themselves to oppression."

She says it curtly, almost like a catechism. It reminds me of discussing politics with Soviet diplomats. They always had a canned answer for any argument.

For the next few minutes she tells me a story about the Prophet Muhammad and a doctor. The gist is difficult to follow because she peppers her Urdu with Arabic quotations from the Quran and the sayings of the Prophet. Like many nonnative, devout Muslims, she employs an Arabic that is learned from reading and prayer rather than from speaking.

When she returns to her diatribe, I'm surprised when I catch the word "Tibet," and ask if she can repeat what she's just said. The translator doesn't bother and tells me she wants to know why in the West we're outraged about Chinese oppression against Tibetans but not against Muslims.

Mrs. Abdul Aziz doesn't wait for my answer, launching into an attack on the United States and American foreign policy. "It was your country who provided the white phosphorous that burned alive the students at the Red Mosque," she says, spitting out her words. "We saw it with our own eyes. And your country also gives F-16s to bomb Muslims in the tribal areas."

I start to say something, but she cuts me off, refusing to be questioned or contradicted. Ten minutes later she pauses long enough for me to ask what she thinks will happen if Obama is elected president.

"He will invade Mecca."

◆

The next morning as usual I go to see Munir in his office. He tells me that just this morning he's put a notice in the newspaper, advertising our petition for guardianship. A week from now the judge will hear our case.

I go back to my original question, asking him his gut feeling on how the guardianship hearing will go. My meeting with Maulana Abdul Aziz's wife reminded me how precarious the country is.

"The judge is a very good man."

"But can you be certain he'll approve us?"

"It will be fine."

"You've talked to him?"

"No. In Pakistan we get our information from the wells."

I think I've misheard him and ask him to explain.

"From the worms," he says.

I have no choice but to trust Munir, and no reason not to. He's been completely aboveboard. In an affidavit to the court he stated his fee. He's been very particular that Reela's father come to the hearing to tell the judge in person that he is renouncing his rights to her.

FORTY-FIVE

A baby bird is hatched while his mother is away. Fallen from his nest, he sets out to look for her and asks everyone he meets—including a dog, a cow, and a plane—"Are you my mother?"

—Amazon.com plot synopsis of P. D. Eastman's *Are You My Mother?*

Islamabad, Pakistan: DAYNA

The United Airlines Boeing 777 tips its wing to put down in Kuwait, only to be met by a rising dust cloud—a *khamseen*, one of the dust storms that announce the arrival of summer in the Gulf. I've been caught in them before, and know how they can close down an airport. I keep my fingers crossed that that won't happen now. I have a plane to catch tomorrow to see my baby for the first time.

Inside the terminal, I follow my fellow passengers to the visa counter. Almost everyone is American, mostly soldiers and contractors on their way to Iraq. Some of them take the hotel shuttle with me, but no one talks; everyone is exhausted from the fourteen-hour flight from the United States. I make a mental list of all the things I want to buy my daughter.

When I ask the receptionist at the hotel what time the stores close, she looks at me curiously, wondering, I suspect, whether I know there's a war next door in Iraq. Kuwait's not the sort of place where you get off the plane and rush out to go shopping. She tells me I still have three hours—good news because I won't have time to shop in the morning before my flight to Islamabad. I take my bags upstairs and come back down to find a taxi to take me to the Salmiyah shopping district.

I still wonder what one buys for a ten-month-old. Will a toy that moves or talks scare her? Will she even care about a stuffed teddy bear? I'm sure she's too young for sweets, but I'll ask the ayah when I get there. Anyhow, Bob should know by now.

The taxi drives down a four-lane boulevard on the water and drops me off in front of a boxy modern building with neon store lights in the windows. The wind has died down, but I still have to cover my face to keep the grit out of my eyes and mouth. I race through the Western-style mall—Zara, Mango, Polo, Godiva— until I find a toy store and buy a play cell phone and some plastic blocks.

Just as I step back out of the mall to look for a taxi to go back to the hotel, I remember something. I go back in and buy chocolates for the ayah.

It's Bob I see first as I push my trolley out of the arrivals hall in Islamabad. He's pointing down at something nestled in his arm, a big grin on his face. I weave through passengers as if racing through a slalom course until I get to him. I'm immediately drawn to this tiny little brown face with black curly hair held back with tiny butterfly clips. She's in a little *salwar kameez*—a tunic that goes down to the knees—with matching pants. They're both made from a white linen fabric covered with small embroidered and beaded flowers. There's glitter on her face—the ayah has dressed her in her best. I hug Bob, and the little bundle in his arms gets squished between us. Her black eyes look up at me calmly, probably thinking, well, now who is *this*?

I take her from Bob and marvel at her tiny little fingers and long eyelashes and latte skin. I rock her gently. I'm completely enthralled.

For the next few days Bob and I stay in the bungalow with Reela; the ayah stays next door. During the first two nights, while

I get over jet lag, Reela stays with the ayah in her room. But first thing in the morning the ayah knocks on the door to come get me. She shows me how to mix the baby formula, feed Reela, and give her a bath. I watch the ayah wash her bottom with cold water and wince when she screams from the cold. When the ayah makes up for it by wrapping her in a furry blanket—outside its ninety by late morning—I think, *The faster I take over, the better.* I'm sure of it when I figure out that the ayah cannot read and has been diluting her formula too much. Still, I realize the ayah loves Reela, and she knows her ways. She shows me how when Reela's tired she pinches her own neck. I look forward to the late afternoon when the ayah leaves me alone with her and we nap together on the bed.

Before I arrived, I worried that Reela would think of the ayah as her mother. But it hasn't turned out that way at all. Reela accepts me as if she's been with me from the beginning, and soon we're inseparable.

Munir's office is in a windowless basement across from the Islamabad District Court, which is at the epicenter of the judicial revolt against Pakistan's president, Musharraf. But today there's no sign of protesting lawyers.

Munir's old salvaged desk is piled with papers. Bob and I sit across from Munir on wooden chairs, Reela in my arms. Munir types at an old squat computer that sits on a rickety gray metal side table on wheels. The whole thing looks as if it's about to tumble over.

"The judge is going to give us a hard time," Munir says, not looking up from his screen.

"Has something changed?" Bob asks, surprised.

Munir doesn't answer and gets up to talk to an assistant who is trying to print something on a printer that looks like an old mimeograph machine. He's in a rush to beat the next rolling blackout. You can set your watch by them, three hours on and one hour off.

Munir comes back and sits down behind his desk, then looks from Bob to me. "This judge is very cautious. He's denied the last three cases to foreigners."

"But you said—" Bob starts.

"He has real concerns about child trafficking."

"Do we look like child traffickers?"

"You must bring a copy of your book to the hearing," he says, "to establish your bona fides."

Bob and I look at each other, thinking the same thing: giving the judge a copy of Bob's memoir, dragging the CIA into a court system with a reputation for Islamic conservatism, can't be a good idea. Can't we just say that we're writers?

"Please bring whatever you can," Munir says.

Neither of us feels we can press it. We're hostages in a foreign legal system, and the smartest thing to do is to follow the advice of our lawyer. Anyhow, as we agreed from the beginning, the adoption is going to be done completely aboveboard, even if it means we have to expose our past.

"Did I tell you the judge is Taliban?" Munir asks.

"There is no—" Bob starts to say, and then stops.

"He went to school in Saudi Arabia. But he's a good man."

We follow Munir across a dusty parking lot, then upstairs and into an office to be fingerprinted. There's a white sheet on the wall with a strange, flowing purple design covering it. I take a closer look: it's smears from where people have wiped the ink off their fingers. Munir seems to know everyone, clerks and lawyers alike. They all clearly respect and like him.

Afterward we go to Saeed's, Islamabad's best-known bookstore, and buy a copy of Bob's memoir, *See No Evil*. Bob also finds a bootlegged copy of *Syriana*, the movie made from the memoir.

◆

It's already hot by ten. Rafiq eases the car into the dirt parking lot and squeezes into a place next to two banged-up taxis. Bob and I are in the back with the ayah, me holding Reela on my lap. Rafiq tells us to keep the baby in the air-conditioning. He leaves the car running, and heads off to find out when our case will be called.

He's back in five minutes, knocking on the car window to tell us it could be a while. He passes us two bottles of chilled water. Reela's fallen asleep. I smile at her, all bathed and dressed up for her big day.

By eleven the parking lot is packed with people milling around, vendors cooking in cut-down fifty-gallon drums, shopkeepers on the raised causeway stacking their wares in front of their stores, men squatting on their heels sipping tea and watching. Most look poor, their salwar kameezes bleached so often they've turned blue. The lawyers in front of the courthouse are talking animatedly on their cell phones.

I see Munir poke his head out of the colonnaded porch of the courthouse. He's in a dark suit, a white shirt, and a narrow tie. He waves at us and smiles, and then disappears back into the darkness of the court.

When Rafiq comes back to the car, he's with Reela's father, Adham. I recognize him instantly from the photo attached to the e-mail Munir's office first sent when we were still in Berkeley. He's a slight man with a tan, weathered face, a black, well-trimmed mustache, and a hawkish nose. The picture was taken on the day he gave her up to the parish. He and Reela both stare at the camera with the same serious expression.

I get out of the car with Reela, and Adham walks shyly up to me. He is wearing a soiled white salwar kameez and sandals. He smiles warmly and offers me his hand. I want to thank him. He holds out his arms to Reela, and I hand her to him. She looks at him quizzically and reaches up to touch his mustache. But I can't tell if she recognizes him.

"You can ask him anything you want," Rafiq says.

But I have no idea what to ask a father who's come here to sign papers forever giving up his child. Finally I ask, "Was her mother small?" I'm immediately embarrassed at how silly the question must sound. When Rafiq translates into Urdu, Adham nods. Then he asks something, and Rafiq laughs. "He doesn't know where you are from, so I just told him America."

A little later, after Adham is gone, I ask Rafiq how he felt about giving Reela up for adoption.

"He cried a little, but he knew it was best for her. He can't feed her."

Just then, his phone rings. "The judge is ready."

The small courtroom is hot, packed, everyone shouting at once. Lawyers wave papers in the air, jostling to get to the clerk. The ceiling fans only stir up the stale air. A man gets up to let me sit down. I watch as three men in heavy shackles are led in by the anti-terrorism police. After ten minutes of this, Munir finally pokes his head out of an office and motions for us to come in.

The judge, sitting behind an old steel desk, doesn't look up at us. He's a slight man, clean-shaven, maybe in his early thirties. He's in a pastel blue salwar kameez. A female clerk in a headscarf stands behind him, silently waiting for him to read through a document. Another lawyer stands on his left, whispering to the judge. Munir motions us to two plain wooden chairs along the wall. I'm just happy Reela isn't crying, and soon falls back asleep.

Munir and the judge talk briefly in Urdu, and then Munir turns to Bob. "The judge would like proof of who you say you are."

Bob pushes across the table the DVD and his book. They

suddenly look very small and unimportant, as if Bob has offered the judge a piece of chewing gum.

"What is this?" he asks in English, looking at Munir.

"There is no anxiety, Your Honor," Munir says. "Mr. Robert wrote this book, and it has no value."

The judge picks up the DVD and then the book, turning them to look at both sides.

"Mr. Bob and his wife were in the CIA," Munir offers helpfully.

The judge doesn't say anything and studies Bob's book. He looks at Munir and asks if he'd mind translating a joke. Munir does after each sentence, but it doesn't matter because I don't understand a thing other than it is something to do with a duck crossing the road and meeting an old friend in the middle. I only know when we've come to the punch line because Munir laughs, holding his sides. Bob and I decide to laugh too.

Munir exchanges a few more words with the judge, and then stands up to leave. We do too, nodding good-bye to the judge.

I'm just getting to my feet when I feel something warm and moist spreading over my whole lap. The sensation is so surprising and unfamiliar that there's a moment of total confusion. I look down to see my salwar kameez has a huge wet spot on it, and I finally grasp that Reela has just peed all over me. *Do diapers leak like this?* There's no time to think about that, and I cover myself with my scarf.

Outside in front of the court, Munir shakes Bob's hand. "Congratulations on becoming parents," he says. "The judge has approved your guardianship. It's just a matter of issuing an order."

So it's all over? I think. *As easy as that?* I can't believe I was so nervous about this all of these months.

As we drive away, everyone's smiling. The ayah changes Reela in her lap, rolls down the window, and throws the diaper out into the street.

◆

That night we celebrate at a little restaurant on Nazim-ud-din Road. At our invitation, Reela's father and the pastor who cared for her join us. We sit down to large shared plates of dal, chicken kabobs, palak paneer, and rice. I start out holding Reela on my lap, but then Adham comes around the table and sits next to me. He motions that he'll hold her so that I can eat. He bounces her on his lap and then says something to Rafiq.

"He says that you will not have any trouble with this little girl," Rafiq says. "He also says that because she is a girl, she would grow up and leave him to live with another family anyway."

Out by the car, I tell the pastor to tell Reela's father that we'll bring her back to visit with her family someday. He bows and makes a sign of praying with his hands.

Adham says something to the pastor. "He wants a picture of you both with her," the pastor says, "to keep in his house." Rafiq takes a few pictures, and then we shake hands and they drive away.

Back at the bungalow, I hold Reela and send e-mails to my father and friends telling them the good news. She's ours, and now it's only a matter of waiting a week for the judge to finish the written orders. We're finally a family.

I should be joyous, and I am, but something continues to gnaw at me. It's just, well, it's all been so *easy*. Years of working for the CIA has taught me to be suspicious of easy.

FORTY-SIX

> To find Osama bin Laden, try Peshawar's smugglers' bazaar on the road to the Khyber Pass. Walk past the small mountains of almonds and lemongrass and green tea. Turn at the stacks of duty-free TVs and cheap cosmetics. Stop at the stalls with the topless women. Down a cramped alley, bearded shopkeepers squeezed behind tiny counters offer a fine selection of fanciful sex products. "Delay sprays" carry the promise of lingering pleasure. For the discerning lover there is Lovely Curves, a product that claims to be a "bust-developing cream." If all else fails, there is plenty of knock-off Viagra at knock-down prices. Worry not about the quality: "Made is Germany" [sic] reads the label.
>
> —*The Guardian*, September 11, 2006

Peshawar, Pakistan: **BOB**

Like any good family with time on its hands, we take a vacation—to Peshawar, the gateway to the Khyber Pass and Pakistan's tribal area. We're thinking about giving Reela an even harder name to live up to, Khyber, and we figure she should at least see the place.

The newspapers are reporting that the Taliban are at Peshawar's edge. A couple of people warn us before we leave that they could seize Peshawar anytime they want, it's just that they don't want to. But the drive to Peshawar seems to belie all the dark talk. Bypassing the Grand Trunk Road, we take the M-1, a modern four-lane divided highway. There's little traffic, and no one speeds because every thirty miles or so there's a police car on the side of the road with a radar gun.

Things get a little ragged when we get off the M-1 at Peshawar, but the Pearl Continental, the only Western-style hotel in the city, is the picture of calm. A uniformed guard at the front gate salutes us smartly as we drive through. Porters run out to help us unload, then take us to the top floor, where an efficient young lady checks us in. A crib is already in the room, and there is a plate of fresh fruit and candies on the credenza. On the wall is a flat-screen TV. That night we eat at the open-air, rooftop restaurant. We keep looking for tracers in the sky, signs of fighting, but it's just a starry, quiet night.

In the morning we come down and I ask for the manager. He's bound to know something about the situation. He comes out of an office and invites me in.

"Is it safe here?" I ask, sitting down in a chair across from him.

He looks out the door at Dayna, who rocks Reela in her arms, and then back at me. "It's perfectly safe."

"Peshawar's safe?"

"The lobby."

I'm not going to let him off that easily. "We were thinking about going to Dera Ismail Khan," I say in the most innocent American voice I can summon. I know perfectly well that Dera Ismail Khan is in the hands of the Taliban and off-limits to us. I'm with family, not serving my old masters in Langley, but why stop trying to elicit information?

"I used to go there a lot in the eighties," I add. "Could the hotel arrange a driver and a car?"

"No," the manager says, "we won't, and you can't go there."

As he stands up to show me out, it's clear that that's all I'm going to get. Before I leave, though, he agrees to find us a driver to tour Peshawar. But he warns us not to get out of the car.

Wander only a few blocks into old Peshawar, and you step back into a dusty, medieval world. Houses centuries old lean into each other for support, their fronts decked with latticed balconies. There are spice and vegetable carts everywhere, and torsos of cows and sheep hang in butcher-shop windows, with people crowding around, bargaining for a good price. We never see another foreigner, which is something considering that not too long ago Peshawar was a tourist destination for young Westerners.

After seeing old Peshawar, I ask the driver if he knows where Osama bin Ladin's house is, the one where he lived in the eighties during the Afghan war. I tell him I think it's in University Town.

"I don't know what that is," he says, looking genuinely confused.

"University Town or bin Ladin?"

"I know University Town."

I make him stop by Peshawar's museum, a big, cavernous, dusty Victorian place so dark you can't see the artifacts in their cases. It's closed for the day, but the door is wide open. I wander around until I find the curator, who's looking through a microscope at what looks like an eggshell. I ask him where bin Ladin's house is.

"I'm sorry. I don't know."

"But you know who I'm talking about?"

"Of course I do. But you say he lived here in Peshawar?"

I promise to come back and visit the museum when it's open.

As our driver pulls away from the museum, I find myself wondering if the curator knows where bin Ladin lived and doesn't want to tell me, or if he really doesn't know. Either way, I think I'm starting to understand better how this man who changed history disappeared like a diamond in an inkwell.

FORTY-SEVEN

Islamabad, Pakistan: DAYNA

Bob is on the phone talking to Rafiq, and I can tell something is wrong. Bob's tone is flat; he's not joking. He keeps asking, "Are you sure? Are you sure?" I haven't seen him this upset in a long time.

Bob gets off the phone and confirms my worst fear: the judge has turned down guardianship. I want to cry, but I don't want Reela to see me upset. I lie on the ground with her, look into her little dark eyes, and wonder what will become of all of us.

Bob says quietly that we'll appeal to a higher court, adding that Munir's already preparing the paperwork. The bright spot is that the denial is only oral. There's a possibility the judge will reconsider.

Everything seemed so clear this morning. We'd made our reservations to leave. I'd e-mailed friends. And now we're prisoners of a legal system I don't understand. I could kick myself. It was stupid to do this on our own, without an international adoption agency. I turn my face away from Reela and cry quietly, for both of us.

The cold truth is that there are no Christian orphanages in Pakistan for her to go to. Her father cannot take her back. I have no idea what the state would do with her. Do we live here forever with her?

The next morning Bob starts making calls as if he were a CIA operative newly arrived in Pakistan, trying to figure out who's in charge. It's his way of coping.

His first call is to the ABC fixer, a contact he's arranged through our friends at ABC News in New York. The fixer doesn't know the judge and can't help with the court system, but his cousin is able to verify that her birth certificate is authentic. In a country awash in forged documents, it's something.

The next appointment is with Hamid Gul, the former head of Pakistan's Interservices Intelligence. Gul was a driving force in the Afghan war, overseeing the arming and training of the Mujahidin. He tells Bob he'd be happy to help if there were a way, but Pakistan's judiciary is notoriously independent. It would take the intervention of the head of ISI to move the courts.

Bob finally goes to see another notorious figure—Colonel Imam, onetime ISI liaison with the Taliban. Nothing comes of that either, other than Bob's getting the man's take on the current war in Afghanistan.

It's fascinating, watching Bob rake the ashes of old history, but I think we both know this is action for action's sake. No one is going to intervene on our behalf. So much for a fat Rolodex. And to think this is Pakistan, a place where one assumes things like this can be fixed.

Munir meets us the next evening in front of his office. We stand in the parking lot because of the blackout. The only light is from kerosene lanterns hanging in the storefronts. While Bob talks to Munir, Rafiq tries to reassure me that Munir will win on appeal. Reela's asleep in my arms. I keep asking what will happen to her if they say no, the same question I've asked over and over during the last two days. Rafiq says they'll take care of her. But I know that's impossible.

Finally, Munir walks over to me and says, "I'm sorry. It seems the judge won't reconsider."

Munir explains that the judge turned down guardianship because we don't have permanent residence in Islamabad, and he won't agree to hand over custody of a child to someone not living in his jurisdiction. "Legally it makes no sense," Munir says. "If that were the law, no one could adopt from Pakistan."

Munir offers his speculation that the judge is afraid to be caught up in a child-trafficking case and wants someone else to make the decision on guardianship. There's no choice now but go to the appeals court, he says. A different judge.

I'm all cried out, and just listen to him. On the one hand, I'm relieved to hear that we were turned down for guardianship for a reason having no basis in law. But I also know that, legal or not, it's not surprising that a Taliban judge would refuse to give custody of a Pakistani child to two Americans who once worked for the CIA.

"We had no choice but to go before a judge from the Taliban," Munir says, reading my mind. "I'm sorry."

I'm filled with second-guessing. It now seems like such a stupid mistake to have given the judge Bob's book and the DVD. But there's no point in telling Munir that. I ask him instead whether he thinks the appeal will work.

"I cannot know, madam. But I'll try my absolute best." Munir insists that he argue the appeal for free.

On the way home we stop at the Marriott hotel, which is in the government cantonment area of Islamabad, near parliament and the American embassy. With its concrete barriers and spotlights, it resembles a fortress. But passing time there is better than spending the night at the bungalow by ourselves, trying to think our way through this. We sit in the café and order juices. I let Reela play in the booth.

There's simply no Plan B if the appeal doesn't work. I know no one's really at fault, but I'm angry anyway. I try to focus on something else and not worry about what could happen. But all I can think about is how the Marriott is a metaphor for what's happening to Pakistan—the fences, metal detectors, drop bars, and armed guards are the only things holding back the boiling chaos.

FORTY-EIGHT

Matter to be considered by the Court in appointing guardian—In appointing or declaring the guardian of a minor, the Court shall, subject to the provisions of this section, be guided by what, consistently with the law to which the minor is subject, appears in the circumstances to be for the welfare of the minor. In considering what will be for the welfare of the minor, the Courts shall have regard to the age, sex and religion of the minor, the character and capacity of the proposed guardian and his nearness of kin to the minor, the wishes, if any, of a deceased parent, and any existing or previous relations of the proposed guardian with the minor or his property.

—Pakistan Guardians and Wards Act, 1890

Islamabad, Pakistan: BOB

People crowd the outside of the appeals courtroom, peering through the latticed brick wall to get a glimpse inside. A guard outside taps his scuffed desk with an oak baton, keeping them at bay. We follow Munir inside and sit on a bench at a long table filled with lawyers, all in black worsted wool suits, stacks of files and papers loosely bound with string in front of them. The appeals judge isn't here yet.

Munir starts to argue loudly in Urdu with another lawyer. He turns around and grabs a piece of paper from his folder on the table to show it to him. They both shake their heads in disbelief. I have no idea whether this has anything to do with our case.

When Munir goes outside in front of the court to talk to his assistant, I follow.

"Is something the matter?" I ask Munir.

"It will be fine."

"But we thought that about the first judge."

"This one is my friend." Munir squeezes my arm. "There are no worries."

We're joined by another lawyer, who says something to Munir, and Munir hurries back into court with him. The assistant and I are left studying the square in front of the appeals court. In the short hour since we've arrived, the streets around the courts are already swollen with vegetable peddlers, police, hawkers, and people just standing around. Two veiled women walk by, holding hands.

"Prostitutes," the assistant says.

The two are as conservatively dressed as any I've seen in Islamabad, and I look at him for an explanation.

"This place is Islamabad's red-light district. Everyone knows who the prostitutes are."

"But why the courts?"

He shrugs his shoulders. It's a mystery as deep as why no one in Peshawar seems to know where bin Ladin's old house is.

I return to the courtroom and reclaim my seat next to Dayna and Reela. Munir is arguing with a clerk, who finally opens the gate to let Munir behind the bench and into the judge's chambers. The other lawyers ignore him, arguing loudly as if practicing their cases in front of the judge.

The judge comes out of his chambers and takes his seat at the bench. Munir follows, but lets himself through a gate and stands before the judge. Without preamble, he starts what sounds like an impassioned oration. From time to time Munir looks over at us, the judge following his gaze. The judge's face is blank. It's as if we're the accused in a criminal trial. This goes on for five minutes.

When Munir is finished, the judge turns to a clerk at an ancient computer terminal and tells him something. The clerk types for a couple minutes before signaling that he's done.

Munir turns to us. "Please, come forward."

As we approach, a lawyer walks up to the bench and hands the judge a pink folder. The judge reads it, and Dayna and I stand there waiting for him to finish. It's the longest minute either of us has spent in our lives.

The judge hands the file back to the lawyer and looks at Dayna and me as if it were the first time he's seen us.

"Thank His Honor," Munir says.

I think I'm beginning to understand what's happened, but I look at Munir.

"The judge has granted you guardianship. His order is being typed now."

I glance at the clerk who's started typing again. I sense that it's real now, and look over at Dayna and Reela and smile. I would kiss them, but kissing is probably forbidden in a Pakistani court.

The mechanics of it all will forever remain a mystery. But none of that matters. We have our daughter.

FORTY-NINE

> Sometimes, if you stand on the bottom rail of a bridge and lean
> over to watch the river slipping slowly beneath you, you will
> suddenly know everything there is to be known.
>
> —Winnie the Pooh

Islamabad, Pakistan: **DAYNA**

The next day there's a little celebration at the ayah's house in
Rawalpindi, the sister city of Islamabad. Rafiq insists on driving us, worried we won't find our way there ourselves.

Just as we come to Rawalpindi, Rafiq turns left across the di-
vide in the highway, scraping the car's bottom. He turns down a
dirt road into a jumble of one-story brick houses. People squat
in doorways with small propane stoves, children play in the road,
and there are goats everywhere, eating garbage. Everyone turns to
watch us go by. I notice the women are in saris, but with their faces
uncovered—this is a Christian slum.

When we're through the village, Rafiq cuts across a field where
men are making bricks from mud, dung, and straw, and then down
a rutted path. We come to a small lake spanning the road. As we
drive across it, I realize it's an open sewer.

Rafiq tells us that this is where Reela lived for the two months
before Bob arrived, with the ayah and her family.

I'm exhausted now and feeling selfish, and just want to celebrate with the three of us. I ask Rafiq if we can just stay for coffee
and go back to the bungalow.

"But she's already prepared dinner," Rafiq says.

We pass a square, unfinished brick house, which Rafiq says is a church. We slow down to a crawl so the SUV can make it over a ditch. I never see another car.

We finally come to a stop in front of another unfinished house. Sheets hang in the spaces where glass is meant to be. Like many structures in this part of the world, this one has an unfinished second floor, rebar poking into the sky, waiting for someone to find the money to finish it. The front door looks like a salvaged piece of old metal. Swarms of mosquitoes hover everywhere.

The ayah opens the door to a clean and tidy house. She steps outside and takes Reela from me, and then introduces us to her husband, mother, grandmother, an uncle and his wife, and three cousins—Reela's first family. They're all delighted we've come.

They show us into a small sitting room with a wooden bench covered in a brightly colored sheet and a half-dozen plastic chairs. Off the room is a closet-size kitchen with a propane stove on a stone ledge. There's no sink, and instead a hole in the floor with a drain. There are buckets of water in a corner—there's no running water in the house. The only light is from a single bare bulb, which flickers. Rafiq sees me looking at it and says that we need to leave before eight when the power goes off, adding it will stay off until the next day. I ask why they don't have rolling power outages like the rest of Islamabad. "Nobody cares about these people," he says.

The ayah's family takes us up concrete steps to the unfinished second floor. There's a good view of the surrounding area, most of it a wasteland where people are trying to grow gardens. Salvaged bricks are piled here and there. On the roofs nearby, other families sit outside among the rows of carefully arranged cow-dung piles being dried for cooking fuel.

As Reela is gently passed among the ayah and her mother and grandmother, I get Rafiq to take our picture before it's too dark. At this point I'm almost broken with gratitude for these people.

Dinner is a feast: chicken, dal, rice, and salad. For dessert there's a *firni*, a sweet rice pudding topped with pistachios. At the end the family gives Reela a blond-haired baby doll that sings the ABCs in English.

After dinner another relative passes by, holding a baby boy the same age as Reela. His head is malformed, and he cannot sit or hold his head up. He's dressed in bright new clothes, and his father is obviously proud of him. I have to wonder what will happen to the boy. It's doubtful he's ever seen a doctor, and he probably never will. For that matter, I'm sure the ayah's husband has never seen a dentist. He has a tooth that sticks out of his mouth at a right angle.

As we drive away, I ask Rafiq if the ayah's house is anything like the one where Reela was born in Faisalabad.

"No," he says, "there's no electricity or water there at all."

I'd like to think this is what we're rescuing Reela from, trying not to admit to myself that something absolutely precious is being transferred from the "have-nots" to the "haves." If only we can love her as much and as well as these people do.

FIFTY

It's all right letting yourself go, as long as you can get yourself back.

—Mick Jagger

Lahore, Pakistan: **DAYNA**

There's nothing like frequent-flier miles—to be precise, 150,000 of them. It was enough to get us to Islamabad and back to California. They rack up fast when you renovate a hundred-year-old Berkeley brown-shingle Craftsman house, and charge everything from the Toto toilet to the Dacor French-door refrigerator with a bottom freezer.

But what we have to look forward to now is thirty-six hours of flying with an eleven-month-old baby we met just six weeks ago. I might have thought it was impossible not long ago, but she's part of me now. I melt at every smile, every giggle, every little acknowledgment that she understands we're going to take care of her, feed and love her. She easily curls up with me and reaches for me like I'm hers, and she's mine.

At the Etihad Airlines check-in counter, we anxiously wait while the attendant checks our tickets. We were on hold for at least an hour with United, trying to figure out how to get us routed back home. Because of Reela's Pakistani passport, she cannot land in Kuwait without an onward ticket, and, traveling as an infant, she has no ticket of her own. But United has seen it before, and issues a "fake" ticket so she can board our flight. It took forever, though, and our phone bill is going to be immense.

Islamabad—Lahore—Abu Dhabi—Kuwait—Washington, D.C.—Chicago—Los Angeles: that's our planned route home. And the last person to have any say over our court-appointed guardianship of this abandoned baby girl we've come to adore is a Pakistani immigration official in a green uniform, complete with felt beret and sidearm.

"Passports," he says officiously, sticking out his hand.

Bob's passport has pages added more than once from all his travels. I'm terrified that somewhere in there is a stamp from Tel Aviv or something else that will cause a problem. The official goes through it page by page, as if looking for a reason not to let us board. Reela studies his face as if she's deciding what he's up to.

The man hands back Bob's and my passports as if he's disappointed, then picks up Reela's brand-new Pakistani passport, empty except for the U.S. visa. And then, page by page, he examines the notarized court documents granting us guardianship. He's like a law student looking for some small anomaly.

"Where are her parents?" he says, looking at Bob and then me.

Bob tells him that her mother died and her father couldn't afford to take care of her.

He looks again through her passport and keeps one page open with his thumb.

"May I ask you something?" he asks.

This is where I wait for the inevitable, where the disdain comes through in his voice and where I feel so guilty for taking a child away from her own country. I'm racking my mind for how I'll explain why we didn't adopt from our own country.

"Why didn't you adopt a Muslim child?" he asks instead.

I start to answer, but Bob does first, explaining how under Pakistani law we can only adopt a Christian child.

The man slowly looks through Reela's passport one more time.

I hold my breath, waiting for him to ask us to step aside so he can talk to his superior, or for him to send us through some unmarked door where all of the past six weeks will suddenly vanish in a small airport interrogation room.

"Take good care of her," he says, and waves us through.

EPILOGUE

It's me who first spots my father at Orange County airport, at the bottom of the escalator. There's a big grin on his face when he sees me with Khyber in my arms. There's no doubt about it: he's delighted for me, for us. But just as we're pulling out of the airport parking lot, he says that he's leaving early the next morning on a trip with his "other daughter."

It isn't the first or the last of painful moments like this. Later, when I find the chance, I tell him that I feel as if I've been replaced. "Well, you were gone," he says. And there it is, the truth.

I lied to myself for a long time that I didn't have to be nearby to keep family bonds. I convinced myself that things would be the way they always had been when I finally came back home. Oh boy, did I get that one wrong.

In the end, family all comes down to what Bob says about spying: you either tend the human element or watch what's really of value slip away.

◈

Khyber is three now. She's loving and happy, a home full of laughter and joy. We keep in contact with her father, Adham, through his bishop in Faisalabad. Adham is now married to his deceased wife's sister. I still stay in touch with my ex–husband, who's happily remarried. Bob's ex–wife was delighted when she heard about Khyber and sends her gifts from around the world (she's still at the State Department).

◈

I read somewhere that an adopted child's life doesn't start the day the child's adopted. Like anyone, the child's history and family began a thousand lifetimes ago. I need to remember that Khyber's mother was her first mother, and that her father made a decision that changed both his and our lives forever. I can't do anything other than plan that Khyber will be able to see him and come to know him and her birth family. The bishop has invited us to stay with him when we come to Pakistan, and I hope we will soon be able to take him up on his offer.

◈

Pakistan continues to struggle. The Marriott, where we often ate dinner and sometimes went just to escape the heat, was destroyed by a truck bomb on September 20, 2008. The Pearl Continental, where we stayed in Peshawar, was destroyed by another truck bomb, on June 11, 2009. Bob's ISI contact, Colonel Imam, was kidnapped by militants in March 2010.

BOB

Two days before we leave Pakistan, I ask our Pashtun fixer why we can't find Osama bin Ladin. It's simple, he says, you never bothered to look for the chicken feathers. He smiles at my confusion and clears it up for me: the Arabs in al Qaeda eat chicken, while their hosts, the Pashtuns, who live in the mountains between Afghanistan and Pakistan, eat mutton. It was a matter, then, of wandering around these mountains looking for chicken feathers outside houses. "In a week you would have found bin Ladin," he said.

◆

The BBC reported in 1999 that "after a long chase" Sheikh Hamad bin Jasim bin Hamad Al Thani was arrested and brought back home to stand trial for attempting to overthrow his cousin in 1996. The question was whether the court would impose the death penalty.

As it turned out, the sheikh was spared execution and even eventually released. At the end of the day, his cousin the emir had the good sense not to shed the blood of one of his own. It's not the way to hold together a family.

◆

I read somewhere that with family the problems start when you never ask the questions you need to, and they never give you the answers they want to. No doubt, there's a certain amount of truth in that. But I think it's a lot more basic: we're just plain dense when it comes to living. And it's all the more ironic for someone like me, who thinks he's so smart dealing with the big questions, like the rise and fall of empires.

Nothing I did in my years in the CIA added or subtracted from the mess out there. But what I do know is that while I was trying to make sense of that mess, there was a mess brewing at home. Very likely I could have done something about it had I stayed put. But what I can tell you for certain now is this: I won't let it happen again.

Authors' photograph: Tara Whitney

ABOUT THE AUTHORS

ROBERT BAER is the author of three *New York Times* bestsellers: *See No Evil* (which was the basis for the acclaimed film *Syriana*), *Sleeping with the Devil*, and *The Devil We Know*. Before leaving the Agency to settle down with Robert, DAYNA BAER was herself an accomplished CIA operative.

Robert Baer is available for select readings and lectures. To inquire about a possible appearance, please contact the Random House Speakers Bureau at rhspeakers@randomhouse.com or 212-572-2013.

ALSO BY ROBERT BAER

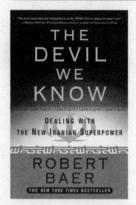

The Devil We Know: Dealing with
the New Iranian Superpower

$15.00 paper (Canada: $18.95)
978-0-307-40867-9

Sleeping with the Devil:
How Washington Sold Our Soul
for Saudi Crude

$13.95 paper (Canada: $21.00)
978-1-4000-5268-4

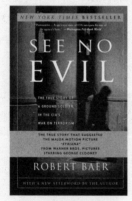

See No Evil: The True Story of
a Ground Soldier in the
CIA's War on Terrorism

$16.00 paper (Canada: $19.95)
978-1-4000-4684-3

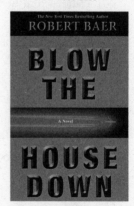

Blow the House Down: A Novel

$14.95 paper (Canada: $19.95)
978-1-4000-9836-1